1999
THE WORLD OF TOMORROW

Selections from THE FUTURIST:
A Journal of Forecasts, Trends, and
Ideas about the Future

Edited by Edward Cornish

WORLD FUTURE SOCIETY

4916 St. Elmo Avenue
Washington, D.C. 20014 • U.S.A.

Published by
World Future Society
4916 St. Elmo Avenue
Washington, D.C. 20014 • U.S.A.

Copyright © 1978 by
World Future Society

Library of Congress Cataloging in Publication Data

   1999: the world of tomorrow

(The Futurist library; no. 1)
Bibliography: p.
1. Twentieth century—Forecasts—Addresses, essays, lecture. I. Cornish, Edward, 1927-   II. The Futurist.
CB161.N56   909.82'9   78-17612

Library of Congress Catalog Number 78-17612
International Standard Book Number 0-930242-04-1

Design: Diane Smirnow
Production Manager: Peter Zuckerman
Editorial Coordinator: Hugh Myers

Cover Art: (taken from covers of THE FUTURIST): 1. "Future Work" by Richard Fanelli; 2. "Transformation" by Sister Jessica; 3. "College Education" by Gerard C. Pilachowski; 4. "Floating City" by Robert McCall; 5. "Lunar Landing" by Robert McCall; 6. "Garden Earth" by Stowmar Enterprises ; 7. "Voluntary Simplicity" by Diane Smirnow and Steven M. Johnson; 8. "Fantastic Megastructure" by Glen Small; 9. "Space Colony" by NASA; 10. "Appropriate Technology" by Diane Schatz and Marcia Johnson; 11. "Visions of the Future" by Sister Jessica; 12. "The Automated Office" by Diane Smirnow with photographer Aboud Dweck; 13. "Bureaucratic Complexity" by Steven M. Johnson and Diane Smirnow

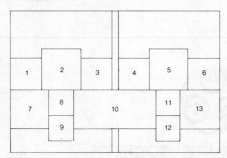

Price $4.95
$4.45 to members of the World Future Society

Please inquire for reduced multiple copy price for classroom use.

Part 4: The Future as Invention

"Inventing the future" has become a popular phrase among futurists.
They do not see the future as something that just happens to people;
instead, people create the future by deciding what they want and then
working to achieve it.

Conclusion

CONTENTS

INTRODUCTION
Welcome to the Future!

The most exciting period of history is right now. Never before have human lives changed faster or in so many fascinating ways. No one can know for certain what may happen in the years ahead, but some people are now thinking very seriously about the future and can give us at least an inkling of what we may witness in the years to come. Even more important, they can help us to decide what we should do today to make the world a better place to live in tomorrow. We must not forget that we jointly create the future by what we do—or fail to do—in our daily lives.

The rapid change that we are experiencing means that the future will probably be more different for us than it was for any previous generation of human beings. The world of tomorrow will seem a strange place unless we prepare ourselves for it, and to do that we must look for glimmerings of what may happen in the years ahead. We cannot *know* what the future holds, due to the inherent uncertainty of events, but we *can* identify some of the possibilities, so that we can decide more wisely what we should do today to create a better future world.

We have inherited a great deal from our ancestors whose contributions through the centuries created the civilization that we enjoy today. But we ourselves must carry forward the human enterprise in the face of many new challenges. We may be nearing the climax of the human drama that began over two million years ago with the emergence of man on this planet. Although we cannot know the final outcome of the momentous period in which we are living, we can clearly see that we have entered a period of fantastic possibilities for good as well as for evil. Some scholars gloomily predict that civilization is about to self-destruct. But others are confident that we have entered a new era in which human beings will not only be happier than ever before but will also create a great and wondrous new civilization that will outshine all the civilizations of the past. We may be entering a Golden Age more lustrous than any that has come before.

Whether we are on the threshold of a Golden Age or on the brink of a global cataclysm that will extinguish our civilization is, I believe, not only unknown and unknowable, but also undecided. The decision will emerge through what we do in the years ahead, for each of us will create a little piece of the common future of all mankind.

To help us carry out more wisely our responsibility for the future, the World Future Society was formed on October 12, 1966, in Washington, D.C. The Society is a nonprofit, nonpartisan association of people who share a deep interest in our common future. The Society does not take stands on what the world will be like or should be like in the years ahead, but serves instead as a neutral clearinghouse or forum for a wide variety of viewpoints. The Society's membership has grown each year since its founding and in 1978 included more than 40,000 people in some 80 countries around the world.

Shortly after its founding, the Society began publishing a regular newsletter, later a magazine, called THE FUTURIST. Since its first regular issue (February 1967), THE FUTURIST has published hundreds of articles on all aspects of the future. The articles in this book are drawn from THE FUTURIST and reflect the great diversity of subjects dealt with in the magazine. This anthology was not designed to offer the "best" of THE FUTURIST but rather to present a selection of recent articles that seem likely to interest newcomers to the future as a field of study.

The first group of articles, "The Future as History," reflects the great interest of futurists in the past: Futurists want to *use* the past to build a better future. Futuristics has even been called "applied history."

The second section, "The Future as Progress," focuses on the continuing story of man's technological achievements. Despite widespread pessimism, progress continues today on almost all fronts, and these articles suggest a few—a very few—of the many fields in which new wonders are being achieved.

The third section, "The Future as Challenge," describes some of the problems that humanity now faces, but also suggests means of solving those problems or at least softening their impact.

The fourth and final section offers "The Future as Invention." Futurists emphasize that we ourselves determine what the future will be like. If we are to mold a better future, we must be inventive and come up with creative new ways to meet problems.

This volume can offer only a tiny sampling of what may happen in the years ahead.* Since the future is the realm of infinite possibilities, we can never know all the things that might come to pass within its domain; all we can do is to make a few forays into that awesomely vast and incomparably fascinating territory.

*Readers who wish to move further into the field should turn to *The Study of the Future: An Introduction to the Art and Science of Understanding and Shaping Tomorrow's World* by Edward Cornish and members and staff of the World Future Society. World Future Society, 4916 St. Elmo Avenue, Washington, D.C. 20014. U.S.A. 308 pages. Paperback. $9.50 ($8.50 to Society members).

Part 1
THE FUTURE AS HISTORY

The past can illuminate the future.

Adam Smith's Vision

Drawing: Tom Chalkley

Smith, Marx, and Malthus— Ghosts Who Haunt Our Future
Three Economic Visions of Tomorrow's World

by James H. Weaver and Jon D. Wisman

Adam Smith, Karl Marx, and Thomas Malthus presented the world with compelling—though mutually contradictory—visions of the future. Today the disciples of each of the three great economists can argue that his vision is alive and well and still foretells the shape of things to come.

One way of exploring the future alternatives of our economic life is by projecting into the future the ideas of the great economists. The rationale for this approach is that, while ideas spring forth from the unfolding of history, they are also exceedingly important in determining the future.

Three economists whose ideas have had a powerful influence on the past and promise to influence the future very profoundly are Adam Smith, Karl Marx, and Thomas Malthus. The systems that they developed represent the most acute awareness of the history of their times— the same history in which our own present and future are rooted.

Adam Smith was an astute student of 18th-century economic conditions. His observations and his Scottish Enlightenment values led him to believe that it was no accident that in 1776 the richest country, England, was also the country in which individuals were left freest to pursue their own self-interest. However, English economic life was still exceedingly fettered by government regulation and intervention in the economic sphere. In consequence, Smith wrote his famous anti-mercantilist treatise, *An Inquiry into the Nature and Causes of the Wealth of the Nations*, which outlined his vision of a good society. A good society would result, Smith argued, if government would leave individuals free to pursue their own specific interests. Individuals know best their own interests, and the competitive social interaction of the selfishly-motivated economic activities of individuals would result in a social harmony, as if guided by an "invisible hand." With competition as the regulator, a "simple and obvious system of natural liberty"—aside from being good in and of itself—would promise the greatest possible material well-being. To be operative, Adam Smith's vision required two basic economic institutions: private ownership of the means of production; and markets through which goods, services, and the factors of production could be allocated.

Karl Marx was equally optimistic, although he had a very different vision of the future. Born almost a century after Smith, Marx observed the seamy side of capitalism as it matured, and he longed for the demise of this system which, through exploitation, created extremes of wealth and poverty. Smith had viewed people primarily as self-interested individuals and thus saw a need for private property and marketplaces to adjudicate between them, but Marx saw people primarily as social beings and thus emphasized cooperation and equality. Humans' exploitation of humans would end as capitalism gave birth to a higher form of social organization. The economic institutions necessary to post-capitalist society were social ownership of the means of production and allocation of goods, services, and factors of production according to the principle of "from each according to his ability, to each according to his need." However, before the latter principle could become effective, "socialist consciousness" must be created and during this transition period the institution of planning and central government control would be essential. Marx's ultimate vision, then, was the possibility of achieving— through socialism—ultimate abundance and the end of alienation—an end to status distinctions between mental work and manual work, between town and country, and between men and women.

In contrast to the optimism of Smith and Marx, the Reverend Thomas Malthus painted a grim scenario of what awaited humanity. Malthus was representative of the reactionary English response to the values of the French Revolution and the growing power of the commercial and industrial class. Unlike Smith and Marx, his fonder sentiments were attached to the past. Believing in original sin, he viewed people as profligate, selfish, and unable to restrain their own appetites. Consequently, they will breed until there is no longer enough food to go around; society is unable to regulate itself, except through the unwilled mechanisms of famine, pesti-lence, plague, disease, and war. Thus, the Malthusian vision of the future was of a nightmare come true.

Let us now look at how each of these visions is faring in today's world and what it may suggest about the future of humanity.

Prospects for Adam Smith's Vision

According to the Smithian vision, social harmony and economic progress result when economic power is widely dispersed among competing economic actors: The means of production are privately owned and the value of everything—from an hour's labor to an ice cream cone—is determined in competitive markets by the "natural" forces of supply and demand. Of course, the ideal Smithian economy does not exist

Adam Smith's followers have produced great wealth for capitalist nations, but his vision of limitless economic growth creates environmental hazards that threaten man's existence.
Illustration: Kathy Sanderson

today—nor has it ever existed. And the degree to which specific economies approximate the Smithian ideal is a source of perennial debate. We are all aware that monopolies, oligopolies, and cartels exist; that labor unions exist; and that governments everywhere are involved with the workings of economies. Still, the Smithian vision continues to act as a powerful guiding philosophy for capitalist countries. Their dominant faith is that the Smithian vision has crucial importance to the well-being of humanity. However poor the fit between the Smithian ideal and specific capitalist economies, it is with and through capitalism that the Smithian vision lives and exerts its influence.

When we look at capitalist economies, we are struck by the fact that in the past 30 years, capitalism has been in one of its most vibrant, vital, dynamic, and expansionist phases. The impact of this expansion has been visible on three groups of countries: the advanced capitalist countries, the less developed countries, and the so-called socialist countries of Eastern Europe.

The developed capitalist countries of Western Europe and Japan recovered with unexpected rapidity from the ravages of World War II, and are now exporting goods and capital to all corners of the globe. The growth rate of the U.S. economy during the 1960s was truly phenomenal: a 3% per capita average annual increase in GNP during the period 1960-1971. This growth came on top of a very high income base at the beginning of that period. Furthermore, capitalism's post-World War II successes have given birth to a dynamic mechanism for spreading capitalist institutions and values throughout the globe: the multinational corporations. These corporations have expanded their operations not only to every part of the underdeveloped world but into the economies of many socialist countries as well.

The less developed countries that are most explicitly following a capitalist path of development—especially those that have opened their doors widest to the multinational corporations—are experiencing a rapid process of industrialization. Brazil now exports manufactured goods of greater value than its coffee. Taiwan, Korea, Singapore, Malaysia, and Mexico are experiencing spectacular gains in industrialization. If we judge these economies on the basis of their governments' goals—that of rapidly increasing the gross national product—they have been remarkably successful.

International capitalism is also launching an expansion in Eastern Europe. In the recent past the countries of Eastern Europe have opened their economies to capitalist institutions such as the market and multinational corpora-

New York Stock Exchange carries on the tradition of Adam Smith.

Photos: New York Stock Exchange

tions. For instance, the Rockefellers' Chase Manhattan Bank has opened an office in Moscow (on Karl Marx Square, no less!). U.S. energy firms plan to purchase natural gas worth billions of dollars from the Soviet Union. Representatives of the USSR and Wall Street are considering raising capital to be invested in Russia. Multinational firms plan to establish operations in Russia, Poland, Hungary, and Czechoslovakia, following several such developments in Yugoslavia.

Thus the socialist countries seem to have succumbed to the lure of consumerism, which is capitalism's mainstay. These countries appear to be gradually accepting Adam Smith's adage that "Consumption is the sole end and purpose of all production." In spite of the fact that the multinational corporation is perhaps the most advanced instrument of capitalism, these giants are being invited in to invigorate the economies of Eastern Europe.

The expansion of the multinational corporations may make the Smithian vision the most likely alternative for future human history but, if so, we should not expect the globalization of capitalism to occur smoothly. At issue is a world-shaking bid for power between the nation-state and the multinational corporation. Ironically, the rise of the multinational corporation has coincided with the development of scores of new nation-states. As increasing nationalist pressures have led to decolonization and to greater national political independence (at least in form), the multinational corporations have grown apace. And these newest repositories of power are mounting an ever greater challenge to the sovereignty, stability, and even the *raison d'etre* of the nation-state.

The multinationals have been able to amass enormous power through their control of four aspects of economic life:

1. Through their control of modern technology, they exert powerful influence over the nature of the process of production and the types of goods and services produced.

2. Their command over long-term finance capital enables them to control somewhere between 300 and 350 billion dollars of liquid assets—one and one-half to two times all the reserves held by governments.

3. Multinational corporations are—at least allegedly—capable of thwarting the countervailing power of national labor unions by threatening to move production to other countries rather than yield to labor's demands.

4. The multinational corporations purportedly wield increasing control over their product markets by psychologically bombarding their clients with the ideology of consumerism—the notion that the good life comes from the consumption of the things they produce. They spend billions on advertising to convince people around the globe that the good life is derived primarily from consumption of goods and services.

The multinationals have in the last few years helped to create domestic and international instability among the developed capitalist countries. For instance, just before the devaluation of the dollar in August 1971, the MNCs helped bring about an enormous flight from the dollar into deutschemarks, gold, and other assets thought to be more devaluation-proof than the dollar. The global giants were instrumental in triggering a balance of payments crisis for the United States that rocked the international monetary system to its foundation.

The MNCs have also posed difficulties for central banks which attempt to use monetary policy to maintain domestic economic stability. In the past, a central bank could affect spending in the economy by changing the supply of money and thereby changing the cost and availability of credit. Central banks could heat up or cool off the domestic economy by intervening in the domestic capital markets. However, large corporations—specifically multinational corporations—have become increasingly independent of domestic credit conditions in their investment decisions. The greatest part of their investment needs is being met from their large stocks of internally generated funds (depreciation allowances and undistributed profits). And if these funds should be insufficient, the multinational corporations can move funds from abroad to meet their investment needs. Thus, as multinational corporations and banks account for an increasing percentage of total economic activity, they increasingly abort the attempts of monetary authorities to stabilize domestic economies. Yet a third area of instability is alleged to be the structural unemployment resulting from the MNCs' practice of moving production facilities away from the industrially advanced countries—where wages are high and unions are strong—to industrially backward countries where unions are virtually non-existent and wages are very low.

Thanks in part to the multinational corporations, the economic system established after World War II on the principles of John Maynard Keynes has changed radically from the 19th-century laissez-faire economy. Today's most distinguished economists, with their panoply of Keynesian tools, don't seem to understand exactly how this new post-Keynesian economy operates, just as economists schooled in classical economic theory failed to understand the Keynesian economy of 1929. The result back then was a terrible depression that lasted for 10 years—a very high price for not understanding the economic system!

Keynes taught us that there is unemployment when there is too little total spending in the economy. The solution is for government to intervene by increasing total spending until everyone is put to work. That worked rather well in World War II, and during the 1950s and 1960s. Keynesian economics also taught us that inflation resulted from too much total spending when we were at full employment, meaning no more could be produced. The role of government was to reduce total spending so as to eliminate the upward pressures on wages and prices.

Thus, we all learned that unemployment and inflation were opposite problems and had opposite policy requirements. At a time of unemployment, the government increased total spending; at times of inflation, the government decreased total spending. In any case, in the Keynesian system, unemployment and inflation could not exist at the same time.

But during the early 1970s the U.S. has experienced unemployment of over 9% (over 8,000,000 people officially without jobs—this is as large as the total work force of Sweden, Denmark, and Norway combined!), concomitant with an inflation rate of 12%.

And what do the Keynesians or neo-Keynesians instruct us to do? Distilling the arcane jargon into lay language, the prescription is: increase total spending to reduce unemployment and decrease total spending to reduce inflation. Such a contradiction reveals the virtual irrevelance of the Keynesian model for current economic ills.

About the Authors

Weaver

James Weaver, Professor of Economics at American University in Washington, D.C., specializes in economic growth and development. He is currently working on a study of the impact of multinational banks on the poor.

Jon Wisman is Assistant Professor of Economics at American University. A specialist in economic thought and methodology, he founded and ran American University's Washington Economic Policy Seminar. In addition, he prepared a study for the White House Conference on Youth, for which he projected the American economy into the future.

. . . the ideas of economists and political philosophers, both when they are right and when they are wrong, are more powerful than is commonly understood. Indeed, the world is ruled by little else. Practical men, who believe themselves to be quite exempt from any intellectual influences, are usually the slaves of some defunct economist.

—John Maynard Keynes
The General Theory of Employment, Interest, and Money, 1936.

British economist John Maynard Keynes explained the causes for capitalist problems of the first half of the 20th century, and offered cures that seemed fairly effective. But changes in the world economy have made Keynesian theory obsolete. Today capitalist economists are struggling to understand the present economy before the world plunges into another war or great depression. Photo: Library of Congress

So far, no new Keynes has appeared on the horizon to set forth a model which suggests politically viable solutions for our current economic woes. We can only hope that a new Keynes doesn't wait 10 years to come up with the needed theory. None of us relishes the idea of living through another Great Depression and world war.

There are three causes making the Keynesian model obsolete for our economy:

First, in the last 25 years there has been a significant increase in monopoly power over practically all markets. The result is that prices and wages have become increasingly resistant to downward pressure. Monopoly power in the more recent past has progressed to the point where prices not only do not fall in response to a decrease in demand—they very often actually rise.

Second, the Employment Act of 1946 committed the U.S. government to maintaining a high level of employment. This commitment seems so politically entrenched that it is unlikely that politicians could permit a recession of the depth or length necessary to squeeze inflation out of the economy. More probably they will ensure a significant amount of aggregate demand, regardless of the inflationary costs.

The MNC is responsible for the third underlying reason why the Keynesian model no longer works. Due to the increasing economic importance of multinationals, U.S. policy-makers increasingly are forced to give more weight to international stability than to domestic unemployment.

Shifting our attention to the problems of international stability, we note that the institutional and power relations which promised to regulate and control the international economy have broken down. The system which developed after World War II was based upon the U.S. playing three roles in the world economy: First, it was the largest trading nation. The U.S. and the other industrialized capitalist nations agreed on a set of rules for trading that were outlined in GATT (The General Agreements on Tariffs and Trade). These rules were, obviously and not surprisingly, beneficial to the people who drew them up—the industrialized capitalist countries. But the OPEC countries have demonstrated the fragility of these rules by using trade both as an instrument of war and as an instrument for bringing about a massive redistribution of income, wealth, and power from the industrialized capitalist countries to the oil-producing countries. It is likely that other raw materials producers will eventually follow suit. Even the U.S. itself has put export controls on soybeans. Thus, *de facto*, GATT has largely broken down and there are no generally accepted rules for international trade.

The second role for the U.S. was that of the world's major banker. The international monetary system established at the end of World War II was based on fixed exchange rates managed in large part by the U.S. and other industrialized capitalist countries. The dollar came to be the principal world currency, and the need for an expanding world currency was met in part by deficits in the U.S. balance of payments. The U.S. spent more abroad than it took in, and other countries kept the dollars and used them as reserves for their own currency. The funds held in this completely unregulated Eurodollar market now exceed $300 billion and pose a great threat to the stability of the international economy.

When President Nixon dropped the international gold backing for the dollar in 1971, the U.S. dollar ceased to play its former role as the primary international currency. The U.S. is no longer able to call the shots as the world's banker, but no new system has emerged and no agreed-upon rules of the game exist.

The third role played by the U.S. was that of the world's largest investor. The U.S. made the rules for its MNCs and multinational banks; other capitalist countries, lacking adequate capital, generally accepted U.S. investments on U.S. terms. But now Western European and Japanese MNCs are increasingly investing abroad, even in the U.S., and the OPEC countries have joined in. The U.S. has become uneasy at the prospect of foreigners owning key American firms, but its diminished leadership role makes it difficult to do much to stop foreigners from buying up America. If the U.S. restricted the realm in which foreigners might invest in the U.S., foreign countries would surely retaliate against American investments abroad.

What are the potential options for dealing with the problems presented by the globalization of capitalism under the driving force of the multinational corporation? The present system seems so unstable that it may provoke investment wars. How can capitalism avoid the seemingly inevitable chaos? Among the options that have been proposed are:

1. **Give the MNCs sovereignty.** They would join the nation-states as equal partners. The President of Dow Chemical went far along this line of reasoning when he argued that his company should buy and locate its corporate headquarters on an unclaimed island—so that it would not be responsible to any nation-state.

2. **Regulate the MNCs through world government.** Some proponents of this approach are encouraged by the recent U.N. conference on control of the sea and its resources as a step in this direction. Some MNCs have themselves expressed the need for some form of world government regulation. They realize that the present international capitalist system requires some type of agreed-upon rules and regulations and governmental intervention from an international body. Some corporate leaders would point to the experience of the 1930s when capitalism broke down in the U.S. and Western Europe and was only revived and sustained by massive governmental intervention. They see the same need on an international scale today.

3. **Regulate the MNCs through regional or special interest groups or blocs of nations.** One could think of the Organization of Petroleum Exporting Countries (OPEC) as one such attempt,

although it is not yet clear that the OPEC countries are regulating the oil companies so much as they are joining them in plundering the consumers of oil around the world. Another example of this approach is the Andean Pact nations of South America which have been trying to come up with a common position in their relationships vis-a-vis the MNCs.

4. **Regulate the MNCs through an international condominium, i.e., joint sovereignty by two or more nations.** Perhaps the nations of Western Europe and Japan will get together with the United States to establish policies which the MNCs must follow. The OECD Committee on Investment and Multinational Enterprise is striving for this sort of solution.

5. **Develop countervailing power through the growth of multinational unions.** These unions would represent all the workers employed by the MNC worldwide and would be able to block efforts to shift production from one country to another to minimize wage costs, break strikes, etc. In Denmark and Sweden, there seems to be a movement toward worker self-management. There are discussions of using the assets of the pension funds in Sweden to buy out the Swedish capitalists, to pay them off with interest-bearing bonds and to turn over management of Swedish industry to the workers in those industries. The workers would then elect workers' councils which would elect management. Since 1973, the membership of boards of all Swedish corporations must, by law, include two representatives elected by the workers. It is hard to know how this will affect the Swedish economy and the Swedish MNCs. But since Sweden has so often been the pace-setter for other capitalist countries, this is a development to be studied very carefully.

6. **Attempt to re-establish U.S. hegemony and control of the mechanism of the international economy.** Discussions are being held on the possibility of breaking the oil cartel, of re-establishing fixed exchange rates and of re-establishing U.S. competitive advantage vis-a-vis the West European and Japanese MNCs. However, it is unclear as to what might be done in terms of concrete measures to strengthen the U.S. position.

Of course, many question the wisdom of any regulation at all. They deny that the world's present course will lead to chaos, and thus they favor a status quo or "do nothing" policy. They argue that there are two kinds of dominant and powerful institutions at work in the world today—the nation-states and the multinational corporations. They ask which is the more dynamic institution? Which is more creative? Which is doing more to enhance human welfare? With which would you wish to identify? It is not clear to many observers that the multinationals come off second best in this comparison.

The technological dynamism of the MNCs is indeed something to be reckoned with, and if technological change is the catalyst for social change, then the MNC promises to be the transforming vehicle of the age. Some proponents of leaving the MNCs unfettered argue that the anti-capitalist, anti-growth, and anti-technology groups today can be compared to the utopian dreamers of the 19th century who established the Brook Farm and Oneida utopian communities. These experiments failed and had little if any influence on the technological dynamism of the capitalist firms that transformed North America in the 19th century.

An analogy can be drawn between the MNCs of today and the large capitalist firms of the late 19th and early 20th centuries, such as Standard Oil, American Can, U.S. Steel, and American Tobacco. At the end of the 19th century, many people and interests opposed the growth and expansion of these large firms. Legislation was passed in the United States to regulate them—the Interstate Commerce Act, the Sherman Act, the Clayton Act, etc. European countries generally did not pass such anti-trust legislation, yet there is little difference in the way capitalist firms developed in Western Europe and the United States.

The giant corporations transformed the U.S. economy just as they transformed the economies of Western Europe and, later, Japan. Proponents of an essentially laissez-faire position argue that the multinationals will similarly transform the economies of the underdeveloped countries as well, and perhaps even the socialist countries. Some observers argue that the Soviet model of development is essentially a state capitalist model, adapted to purposes of rapid development. Another way of putting this would be to view the Soviet Union as going through a stage comparable to mercantilism in Europe; now nearing the end of that stage, the Soviet Union stands poised and ready to take the last steps necessary to join the capitalist countries. In this view, the Soviet Union is ready to learn the lessons of Adam Smith concerning the virtues of private property and competitive markets.

Viewed from this vantage point, the Smithian vision appears alive and well, vigorous and dynamic. The alleged problems are merely bumps in the road of capitalist progress. Capitalism, rather than declining, is actually gaining speed in its conquest of the world. And those who anticipate the death-knell of capitalism merely fail to see the road continuing on the other side of the bumps.

Prospects for Marx's Vision

Karl Marx thought that capitalism was merely a necessary stage in the progress of history and that the demise of capitalism was imminent. Although the international capitalist system appears quite dynamic, many Marxist observers remain convinced that it is emitting its last gasps. In the Marxian view, the 19th century was the heyday for capitalism, but the 20th century belongs to socialism.

The ineptitude of the capitalist countries in getting themselves involved in World War I paved the way for the triumph of socialism in Russia. The still greater chaos generated by World War II made it possible to establish socialism in China. And, in the eyes of many observers, the momentum gained by the establishment of socialism in these two giant countries has made socialism in the Third World seem inevitable.

In particular, the development of China presents a very attractive alternative to many in underdeveloped countries. For centuries, Westerners had thought that there would always be the pathetic and hopelessly poor in China. Yet in a short 25 years China seems to have transcended its historical plight.

Karl Marx envisioned a society in which man does meaningful work and lives in harmony with his neighbors. But his disciples have often created large and repressive bureaucracies. Illustration: Kathy Sanderson
Copyright 1978 by World Future Society

With a very modest level of per capita income, China has been able to overcome problems of unemployment, hunger, poverty, illiteracy, and inadequate or nonexistent medical care and housing for its 800 million people. None of these problems has been solved or is even very far on its way to solution in any of the underdeveloped countries following a capitalist path. The Chinese experiment has attracted many admirers.

What is unique about the Chinese model? First, unlike the capitalist and Soviet experiences, development in China does not favor the cities over the rural areas. That is, agriculture is not being bled to subsidize urban industrialization. Instead, there is an attempt to bring about development so as to minimize rather than maximize city-country distinctions. Services and amenities such as the "bare-foot" doctors, teachers, and cultural events are spread throughout the countryside. The decentralized pattern of development has enabled China to avoid the social and psychological tensions which normally accompany rapid urbanization.

A second important characteristic of the Chinese approach is its emphasis on intermediate technology. The history of Western development has taught that a country must develop by utilizing the most advanced, sophisticated, and large-scale technology available. This has normally meant that development must initially result in a high rate of unemployment, exploitative wage rates, and an increasingly skewed distribution of income. China, on the other hand, has implemented only those forms of technology which promise to take maximum advantage of present resources, while simultaneously promoting desired social goals. In addition to some heavy industry, China has developed a small-scale and labor-intensive technology which has yielded full employment and a more equally distributed income.

A third characteristic of the Chinese development model is that it seems to be less threatening to the environment than the development models pursued in the West. There are several reasons for this: First, the wide geographical dispersion of development effort means that strains on the environment are widely dispersed. Second, small-scale, labor-intensive technology also means that demands on the environment are less concentrated. Third, by de-emphasizing the importance of markets, all costs—including those to the environment—are more likely to be given attention. Finally, by emphasizing social rather than individual consumption, relatively more importance is given to such public goods as clean air, clean rivers and lakes, etc.

The fourth characteristic of the Chinese development model is its great suc-

Farm commune in mainland China is run by people striving to realize the vision of Karl Marx. These rice paddies are part of the model commune at Tachai in the Shansi province.
Photo: H. Henle, U.N. Food and Agriculture Organization

cess in inspiring and mobilizing the people. Studies abound on the positive relationship between motivation and productivity, and this is by far the most striking characteristic of the Chinese experience. Bureaucrats and intellectuals are thought to serve the people. "Elite" cadres work side-by-side with workers and peasants for periods of time. In addition, positions of responsibility and admission to universities are obtained more on the bases of work dedication and peer-group selection than on the bases of class background and purely intellectual endowments. The result is to encourage work diligence and cooperation. People are encouraged to be self-reliant and to share. Evidence indicates that everyone is fed, clothed, housed and medically cared for. Although China is a poor country, there is no poverty.

But aside from the Chinese experience, there are many other reasons why the Marxist vision might be the best guide for our future history. For instance, the ability of the Vietcong and the Khmer Rouge (with the aid of the U.S.S.R., North Vietnam, and China) to resist the largest and the most powerful military machine in all history has given great encouragement to socialists around the world. Furthermore, the socialist vision has come to be shared by many of the world's intellectuals, both in the developed and underdeveloped countries. Marx, Lenin, Mao, Fanon, Sartre, and Che Guevara have developed a significant body of socialist literature to inspire revolutionaries everywhere.

The mass movements which have sprung up around the world in this century are socialist in nature. For the most part, the causes for which people have been mobilized and for which they have given their blood have been socialist causes. No mass movement of which we're aware has as its slogan "Build Capitalism!" This is not to say that there aren't people who are fighting in defense of capitalism—but not as a mass movement of people.

These mass movements seem to thrive on the economic woes of the capitalist world. As the capitalist economies become increasingly interdependent, international economic instability comes more and more to affect individual capitalist economies, and hence the power structures within individual countries. The recent socialist triumphs in Angola, Mozambique, Portugal, and Ethiopia may have been triggered in some part by the international economic instabilities of the past few years. Socialist parties are gaining influence in France, Italy, and other capitalist nations because the socialist countries are not experiencing the unemployment, inflation, and balance of payments problems that are plaguing the capitalist countries.

The Marxist vision is one of unalienated people working and living together in egalitarian harmony, not just with each other, but with nature as well. Yet in many respects the trend in many so-called socialist countries—especially those in Eastern Europe—works against this vision. This can be seen most clearly in the extent to which these societies have become hierarchical. In the political sphere, this has meant government by hierarchic rather than democratic principles. Instead of decentralized participatory decision-making, large centralized bureaucracies wield ultimate

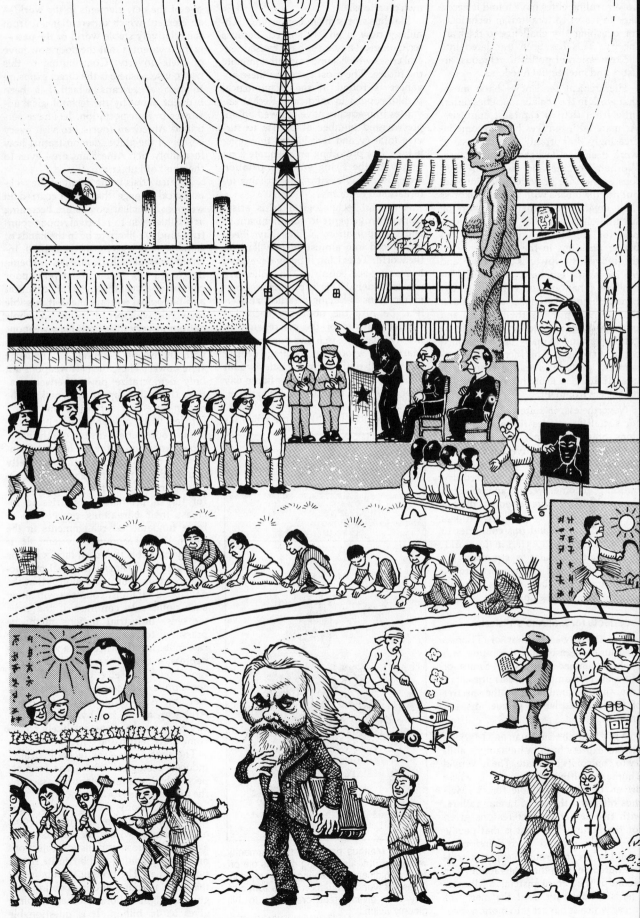

Karl Marx's Vision

Drawing: Tom Chalkley

power. Striving to legitimate this power, ruling elites have found it necessary to resort to totalitarian techniques for quashing any challenge to their authority. This has been translated into the repression of political, religious, artistic, and intellectual freedoms.

Hierarchical tendencies have meant that work in the socialist societies differs little from that in capitalist countries. As material incentives have become increasingly important, the process of work itself has declined in importance. Workers become alienated from their jobs as they are provided with incomes but not the means with which to express their creativity. Rather than working harmoniously together, workers compete for greater material rewards and higher positions in the hierarchy. And the movement towards hierarchy and the increasing emphasis on material incentives enhances, and is enhanced by, consumerism. The capitalist contention that "consumption is the sole end and purpose of all production" seems to be gaining ground in many of the so-called socialist societies. This increasingly consumerist attitude gives the economy a goal of limitless growth which bodes ill for the environment.

Nevertheless, in spite of the tendency for socialist societies to become something other than what was hoped for, the Marxist vision is alive and well. The socialists have identified themselves with those who are calling for a redistribution of income, wealth, and power in the world. They have supported the call for a new and more just international economic system and this continues to win them many supporters in the world. The socialist impulse is strong in the world today, and there appear to be many more Russias, Chinas, Cubas, and Vietnams on the horizon.

Prospects for Malthus's Vision

The third vision—that of Thomas Malthus—suggests that the future will be far grimmer than either Smith or Marx ever dreamed. Malthus presents a cruel future, dominated by the spectres of famine, pestilence, plague, disease, and war.

While both the Smithian and Marxian visions express faith in humanity's ability to control its own fate, The Reverend Thomas Malthus envisioned a world driven by uncontrollable forces. Malthus offered a theory of human failure, with two rather distinct reasons given for the failure: The first is that people are simply wicked and therefore it would be preposterous to expect a positive outcome from their interaction. The second is the "Frankensteinian Monster Thesis"—humanity is at the mercy of forces which it has set into motion; people simply do not possess sufficient

awareness and strength to control their own creations.

Malthus's pessimism concerning technology now is widely shared, because technological advances have caused several crises which some say will dominate the future. The most ironic of these advances is found in the technological breakthroughs in medicine. Recent advances in medicine have allowed an unprecedented number of people to survive infancy and live longer than ever before. But providing an adequate food supply to the rising world population seems impossible within the existing international economy.

A second technological crisis arises from improvements in communications and transportation. Radios have been introduced into almost every village in the world. Television is being developed in many poor countries, and films are shown widely. This explosion in communications is having a radicalizing effect, because the poor are becoming painfully aware of the discrepancy in life-styles among rich and poor nations. Marx once wrote that a cottage doesn't seem small until a great castle is built beside it. The peasant comes home day after day and rejoices in his cottage. When a castle arises, the peasant says, "Why should I live like a pig when it's

Thomas Malthus predicted that humanity will breed until its teeming millions die off from war, disease, and hunger. The rapid increase of world population in the 20th century has given great credibility to his gloomy vision.
Illustration: Kathy Sanderson
Copyright 1978 by World Future Society

possible to live so much better?" Thus one of the new elements in the world—an element which differentiates it from the relatively stable world of the past—is the awareness that the poor now have of their poverty. Contributing to this new consciousness is the direct exposure to rich Americans which has been brought about by the technological advances in transportation. Jets have permitted American tourists to visit every corner of the globe, demonstrating how incredibly rich Americans are—even to the point of vulgarity.

A third crisis is the result of the technological change that has occurred in weapons. Nuclear bombs are becoming accessible even to relatively poor countries, and are likely to be in the hands of some 30 countries by the year 2000. Intercontinental ballistic missiles are being developed by some relatively poor countries. Breakthroughs in chemical and biological warfare make it possible to wreak widespread havoc on whole nations at very little cost. New weapons technology will provide terrorist groups with increasing potential to challenge state power. Thus, the new weapons not only democratize power between nations; they also appear to be making the nation-state less defensible and therefore less viable as a political unit.

The fourth crisis arises from the enormous expansion in the use of modern industrial technology, which has greatly increased the need for energy. The resulting energy crisis has pointed the way for the oil-producing countries to increase their bargaining power and to force fundamental realignments in the international economic system. It is highly probable that such tactics will be emulated by other raw material-producing countries, but it is doubtful that the developed capitalist countries will allow such policies to continue. If the crisis worsens, industrial nations might be pressured to use force to take over the raw materials they need. If a worldwide depression comes, there will be an enormous push to seize the oil—through some pretext, of course: an Arab-Israeli war, an Arab-Iranian war, an Arab-Arab war, a coup in Libya, etc. As scarcity increases, nations are likely to become more selfish and nationalistic.

The sixth crisis—the technologically-induced ecological crisis—has four aspects which are important for assessing the future of the world economy:

1. **Food.** Many demographers argue that world population is going to double and re-double within the next century, even if the most optimistic projections on family planning and birthrate reduction are met. The present population of the earth is four billion; doubling that gives us eight billion; another doubling gives us 16 billion. It is questionable whether we can even feed that many

Children at a day care center in Bangladesh.

Photo: United Nations

people, much less increase their level of consumption of other goods. Optimists point out that we can count on more green revolutions, hydroponics, and synthetic foods to feed us. However, even if we do manage to feed ourselves, the cost in lost liberty may be exceedingly high. India's actions in implementing forced sterilization may only hint at what lies ahead.

2. **Energy.** Events of recent years have also heightened our awareness of the scarcity of energy. There is serious concern as to whether we will continue to have sufficient fuel to propel industrial growth. Projections for petroleum show demand increasing at the rate of 10% per year. Experts project that at the present rate of industrial growth, known and foreseeable oil reserves will be exhausted by the end of this century. We can assume that the estimates of reserves are low; perhaps we really have four times as much oil in the ground as the experts project. But even that would only allow us to keep on using oil for an additional 14 years at present rates of

growth. Again the technocrats argue that we will find alternative energy sources. They cite the disappearance of wood and its replacement by coal, which was in turn replaced by oil, and now they confidently predict oil will be replaced by atomic, thermal, solar or yet unknown forms of energy. However, even if they are right, there are still the very serious problems of heat and wastes to be dealt with before such happy solutions really become viable.

3. **Metals.** Experts tell us that a vast number of essential metals are simply not going to be available to support continued industrial growth. Some projections suggest that many of these metals (silver, gold, copper, lead, platinum, tin and zinc) will simply be unavailable within 20 years, if present rates of use continue. Of course, there are optimists who contend that we will be capable of adjusting to such shortages. Technocrats assure us that technology will devise synthetics for these scarce resources, citing the case of synthetic rub-

ber in World War II. And market economists argue that as scarcity pushes the prices of resources up, producers will substitute other materials for those that are scarce, while consumers will shift their consumption from resource-using goods to services—more plays, concerts and psychiatrists, fewer cars and planes (indeed, we can already observe a shift to services in American consumption patterns). Nevertheless, it is difficult to imagine such adjustments occurring without substantial social disruptions.

4. **Waste disposal.** The fourth aspect of the ecological crisis concerns our capacity to dispose of the wastes which are by-products of our continued economic growth. The earth, air, and water are heavily polluted now and we have no way of knowing when the level of pollution may make future human life on the planet impossible. For instance, there is growing evidence that pollution is causing irrevocable damage to our seas; that we are destroying our atmosphere's ability to shield us from carcinogenic ultraviolet rays; and that we might be changing the earth's climatic conditions. Of course, the technocrats optimistically respond that non-polluting technologies will be developed and re-cycling can take care of our problems.

When we turn our attention from the relationship between technology and the ecological crisis to the institutions available for dealing with the crisis, it is difficult to be optimistic. Western institutions have been built on the attitude that nature is an adversary to be tamed and dominated. Indeed, the spread of this attitude was undoubtedly a key factor in the phenomenal growth and development of the West in the past four or five centuries. Yet, ironically, we seem to have reached a juncture where the persistence of this attitude threatens our very survival. Our institutions operate as if nature's bounty were boundless. Hierarchy, inequality, and alienating work are made socially palatable by the promise of more material wealth for everyone. Indeed, Adam Smith's famous dictum that "Consumption is the sole end and purpose of production" appears to have been changed to: "Consumption is the sole end and purpose of life." Hierarchy, inequality, and boring jobs are tolerated because practically everyone can have more income with which to buy "the good things in life." Non-material values such as a sense of community, political participation and clean and safe neighborhoods are also tossed into the trade. For a sense of identity, purpose, or life goal, all that many people have left is consumption. Understandably, they now believe that their societies can only be kept going by creating an ever-increasing flow of goods and services. If, for ecological reasons, economic growth were halted or drastically slowed, political turmoil would likely follow. Therefore, for reasons of domestic social stability, it seems unlikely that politicians will be capable of implementing significant measures to avert further ecological deterioration.

On an international plane, the existing institutional framework offers little hope for dealing successfully with the ecology problem. In their suspicious and hostile international environment, nations can ill afford to limit technological change and economic growth. The technologically and economically weaker nations are vulnerable to military conquest and domination by the stronger nations. Consequently, for mere survival, nations see themselves with no choice but to forge ahead at full speed. International agreements to limit ecologically destructive activities, would likely be honored only in the breach. And the poorer nations have yet an additional reason to resist international accords to save the environment. The rich countries greatly benefited by being able to pollute freely during their industrialization. Understandably, the poor nations believe that without the same advantage their potential for joining the industrialized countries would be severely restricted. Even if international ecological accords can be agreed upon, the problem of effectively enforcing them seems virtually insurmountable.

Consequently, world ecological balance seems to require an end to the na-

Indian woman toils to grow the rice she needs to survive. The gloomy vision of Thomas Malthus is alive and well in most Third World countries.

Photo: Carl Purcell, Agency for International Development

tion-state system as we know it. We are now coming to realize that we have only one worldwide energy supply, only one worldwide food supply, and only one biosphere in which to dump our wastes. Our very survival requires that we think in global terms rather than in terms of nation-states. Just as the invention of gunpowder and artillery made the city-state indefensible in an early age, so has technological change today made the nation-state an anachronism, ready to be dumped into the dustbin of history. But recent history gives us little reason to expect an end to the nation-state. If anything, nationalism is on the upsurge; around the globe, nations strive to assert their independence and sovereignty. Perhaps just as the city-state was ended through violence, only violence can bring an end to the nation-state. But an unleashing of today's weapons might end all human life as well as nation-states! We may be trapped between an ecological apocalypse on the one hand and nuclear holocaust on the other.

So perhaps the most likely alternative for the future is the Malthusian spectre. The forces which humanity has set into motion seem beyond control. We appear to be incapable of limiting our population growth or of providing for even the basic needs of our population. We appear to be transforming the earth so that it is becoming hostile to human life. We threaten ourselves with total annihilation. The most materially privileged among us appear to suffer increasingly from a lack of purpose—a collapse of spiritual values. We are haunted by the prospect that should humanity survive, it will do so in a sterile and regimented world. Understandably then, to many, the Malthusian spectre seems perhaps the most likely alternative future of all.

Toward a New Vision

In reflecting on these three alternative futures, one cannot help feeling that yet undefined alternatives might be lurking on the horizon. The three alternatives which we have outlined evolved out of an essentially Western historical context, and were formulated during the progress-tinged rationality of the Enlightenment. (Malthus did not stand outside of this context, rather he reacted against an aspect of it.) But consciousness, like institutions, is in constant flux. We now recognize that human consciousness reflects the prevailing institutions and material conditions. We also admit to the power of human consciousness to transform our institutions and material conditions. In the past, institutions and material conditions seem to have been dominant in determining the course of history, but social consciousness might possibly take over that role in the future. Such a hope has always motivated the more optimistic visionaries.

History offers few instances in which a new social consciousness has sprung not from changing material conditions, but rather from a central human or social purpose. But one instance is the Chinese revolution. The Chinese appear to be engaged in the most massive social experiment ever. They are attempting to elevate social consciousness into command of their society's future. The Chinese experiment represents a new dimension in social freedom: the ability of one-quarter of humanity to transcend—through cultural revolutions—the dictates of their socio-economic institutions. Whether such social freedom can be made consonant with the individual freedom which Westerners have sought and cherished remains an open question. But if the Chinese experiment succeeds, we will have seen the force of social consciousness in changing the course of history.

But even if social consciousness succeeds in transforming societies, there seems to be no compelling reason to expect it to function for greater human welfare. Using rational social organization, humanity may be on the technological brink of solving the problem of insecurity caused by the niggardliness of nature, but that same technology threatens to abet ever more complete forms of human enslavement. If current technology were ever to fall into the hands of truly demonic forces, then nightmares far surpassing those envisioned by George Orwell could await humanity. Even without such demons, increasing population and technological sophistication require ever greater social control. Such control must be carried out through the proliferation of rules and other organizational mechanisms that constrain individual freedom.

But we can also look at our prospects more optimistically, from yet another perspective. People are becoming increasingly aware of our planet's smallness. Unlike the progress of the past, which has been based on looking outward to new external frontiers, the progress of the future might be based on looking inward—to creating social institutions which provide an environment supportive of self and social realization. As individuals, rather than striving for knowledge with which to exert ever greater control over the world about us, perhaps we will progressively redirect our attentions inward toward discovery and mastery of ourselves.

The world today differs dramatically from the world that moulded the visions of our three great economists. Yet their visions remain surprisingly powerful and still have the power to shape our thinking about the future. In the years to come, however, perhaps new visionaries will appear that will offer more appealing and realistic concepts to help us interpret our future prospects. ❧

Thomas Malthus's Vision

HOSPI[TAL]

Drawing: Tom Chalkley

You Will Think This a Dream
A 1915 vision of tomorrow

by Charles P. Steinmetz

Forecasts of things to come have sometimes been startlingly correct—and sometimes ludicrously wrong. THE FUTURIST here reproduces a forecast made in the September 1915 issue of The Ladies' Home Journal, by Charles P. Steinmetz, one of the greatest scientists and inventors of his time.

Following Steinmetz's article is a commentary by Joseph Martino, Technological Forecasting Editor of THE FUTURIST, who finds the 1915 effort "a remarkable piece of forecasting."

THE time is coming when the cost of electricity will be infinitely lower than now, and when that time comes it will revolutionize all our domestic life.

First of all, when electricity becomes universally used, it will be against the law to have a fire of any kind within the city limits. The Government will not allow fires because they are dangerous, dirty and insanitary: dangerous because of conflagrations, dirty because of handling the coal and ashes, and insanitary because of the smoke and gases in the air. No fires will mean no cellar furnaces, no kitchen ranges, no illumination by gas, no steam-power plants, no gas engines.

When we use nothing but electrical power for heating as well as for other purposes the supply will come through transmission lines from big central stations of many million horse power. These stations will be located wherever power is available, such as at waterfalls, coal mines and oil and gas wells. This will do away with the wasteful process of hauling coal from the mines to the relatively small power houses scattered all over the country.

It may be that at the coal mines, instead of taking out the coal and burning it in the way we do now, steam power will be generated in the mine itself by setting the coal in the veins on fire. No—this is not beyond the dream of possibility. It has already been seriously proposed by an eminent English scientist.

Charles P. Steinmetz (1865-1923) served as Chief Consulting Engineer of the General Electric Company for many years. He is considered, along with Thomas Edison, to be one of the fathers of the technology used by modern electric utilities.

Startling will be the changes effected by such a supply of electricity. At present, when we wish to keep warm in cold weather, we use a furnace fire, steam heat, stoves, open fireplaces and other unsatisfactory and insanitary methods. At other times in the year, when the temperature is above normal, we are helpless and have to suffer.

As a matter of fact, when the weather is very cold our extremely crude method of heating does not give us a desirable and uniform temperature; and, besides, we are bothered by dirt and ashes and by gases and the nuisance of taking care of fires.

Nothing could be of more trouble than a furnace fire, because the heat energy from coal is very difficult to control. It takes much time and attention to keep the fires regulated.

Heating and Cooling Our Houses at Will

WHEN heating is done electrically, if I want seventy degrees in my home I shall set the thermostat at seventy and the temperature will not rise above that point. This temperature will be maintained

---

Living room of the future: A 1911 conception. Four years before Charles Steinmetz's article was published, artist Harry Grant Dart offered this view of things to come. The gentleman in the drawing pushes a button on his Observiscope to see his son Willie (revealed in an amorous pose). A wind-up mechanical butler on wheels waits with a decanter and glass. Other amenities include air from Pike's Peak, Newport, and Atlantic City as well as stored sunlight. This drawing, from the New York Public Library, appears in the PERPETUAL CALENDAR OF THE FUTURE (1975-2001) prepared by Future Research Associates. The calendar, which can be used up to the year 2001, is available for $2.95 from the World Future Society's book service.

uniformly without regard to the temperature outside.

If it is very cold electric heaters will hold the temperature at seventy. If it should be ninety or one hundred degrees outside, the same electrical apparatus will cool the air inside. In this way we shall have a uniform temperature in our homes throughout the year.

Besides temperature, we have to suffer from humidity, or from dryness of the air. This is especially true with the present-day furnace. With electric equipment we shall be able to control this and have the humidity normal at all times. This electric equipment will have an absolutely automatic control of both temperature and humidity.

Ventilation doesn't exist in the average home today. At present we have to depend upon the windows and doorways, or we turn on an electric fan to blow the bad air out. When electricity is developed we shall have apparatus that will destroy the bad air, bring fresh air into the home, and, when the air outside is not sufficiently invigorating, automatically arrange a distribution of ozone. We shall constantly have good, fresh, pure air indoors.

When We Shall Cook on the Table

OF COURSE there will be no more coal or gas kitchen ranges. All cooking will be done by electricity. A great deal of our food will be cooked on the table, so that with the elimination of the coal stove the kitchen will be very small, compact and efficient.

Cooking by electricity will be very much more satisfactory and under perfect control. By adjusting the regulator the food will be perfectly cooked automatically.

For example, should the directions for baking a cake call for heat at a temperature of two hundred and eighty degrees for forty-five minutes, you would simply adjust your regulator to "280-45," and automatically the heat would rise to the temperature indicated and automatically turn off at the expiration of the time.

Hearing Concerts in Our Homes

THE telephone will be improved. If we want to hear a concert we shall not have to go out in the crowd and sit in an unventilated room. By means of the improved loudspeaking phones, we may listen to the concert in our homes. That will mean that unlimited numbers can listen to such concerts, even if they are living many miles away in small cities and villages.

With wireless telephones, if a great singer should be singing in an opera in some European capital, we should be able to listen to this opera in our own libraries in America. The new telephones will make it possible for millions of persons in moderate circumstances to hear the finest concerts in the world without crossing their thresholds.

With the motion picture and the talking machine perfectly synchronized, as they will be, it will not be necessary to go to the theater for our amusement. These machines will be made for use in the home. We can have the best and finest productions in this way. Both the films and records will be greatly improved.

Automobiles in Cellars

FOR local transportation the majority of people are now dependent upon rapid-transit systems or trolley cars. These require subways, elevated structures in the heart of the city, rails in most of our streets and almost an endless amount of noise. The automobile is very convenient. When fires are not allowed within city limits electric automobiles, bicycles and tricycles will be developed, and, on account of the low price, will be available to almost everyone.

These electric cars will be kept in our cellars or basements, where now we keep the furnace and the coal and ashes. We shall have a driveway going right under the house, and this will make a convenient place to store our cars in, from the big family or touring car to the small bicycle or tricycle. This will eliminate the need for garages. While the cars are in the basement they will have their batteries charged.

Evergreen Trees Will Grow in Our Cities

ALL these changes in our domestic life will revolutionize the appearance of our cities. In the first place, cities will become sanitary—no dirt, dust or smoke will be possible. The streets will be beautifully clean. There will be no reason for dust or dirt. Without fires, and with no animals for tractional labor, there will be no dust and dirt.

The atmosphere will be perfectly clear. Today it is bad enough in the city when only anthracite coal is burned, but in places where soft coal is used the people cannot see the sky on account of the smoke and gases in the air.

With clean, pure air we shall be able to raise evergreen pine trees in the city, and it is healthful to have pine trees where you live. There are no pine trees in cities now; all trees are deciduous. The reason for this is that trees and all plant life need air the same as human beings. With an evergreen tree the needles are the leaves or lungs. The dirt, gases and smoke that we now have in the air of our cities clog the breathing spaces in the needles, and in a few years the tree dies from suffocation. Evergreens have only one set of needles. The deciduous trees have a chance to live in cities because their leaves or lungs drop off each autumn and they get a fresh set each spring. That is their only salvation.

The industries in the city, of course, will be operated by electrical power, which means no dirt and smoke. The tendency will be to move all industries as near the source of supply of raw material as possible, the same as the power houses will be moved to the various sources of power.

The Cost of Living Will Be Less

NATURALLY, the question arises: "How will all these changes affect the cost of living?" In the first place, today the farmers are almost entirely dependent upon manual labor. With electrical energy available and with the application of scientific methods and the production of quantities of nitrogen fertilizer from the air—the same as is now being done in Sweden and Germany—the cost of raising food supplies will be very materially decreased. This should result in a corresponding decrease in the cost to the consumer.

The use of electricity will so facilitate labor that the hours of labor will be shorter. This means that workers will have more time to carry out their hobbies. Vegetable gardens and raising chickens are the outdoor hobbies of many men. These occupations bring returns to the home, and, as the work under these conditions is pleasant, the cost of food will be reduced.

Of course there will be many other hobbies that men will be following, and all kinds of articles will be produced as a result of this work. One man may enjoy making brass lamps by hand. After he has supplied his own home with lamps he may make some for his neighbors, who, in return, will furnish him with vegetables from their gardens, with eggs or with some articles which have been made as a result of their hobbies.

In some respects this will return us to the days of barter and trade, and it will be a good thing, because the articles will be produced very cheaply.

Turning Our Hobbies Into Money

WE OFTEN lose sight of the fact that when a man has a hobby and produces something as the result of that hobby the labor does not cost anything. Hobby labor is the cheapest labor in the world. It is also pleasure and recreation.

You will frequently see a man who has developed a hobby for raising chickens. He takes a lot of pleasure and pride in looking after all the work himself. He finds that raising chickens on a small scale is profitable. This is true, but the profit lies in the fact that the labor is cheap; it does not cost him anything. But he doesn't figure on this, and, thinking that the business itself is profitable, he invests in a larger plant, employs his labor—for which he has to pay—and then loses his money.

The production of a great many things by people carrying out their hobbies will greatly affect our economic life.

Another effect in the cost of living will be that, as the result of clean, pure air and even temperature in our homes, materials will have a very much longer life. Curtains and carpets will not have to be cleaned so frequently. This means less wear and tear.

Furniture will last almost indefinitely because of the even temperature and no excess humidity or very dry air to warp and crack the woodwork. The cost of renewals will be very greatly reduced and we can afford to pay more for our household goods in the first place. The standard in our homes will be raised.

Electricity Cost by Tax, Like Water

ELECTRICAL power will be used so generally that it is very likely the cost will be on the basis of a tax, like our water tax. For example, so much a plug, as we are now charged so much a faucet. It will be very cheap and it will not pay to install meters and have them read and keep the accounts in the offices of the electric companies, or in the Government building if the power is being generated by the municipality or the Government.

Today water is used universally and no one would think of making a charge to a friend or even a stranger for any amount of it. It will be the same with electricity. If you make a call in your electric vehicle the vehicle will be run into the friend's basement and the batteries will be charged while you are making your call. It won't make any difference whether you get your electric current from your friend's plug or from the plug in your own home—the tax will remain the same.

We Shall Live Easier but Better

WHILE making life very much more pleasant, easy and worth living, naturally the question will be raised: "Will not the human race degenerate because of the removal of so many means of resistance?" I think the contrary will be true. In the first place, human nature will always demand a change, and for recreation we shall go out into the wilderness and live like our ancestors, the same as many of us do now when we enjoy camp life; but even in camp now we have very many modern conveniences to make the life easier.

It does not reduce the physical ability and endurance of man to have him take the best possible care of himself. We have a splendid example of that today in the European war. Look at the physical power and endurance of the men who are spending and have spent so much time in the trenches. This sort of thing calls for far more endurance than any of the labors put upon the soldiers in Napoleon's army; and many of these men are clerks, industrial workers, college professors and professional men who are unaccustomed to the rigors of outdoor life.

Another example we have is the contrast between the street urchin and the boy of well-to-do parents. When it comes to a test of endurance, as in an athletic contest, the rich boy is almost always superior, because he has been well taken care of all his life.

The means for all these things are here now. No difficult scientific or engineering problems are presented. Of course, no one can predict exactly what is going to happen, because of new devices that may be invented. What I have said is based on what we have today. ■

On Charles P. Steinmetz as a Prophet

by Joseph P. Martino

The Technological Forecasting Editor of THE FUTURIST finds much to praise in the 1915 forecast.

Steinmetz's 1915 prophecy must certainly be given high marks for boldness. However, Steinmetz, a towering genius in the electrical engineering field, made a career of bold innovation. Indeed, in this prophecy, he is simply applying his bold vision of the potential of electricity to the mundane needs of the household. How well did he do, with his combination of knowledge and boldness?

His opening prophecies seem to be grossly in error. We still have fires in cities, and power plants are located near the consumer,

not near the source of fuel. It turns out that electricity is one of the most expensive forms of energy to transport. Not only are the facilities (high-tension lines) expensive, but the losses are high. From the overall economic standpoint, it is cheaper to transport energy in the form of coal or oil from the source to city, than to transport energy in the form of electricity the same distance. Moreover, Steinmetz did not foresee natural gas whose price was artificially held down by government action, thus providing a clean and low-

direct-cost alternative to electrical heating (as well as leading inevitably to today's shortages of natural gas).

From there on, however, his performance improves dramatically. While not all houses are electrically air-conditioned, we are well on our way to that stage. Cooking at the table is already a possibility, with electric hotplates, etc. Ovens are too big and bulky to be portable, because of the necessary insulation, hence the electric (or gas) range has not vanished. Such ranges, however, have for years had automatic controls of varying degrees of sophistication. We do indeed have concerts in the home. While operas and orchestra performances have been broadcast "live" by radio, it turns out that the recordings are more convenient and permit listening at will. The electric car is still awaiting adequate battery technology, but that now seems to be only a matter of time. Overall, the cost of living has declined as a result of cheap energy, including electricity.

Steinmetz's final forecast—that hobbies would be converted to useful production through barter—again misses the mark widely. Here he evidently overlooked the fact that money was invented simply because barter was so inconvenient and undesirable. Society is not now going to go back and "uninvent" it.

Overall, Steinmetz can be given credit for accuracy where his prophecies depended largely on technological feasibility. Where economics entered the picture, however, he seems to have gone badly astray. Perhaps this is simply one more illustration that technology is driven by economics, not vice versa, and the would-be technological forecaster must take economic feasibility and competition among technical approaches into account.

Col. Joseph P. Martino, Technological Forecasting Editor of THE FUTURIST, is Director, Engineering Standardization, Defense Supply Agency, Defense Electronics Supply Center, Dayton, Ohio 45444.

Charles P. Steinmetz, who ranks with Thomas Edison as one of the greatest inventors of his time, envisioned future cities powered almost entirely by electricity. He predicted that air conditioning and electric cars would become commonplace, and that city dwellers would enjoy pure, clean air.

The Future in Retrospect
The Foreseeable Future Revisited

Sir George Paget Thomson, author of *The Foreseeable Future*, died in September at the age of 83. Sir George won the Nobel prize in physics in 1937 for his work on the diffraction of electronics in crystals. He was the son of another Nobel laureate, Sir J. J. Thomson, the discoverer of the electron.

Photo by Edward Leigh

by Robert W. Prehoda

In 1955 the Nobel prize-winning British physicist Sir George Thomson published a book forecasting future technological developments. Recently, another technological forecaster, Robert W. Prehoda, examined the book to see how Thomson's forecasts are faring. In the following review, Prehoda reports that the Briton's decades-old forecasts have generally turned out to be remarkably accurate, with a few noteworthy exceptions.

Those of us engaged in the broad arena of futures studies are basically trying to refine more accurate means of projecting critical trends and delineating the desirable options that can be tomorrow's reality if the requisite changes in policy and priorities are made today. There is no sure guide to enduring value except time and hindsight, and this dictum is absolute in evaluating forecasting methodologies. Consequently, a review of past forecasts provides unique insights that may allow the emerging art of futures studies to evolve into a more precise discipline.

A book that can be classified as the first systematic approach to technological forecasting was published in 1955. After 20 years, Sir George Thomson's *The Foreseeable Future* remains a work of stunning brilliance offering insight into the favorable options open to humanity through selective refinement made possible by science. He began with the assumption that "technology is governed by scientific principles, some of which are understood, and there is accordingly a basis for prediction ... I have supposed that developments which do not contradict known principles and which have an obvious utility will in fact be made, probably in the next hundred years. No doubt there will be discoveries which will transcend what now appear major impossibilities, but these are unpredictable, and so are the practical developments which will follow from them."

The reason Sir George restricted his forecast chiefly to the future of technology was his conclusion that "sociology has still to find its Newton, let alone its Planck, and prediction is guesswork." Remarkably accurate projections of the social consequences of technology, however, are included in the book.

Erred on Population

In revisiting *The Foreseeable Future*, and carefully analyzing each forecast, the reader finds only one area where contemporary reality represents a significant departure from what the book anticipated: "Careful estimates suggest that the population may be expected to rise from its present 2.5 billion to 6 or even 8 billion by 2050." We now know that the global population has exploded, reaching 4 billion in 1975, and it will expand to the 6 billion level by 1994 if present trends are not changed by birthrate reduction or famine. However, Sir George also wrote: "One of the hardest things possible to predict is the course of population." After analyzing the failure of demographic projections made in the decades prior to 1955, he concluded that "scientific prediction becomes impossible" in the population area.

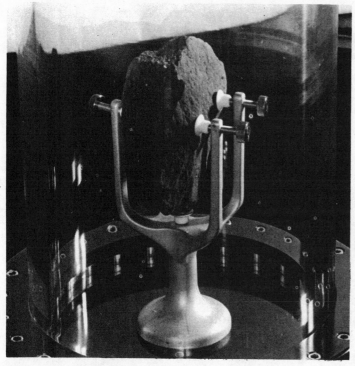

Space exploration has occurred much more rapidly than Sir George Thomson forecast in 1955, reviewer Prehoda reports. Except for timing, however, Thomson's astronautics forecast was quite accurate. Rock from the moon was displayed at the Smithsonian Institution in Washington, D.C., in 1970, far sooner than Thomson imagined. Still in the future are large space bases like the orbiting laboratory shown in an artist's conception at right.   Photo: NASA

In fairness to Thomson, it must be pointed out that he simply summarized population data believed to be correct in 1955. Demographers then said that world population was "increasing by about 25 million a year." The rate of increase was probably much higher at that time, and such uncertainty is reflected in the fact that authoritative estimates for global population increase in 1975 range between 70 and 90 million. I have reviewed countless demographic forecasts, and every one written before 1960 has been in error on the low side, usually by a considerable margin.

Breakthroughs in plant genetics were foreseen, and what is now called the Green Revolution has developed in the precise form anticipated by Sir George. He also recognized the Malthusian implications of population growth and warned that the citizens of India, Indonesia, China, and Africa "probably soon will be pressing hard on the immediately available food supplies."

The remarkable accuracy of Thomson's technological forecasts can be explained by the fact that he devised a systematic approach to replace, or at least improve, the "educated guess" intuition of traditional prognostication. In making future projections, he observed:

"It is because major discoveries are likely to be based on scientific principles rather than on mechanical ingenuity, and because these principles have limitations, that it is reasonable to hope to be able to predict in a general way the trend which these discoveries will have. For this reason, it may not be too rash to regard certain kinds of technical progress as foreseeable, though one will certainly miss a great deal."

"Principles of Impotence" Offer Key

Sir George points out that scientific principles are frequently "principles of impotence." They say that certain things *cannot* be done, but they do not say that everything else *can*, for that would imply that there are no more fundamental principles to discover. From the discoveries of the past 300 years, he identified eight principles based on our current understanding of the laws of nature which can aptly be called "principles of impotence." They include restrictions such as the speed-of-light barrier, the second law of thermodynamics, and the conservation of mass and energy.

The validity of this forecasting methodology is demonstrated by the fact that only one of these eight principles of impotence has been modified since 1955. This year's discovery of the magnetic monopole means that magnetic charges need not be inseparable north and south poles on the same body. The monopole is the magnetic equivalent to the positive proton or negative electron that exist independently in nature.

If any principle of impotence is added or discarded, or even radically changed, the unforeseen—and a new scientific era—will be upon us. For example, the discovery of the monopole could revolutionize the field of electronics, allowing new medical therapies in the fight against cancer, new sources of energy, extremely small and efficient motors and generators, and new particle accelerators of much higher energy than any yet built.

Foresaw Today's Energy Crisis

Our present energy crisis is one of Sir George's fulfilled prophesies, since he expected restricted oil supplies within 25 years. His overall review of foreseeable energy options was especially accurate, as well as his preview of the energy conservation dilemma: "The power needed for a given standard of living is by no means a fixed quantity." He defined the promise and restrictions of solar energy, and forecast—perhaps for the first time in a popular book—that thermonuclear fusion could eventually provide an inexhaustible source of clean, low-cost energy.

Sir George expressed high hopes for the automated future, but his hope was tinged with judicious regard for the limitations of science and society. He realized that technology's appetite for industrial materials—copper, lead, zinc, etc.—would lead to the shortages which are now beginning to appear, and made highly imaginative suggestions concerning substitution and new sources of supply.

As the sources of industrial materials change, so will their form, Sir George predicted. They will become remarkably light and flexible. Designers of buildings may copy the structure of butterflies and other insects: "The world of the future may be expected to look more ethereal, more like fairyland ... "

Predicted Computer's Triumph

The book includes accurate forecasts of computerized weather forecasting, advanced materials including ultrastrong composites, automation in factories, forms of synthetic food recently added to our market shelves, supersonic aircraft, advances in surface transportation along with various systems presently emerging from the laboratory. Thomson also foresaw in vivid detail the all-encompassing role of the computer throughout commerce, administration, and research. He expressed hope that a better understanding of cybernetic systems would shed light on some of the mysteries of the human mind.

Before his death, Sir George told me that the advance of space exploration occurred at a much faster rate than he expected in 1955. Except for timing, however, his astronautics forecast was accurate. He was correct in believing that "space travel will be an outlet for communal effort," allowing vicarious participation on the part of the general public. A hope was expressed that astronautics would be a "safety valve for man's war-breeding cravings for adventure," which can be expected to mount as the world becomes more mechanized.

The Foreseeable Future stated that no species of animal had been tamed since Hannibal and the Carthaginians domesticated the African elephant and suggested that "other species could be usefully domesticated." This suggestion has since been fulfilled by the successful domestication of the Arctic musk ox and the use of cetacea (dolphins and killer whales) to engage in useful underwater tasks. Thomson also anticipated African game ranches, which are now stocked with recently domesticated eland and oryx.

Forecasts must have intellectual coherence and scientific plausibility, as well as societal acceptability. Thomson's remarkable 1955 book fulfills each of these requirements, and expresses a sincere concern for the welfare of individual men and women—a rare

Struggle for power today was accurately anticipated in *The Foreseeable Future.* **Writing in 1955, Sir George Thomson accurately forecast restricted oil supplies within 25 years.**
UGI Corporation

degree of compassion in a technological forecast.

Writing years before Sir Charles Snow published *Two Cultures and the Scientific Revolution* in 1959, Sir George said: "People's minds tend to fall into one of two classes, the humanistic—interested mostly in people and words—and the scientific and engineering—interested mostly in things and ideas." But Thomson himself was a modern Renaissance man who

Sir George Paget Thomson, one of the preeminent scientists of the 20th century, died on September 10, 1975, at the age of 83 (after the accompanying article had been written). He was awarded the Nobel Prize in physics in 1937 for work on the diffraction of electrons in crystals—experiments which are fundamental to the quantum theory. He was the son of another Nobel laureate, Sir J. J. Thomson, the discoverer of the electron. In World War II, Sir George was Chairman of the First British Committee on Atomic Energy, which defined the theoretical foundations which culminated in the success of the Manhattan Project in 1945. The recipient of many awards in science, he served on the British delegation to the U.N. and was master of Corpus Christi College, Cambridge, for many years. He was the author of a diverse variety of technical monographs and popular books.

bridged the two cultures. He was both a scientist and a humanist. Consequently, *The Foreseeable Future* possesses a timeless quality which will cause it to be as stimulating and thought provoking in the decades to come as it was 20 years ago.

Many of Thomson's humanistic visions are not yet part of our contemporary world, but now seem much closer to realization than they did in 1955. He cautiously suggested that the parapsychologists' research in extrasensory perception may prove vitally important, and "if true, it will produce a revolution in thought." Concern for the dehumanizing effects of commuter traffic in large cities was answered with the hope that the videophone and other communications breakthroughs would allow us to break up our large cities into livable urban units of about 50,000 people—an optimum size allowing one to walk or cycle to his workplace.

Sir George's approach was analytical; by seeking the deepest and simplest underlying principle, he makes the familiar seem strange and the strange appear acceptable. More sober than science fiction, his book remains just as exotic and exciting. Judged as a work of popularized science, it has yet to be excelled.

The concluding paragraph of the book reflects the fundamental optimism of its author and deserves careful consideration in a time dominated by the apocalyptic mood in futures studies:

"There is no reason to anticipate that anything irreparable will go wrong with the earth physically for many millions of years, and are there not other planets and other stars? It is difficult to exterminate a species once well established, and man's best efforts to kill himself are unlikely to be more successful than those of the plague bacillus or the influenza virus. Even with the present brains of intelligent people Man may expect a glorious future. Who will dare to set limits to what he may reach as his brain improves? This future is not foreseeable!"

Reviewer Robert Prehoda is one of the pioneers in technological forecasting and the author of *Designing the Future: The Role of Technological Forecasting* (Chilton, Philadelphia, 1967). His address is P.O. Box 2402, Toluca Lake Station, North Hollywood, California 91602. Sir George died September 10 at his home, Little Howe, Mount Pleasant, Cambridge, England.

The Foreseeable Future by Sir George Thomson. Cambridge University Press, Cambridge, England. 1955. Out of print.

Part 2
THE FUTURE AS PROGRESS

Technology continues to advance on all
fronts. Here are some reports on what may be
in store for us in the years ahead.

The Automated Office

by Hollis Vail

Automation has already revolutionized the factory. Now it is about to revolutionize the office—freeing workers from rigid schedules, busy work, and the aggravations of commuting.

In Washington, D.C., the representatives of 10 government agencies take a few minutes once a week to check in with each other. They discuss the timing of upcoming meetings, comment on drafts of proposed documents, report what they are doing, and even vote on issues. Yet, they do it all without ever leaving their own offices, and at whatever hour of the day or night seems most convenient.

The weekly "meeting" of 10 people is made possible by a typewriter-like terminal that connects each office to a central computer. A message typed into the terminal travels by telephone wire to the computer where it is stored, together with the messages sent in from the other terminals. Any member of the group can use his terminal to call up the computer and ask for messages. The computer will then respond by activating the keys of the caller's terminal, causing them to type out any messages the computer has received up to that time.

Here is what such a sequence of messages might look like after one of these representatives—let's call him "Bob MacAbee"—starts the ball rolling:

```
1.      MacAbee—12/9/78—Please let me
2.   know if Jan. 25, 1979 is OK for a
3.   meeting at the Alfry Building, Rm 309
4.   at 9:30 am. Also, please comment on
5.   the following agenda items:
6.
7.      a. Progress report for year
8.      b. Establishment of divisions
9.      c. New business (suggest items)
10.      —end—
11.
12.      Henry 12/13/78—Date OK. Suggest
13.   we discuss meaning of voluntary
14.   metric conversion in all our agencies.
15.      —end—
16.
17.      Allen 12/13/78—Date NOT OK. Will
18.   be out of town. Can meet any other
19.   day that week or following week.
20.   Agenda OK.
21.      —end—
```

Using this method, the date and agenda can be agreed on, draft documents reviewed in advance, and possible problems identified so that each representative will be prepared to get maximum benefit from the actual meeting. And, all of this can be done at each representative's convenience in whatever spare minutes may be available during a busy day.

Telephone Provides Key Link

This use of the computer in the office is made possible by another electronic device—the telephone—which has been around for so many years and is so common that we seldom think of it as an electronic instrument. The telephone now is speeding the development of the electronic office.

Today's worldwide telephone network means that portable computer terminals can be carried and used almost anywhere. For instance, a management consultant located in Washington, D.C., can use a telephone-plus-computer system to keep in touch with his employers thousands of miles away in Menlo Park, California, just as easily as Bob MacAbee did to contact his colleagues located in different buildings around Washington, D.C.

Bob could have arranged his meeting by telephone without the computer, but someone would have had to call each person separately. Many calls would have been needed to reach a group of busy individuals, get their ideas, and pass them along to others. By contrast, a single call to the computer enabled each person to review all previous messages and to give unhurried thought to the issues before responding with comments or questions.

Besides telephones and computers, an electronic office may use copying equipment, facsimile transmission devices, television, tape recorders, and countless other electronic devices. New electronic technology offers so many opportunities for startling and productive innovations that it is safe to forecast that the many innovative experiments taking place now will multiply in the months and years ahead.

To understand what tomorrow's electronic office may be like, let's look at how an office functions and at current trends in office automation. First of all,

typewriters are being integrated with small computers to create "word-processing" equipment that is revolutionizing the way in which letters and other documents are written, corrected, and reproduced. With the new equipment, a typist can dash off a rough draft, pass it back to the boss for approval, retype only the specific words that need correction, then hit a button and watch the word-processing machine automatically type out a flawless final copy at 400 or more words per minute. The secret? As the rough draft was typed, the letter was also recorded and stored in the computer; when corrections are typed over the original, the computer record of the letter is also corrected. The computer then can print out a perfect copy of the letter as fast as the machine's typing element can move.

Word-processing equipment is an important transition step toward the electronic office. Besides speeding up and simplifying the job of typing, the automatic editing features of these machines enable writers to "cut and paste" their drafts electronically. A manuscript can be revised and rearranged many times without becoming an unreadable mess of penciled notes and sticky scraps. Instead of typing directly onto paper, a word processing machine can display the text as it is written on a TV-like viewing screen called a CRT or Cathode Ray Terminal. At the same time, the text is being recorded in the machine's computer memory. Later the changes and additions are also stored in the computer, replacing the former text. When all the desired changes have been made, the author can have the machine type on paper a neat, clean, corrected draft.

Automatic typewriters do more than speed up the drafting and finalizing of textual material. They also open the way to a new era in the transmission, storage, and retrieval of information. Already, a growing number of offices are beginning to tie automatic typing equipment at many locations into a central computer. The typist goes through a simple routine to get on-line with the computer, then types the material just as on any typewriter. The difference is that the text is now being recorded and stored in a central location and can be "called up" by anyone else tied in to the same computer.

The advantages of such an arrangement are shown in the following scenario, describing how a government office in the near future might respond to a letter from a congressman. While the names and agencies in the scenario are fictional, the incident is based on an actual occurrence.

The Congressman and the Eggs: A Scenario

Our future scenario begins in the office of David Brier, chief congressional liaison officer for the Federal Farm Bureau (FFB). Looking over the morning's mail, David finds a letter from a congressman transmitting a constituent's complaint. The constituent is angry because a local FFB farm is selling eggs in competition with him.

After reading the complaint, David turns to his office computer terminal and queries FILE (a computerized storage and retrieval system) to see if there has been any previous correspondence involving the constituent or the FFB farm on the subject of eggs. It turns out that this is the first letter from the constituent during the last five years, and that there is no correspondence involving eggs and the FFB farm.

David then queries REF (another computer file) to get the name of the FFB representative stationed nearest to the site of the FFB farm in question. This turns out to be Mary Westerly. David then tags the constituent's letter for facsimile transmission to Mary. He also advises her of the complaint by means of MESSAGE, the computer's message routing program.

Mary receives David's communication that afternoon when she turns to her computer terminal and queries MESSAGE to see if there are any messages for her. Among the messages is the one from David. She immediately calls the mailroom and finds that the facsimile copy of the constituent's letter has arrived; so she goes there and picks it up.

To find out more about the situation, Mary phones a local government official to inquire if the farm is selling eggs, and if so why. It turns out that the FFB leases its research farms to local families who run them as ordinary farms except when the FFB has a research project for the farm to participate in. These farm families sell their produce in the usual way to pay their lease and earn an income.

She drafts a reply letter to the complaining constituent using DRAFT, the central computer's text-editing pro-

To write this article about the office of the future, Hollis Vail used some of the very equipment he describes. The telephone connector unit pictured here allowed him to type a rough draft via telephone lines directly into a computer, make revisions and corrections, and then instruct the typewriter unit to print out a clean final draft.

Photo: Elizabeth Vail

gram, and passes this along to David through MESSAGE.

David receives Mary's draft letter the next morning when he checks his computer terminal for incoming messages. He decides to make a few changes in the text, then refers the revised draft via the computer to those officials who need to concur with it. As soon as the concurrences are recorded in the computer, the draft letter automatically comes back to David for his signature.

David's secretary has the computer run the letter in its final form, David signs it, and it goes out in the mail. The secretary than amends the computer record to indicate that the letter was signed and the date.

Finally, the constituent's original letter is microfilmed along with many other pages of material, on a special microfiche, that is, an index card-sized piece of microfilm. By entering the reference to the microfiche in the central computer's FILE program, it can easily be retrieved for later reference. Once on microfiche, the letter requires only a fraction of the space needed for paper records.

In the scenario just outlined, David Brier quickly located the person he needed to contact by consulting REF—a private data file which he had set up for his own use in the computer. He also queried the general files of the computer to see if any prior correspondence on the subject of egg sales by FFB farms existed.

A large organization needs many different data files. Some may be highly specialized and confidential, such as accounting records and personnel data files. Others may be compared to the reference room or "open stacks" of a public library—containing massive quantities of information that must be accessible to many different kinds of users for many different purposes.

One example of this kind of data file is MEDLARS, the computer-based **M**edical **L**iterature **A**nalysis and **R**etrieval **S**ystem at the National Library of Medicine in Bethesda, Maryland. MEDLARS' vast data base of current articles from more than 2,200 medical journals around the world is now available to physicians and medical libraries throughout the United States via MEDLINE (MEDLARS On-Line) for instant retrieval from any compatible computer terminal.

Data systems of all kinds are now being adapted so as to be accessible through long-distance telephone lines. At the same time, the procedures for gaining access to these data systems are being simplified so that people can use them without the help of professional computer programmers.

In the past, programmers were needed to prepare even the simplest computer routines. Today more and more general-purpose computer programs are becoming available. These computer programs allow ordinary individuals to

About the Author

Hollis Vail is a management consultant for the Department of the Interior, Washington, D.C.

select the data they want to store, load the data in the file by themselves, and later query the computer and have it print out or display the specific information they need.

David Brier, for instance, needed an easy way to keep track of people he might often deal with in his work. He therefore set up a general-purpose computer program that let him file in the computer the names, addresses, phone numbers, areas of responsibility and other work information about his colleagues and associates. To locate Mary Westerly's name, all David had to do was to enter the location code he had set up in the file and Mary's record was immediately found and displayed for his use.

A similar program is being used today by at least one Washington official (let's call him Bill Gregg) to help him keep track of metric conversion activity in his agency. Bill knew that several bureaus in his agency were converting various areas of their work to use the metric system. But he did not know which areas; so, he made up a simple form which was to be filled out for all conversion projects. As the forms came in, he entered them in the computer, where they are available whenever he needs to query them. He may, for instance, get a call from someone in another agency who wants to know whether Bill's agency is converting any of its signs to the metric system. Bill queries the computer for any information classed under *sign* and certain other reference terms. His queries quickly turn up any reports that show sign conversion activity.

"Garbage in, garbage out" has long been a classic axiom in the computer world. But in the new world of the electronic office, this axiom is becoming less applicable. David Brier and Bill Gregg can live with less than perfect records. What they need is quick set-up and easy use, and, with the improvements now taking place in computer technology, they can get it.

Bringing the Office into the Home

In recent years, many offices have moved the job of typing away from the immediate office area to separate "word-processing centers" that utilize remote dictation and automatic typewriting equipment. Since it is now clear that the typing function can be performed efficiently at a location physically removed from the author and from the site of other office activities, tomorrow's word-processing centers could easily be in one's own home. Consider the following scenario:

Since 1980 (three years ago) Jane Adams has worked for the Afgar Company. During this period she became familiar with the typing and filing routines of the office. But this spring, after she had her first child, she decided she would rather remain at home. Once this might have meant that she would have to give up her job. But not any more!

The company simply arranged to have a remote dictation unit and a computer terminal installed in Jane's home. To avoid tying up her family's phone line, Jane's company also had a separate phone line installed.

Today, Jane attends to her household chores, mothers her new daughter, and periodically checks the incoming dictation unit to see if any typing needs to be done. When there is some, she sits at her terminal, transcribes the dictation, and then registers its location in a computer file so that her boss can find it.

Everyone likes the new arrangement. Jane normally works the equivalent of a 40-hour week, but on a very flexible schedule. The arrangement she has with her company is that she will get the work out in a reasonable period of time. Only occasionally does her boss call to tell her something is urgent. Thus, if Jane wants to use a weekday afternoon for shopping, she can do some of her work at night. Or she may prefer to work on Sunday and take Monday off.

One may wonder how Jane's work gets on paper. The answer is that much of it never does! Her boss usually reviews the material that Jane enters into the computer using the video display unit (CRT) of his terminal. Using the terminal keyboard, he can enter any needed corrections himself, or, where more extensive changes are called for, he can phone these in to the remote dictation unit for Jane to type later.

Even when the document has been put in final form, it may remain in the computer and be "passed along" to others in the Afgar company via the video display units of their individual computer terminals. If paper copies are ever needed, of course, they can be easily produced by means of an automatic printer that operates at speeds of 1,500 words or more per minute. (This is a considerable improvement over the "automatic typewriters" and "hard copy printers" attached to computers in the 1970's which turned out a mere 450 words per minute!) The computer program that Jane and the others use includes routines that automatically break the text into properly numbered page-length sections.

Of course, none of this paper gets into Afgar's files. The company shifted to a magnetic tape/microfiche system of record storage back in the late 1970s. Today, in 1983, all Afgar's active records are maintained in on-line, random-access computer storage facilities. Certain of these records, such as the company's product catalogs, are also produced on microfiche by the computer. One advantage of this system is that the entire active file can be queried from any terminal in the company, and letters, reports, catalogs and other records can be located in seconds and displayed for use.

Jane no longer has an "office" in the sense of a desk in a room downtown. But neither does her boss. He travels a great deal, so he carries his "office" with him. It fits inside his briefcase and includes: a portable computer terminal that can be hooked up by any telephone to the company's central computer, a microfiche viewer, and a pocket-sized dictation machine that he uses on planes, in cars, and—whenever possible—alongside hotel swimming pools. A special attachment to this unit stores his dictation and can transmit it on command at high speed by telephone to Jane's recorder.

Jane and her boss still meet face to face occasionally to talk over problems, and, of course, to attend office parties. Even in this modern age, "electronic parties" are not yet in sight.

Fast-Talking Machines

So far, we have discussed the linking-up of offices and office functions via central computers. We have seen that the telephone system's ability to connect one machine to another has become just as important as its power to carry human voices back and forth over great distances. We have also briefly referred to the microfiche as a convenient way to compress mounds of paper records into a size and format that permits easy storage and quick retrieval.

But other technologies will also have an impact on the office. One interesting possibility is the speech compressor. This machine speeds up the rate of recorded speech without increasing its pitch, thus avoiding the "Donald Duck" sound we commonly hear when a tape-recording is run fast. With a speech compressor, the listener hears the person on the tape talking faster but sounding much the same otherwise. Models in use today can produce speech rates of 300 to 400 words per minute, which is as fast as many people read. Many blind persons already are using speech compressors to speed up their "reading" of voice recordings.

A speech compressor can enable a busy executive to listen to a tape-recording of a conference in half the time it would have taken to attend in person. Recorded telephone messages could be played back at high-speed to save time. Many reports and information memos now put on paper could be recorded and retained in audio form, since they could be listened to as rapidly as they could be read. Also, recorded information could be played back while traveling, or at other times and places where reading might be inconvenient or impossible.

Television, calculators, photocopying machines, and other technologies are also finding new uses in the office. At one U.S. government agency, for instance, engineers located in Denver can inspect structures hundreds or even thousands of miles away without ever leaving their offices. Cameramen at the site to be inspected transmit television images via satellite to the engineers. The engineers can tell the cameraman to focus on a particular part of the structure, or switch from a close-up to a long-range shot as needed. They can also record the pictures being sent, freeze them on the screen for a detailed examination, or store them for later reference.

The physical appearance of tomorrow's office may be impossible to predict, but we can feel confident that it will be electronic. Just as the electronic devices in common use now—the electric light, the telephone, the electric typewriter, and the photocopier—distinguish the office of today from the office of a century ago, so it seems nearly certain that the new electronic technology—computers, speech compressors, two-way television links via satellite, etc.—will play key roles in the office of the future.

New Attitudes Will Also Shape Tomorrow's Office

New attitudes toward work and the workplace may prove even more important than new technology in determining how and where "office work" will be done in the future. The concept of the office as a set of connected

rooms with people working in them owes as much to persistent custom as it does to efficiency or practical convenience. Afgar Company's decision to let Jane Adams take her dictation units and computer home with her would represent an important change from today's attitudes as well as a change in office procedures.

Furthermore, technology itself will influence attitudes. Computer-conferencing makes it not only possible but *practical* for a hundred or more people located thousands of miles apart to work on the same project and to be in daily contact with each other. Computer programs like MESSAGE can not only shorten the time it takes to communicate with others but also encourage informality in such communications. This may radically change the traditional administrative structure or "chain-of-command" found in offices today. In today's large organizations, communications tend to move vertically between the different hierarchies: reports and requests move up the ladder stage by stage until they reach the top management. Decisions and orders tend to move downward from the top managers to the next level below, and so on. But computer technology and electronic communications facilitate "violations" of this step-by-step routing. David Brier, for instance, knows that he can get a faster and more complete response to his inquiry by dealing with Mary Westerly directly rather than trying to pass his

message on "through channels." The central computer, with its information storage files and remote terminal links, makes direct contact easy and reliable.

Another possible change in attitude brought about by changes in office technology may be that many office workers will choose to be independent contractors rather than employees. Jane Adams might decide to buy her own computer terminal so she could work part-time for many different companies rather than full time for a single employer. And, when Jane wasn't working at her computer terminal, her children could use it for their school assignments.

The routines of the traditional 9 to 5 office day may disappear completely as new electronic technology makes it possible to perform all kinds of "office work" in one's home or out of a suitcase anywhere in the world. Office support services are among the most likely areas to experience change. Electronic message transmission will impact heavily on messenger and mail delivery systems. Written material that must travel by traditional modes will be speeded on its way by computer-controlled mailing equipment that automatically prints out the address, stuffs, stamps, and seals the envelope, and sorts the material by destination even before the postman comes by to collect it. More often though, written messages will be sent electronically from the company computer to the computer of the receiving party—perhaps through an intermediary satellite-linked message routing service.

The electronic innnovations in tomorrow's office will help executives compose their letters and reports as well as copy them faster and more easily. Computers with built-in dictionaries will check spelling automatically, and search their encyclopedia-like memory banks to locate needed statistics and apt quotations.

With all this change, will the office as we know it now—that is, the room downtown with desks, filing cabinets and people—disappear completely? Perhaps not. People's need for contact with others may never be fully satisfied by electronic means, however sophisticated. Many homes are not suited to work needs because of inadequate space or privacy. Furthermore, we still lack good measurement systems for many types of work, and the traditional office helps us to watch how "busy" others are.

It is clearly too soon to write off the traditional office completely; but, just as clearly, "office workers" in the years ahead will be spending more and more of their time in a variety of new environments. ❧

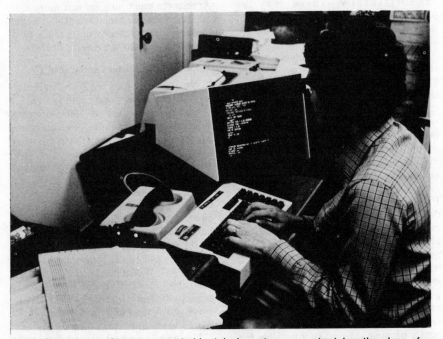

Word processing equipment connected by telephone to a computer takes the place of a conventional typewriter. As each word is typed, it appears on the video-display screen and is simultaneously stored in the computer's memory. Corrections can be made by simply back-spacing and typing over any misprints; then a perfect copy can be run off. In offices of the future, letters, memos, and reports will circulate electronically from one display screen to another via a central computer.
Photo: Hollis Vail

BEYOND 2000 ARCHITECTURE

by
Roy Mason

In the decades ahead, architects will have at their disposal a wide variety of new materials and techniques that will free them to create buildings dramatically different from those known today. In the following article, a future-oriented architect suggests the possible structures that man will build on earth, beneath the sea, and in outer space.

Architecture has always been one of man's primary means of satisfying his basic needs and expressing his highest aspirations. Houses, fortresses, cathedrals, and rocket gantries offer examples of the many ways in which man has modified his environment to protect himself from the harshness of nature and provide a means of achieving his aspirations.

New technology has freed the architect from many past limitations. Hence, the architecture that will develop in the next few decades may be excitingly different from the types of structures that now are familiar. To get a glimpse of tomorrow's architecture, we must look at the possibilities opened by the new materials and systems and at people's physical and social needs during the years ahead.

One enigma of an architectural forecast is the city. Traditionally, the city has been the primary context for architectural expression. But the future of the city is now heavily clouded. With world population expected to double in the next 35 years, cities will likely experience explosive growth. Skyscrapers of 100 to 150 stories may become commonplace as cities seek to pack more and more people into the available space. At the same time, urban sprawl may continue unabated, yielding subcontinental megalopolises like

"Boswash" (the urbanized area running from Boston to Washington) and "Sansan" (the San Francisco-San Diego corridor). Whether cities grow vertically or horizontally, there may be phenomenal increases in all types of pollution with diminished prospects for a high quality life.

But the mounting problems within the city raise the question whether the city will actually continue to grow as the population and urbanization trends indicate. There is even a question whether the city will survive at all, at least in its present form. Already, many people view cities as unmanageable and virtually uninhabitable monstrosities and are fleeing to the countryside. (See articles in the August issue of THE FUTURIST.) At the same time, new developments in technology eliminate many of the reasons for maintaining the physical proximity of large numbers of people.

Though the continued existence of cities can no longer be taken for granted, I believe that cities will survive, partly because so much of civilization is now concentrated in them and partly because they make it possible for people to realize deep needs for high quality personal interaction.

But if the city is to be a truly desirable place to live, its growth must be guided more effectively than in the past.

Architects must recognize the growing need to protect people from unpleasant sights and noises and to provide simpler and more flexible personal space. Architects must also consult more frequently with the social scientist, so that the needs of the user can be more fully incorporated into the design process.

Impact of Computers and Cable TV

New technologies will have major impact on the cities—and could even make them obsolete. Just as electric lights, telephones, automobiles, and elevators have all had important effects on urban form, so computers, lasers, and two-way cable television systems promise further major changes. The new communications technology can bring entertainment, shopping, employment, education, and medical services into the home, thus depriving the city of many of its reasons for existing. But if the city continues to exist anyway, how will it change? Will it perhaps decline as a desirable place to live, and consequently tend to become increasingly the residence of the poor and needy? Or will the city develop important new functions?

Energy production constitutes another major area of concern for the city. The United States currently uses one third of its energy for transportation and one third for heating and cooling its buildings. Will we continue to

Author Roy Mason stands in front of an environmental school he designed and built in Virginia. An example of ecological architecture, the structure is made of urethane foam sprayed onto a framework of metal laths. Crushed aggregate applied to the surface makes the building almost indistinguishable, at a distance, from the surrounding natural rock formations. A Washington, D.C., architect, Mason has designed a variety of homes and apart-ments, often exploring the possibilities of innovative materials such as plastics, recycled materials, and alternate energy systems.

Mason has served as the World Future Society's Art Director since 1966, when the Society was organized and he designed its symbol. Recently named Architecture Editor of THE FUTURIST, Mason is planning a series of articles (of which this is the first) on the various directions that architecture may take in the years ahead. Readers wishing to contribute to the architecture series are invited to write: Roy Mason, Architecture Editor, World Future Society, 4916 St. Elmo Avenue, Washington, D.C. 20014. Mason is also Co-founder and Director of Planning of the Future Options Room, which seeks to distill and simplify options in various fields. FOR is located at 2216 Fortieth Street, N.W., Washington, D.C. 20007.

Photo: Peter Vote

plan to use large nuclear reactors and coal-fired generators as our primary future sources of energy?

Among the alternative sources being discussed are wind, tidal, geothermal, and solar energy. Solar energy appears to be the most stable and widely distributed source of supply. With solar collectors to provide for heating needs, a building could become an energy producer, rather than just a consumer. Solar systems can readily be constructed in all structures ranging from the smallest to the largest. Locating structures underground could reduce energy demands by virtue of the superior insulating qualities of earth. (An underground location might also alleviate some of the problems of visual pollution.)

One problem posed by urban and suburban sprawl is that the land available for agricultural use is reduced. But buildings could produce food as well as energy. Greenhouses and hydroponic facilities, in combination with solar energy, could ultimately produce the bulk of the inhabitants' food. Computers could supervise the germination of seed, the distribution of nutrients, and the harvesting of the fruit as they do the production of industrial goods. It is not difficult to imagine that an acre of apartment complexes may someday

Solar house in Tucson, Arizona, has laminated copper roof panels and a solar collector, which is expected to provide 75% of the cooling and 100% of the heating needed for the house. Silicon solar cells will convert the sun's energy to low voltage power for small appliances. Major appliances will run on conventional power. This prototype house, designed by M. Arthur Kotch, is being built by the Copper Development Association.
Illustration from *Progressive Architecture*

In this combined building and life-support system, homegrown fruits and vegetables nourish the residents. Bioshelter enthusiasts believe that a home can grow even more food than if the land were devoted to regular agriculture. This domed structure with an outer membrane that becomes opaque when exposed to direct sunlight was designed by Sean Wellesley-Miller and Day Charoudi with Marguerite Villecco.

Drawing from *Architecture Plus*

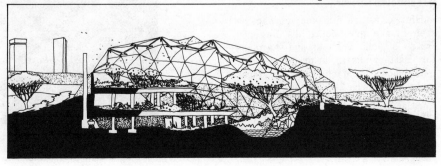

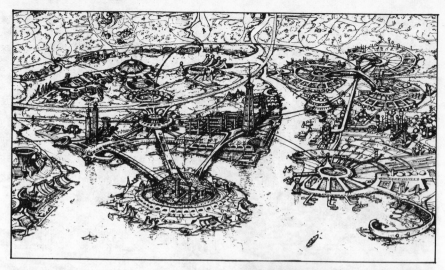

Transportation needs may shape tomorrow's city. The author, Roy Mason, prepared this concept of a port city designed around a transportation center that brings to a focus the train, bus, helicopter, and monorail systems circulating throughout the entire city. Automobile traffic is completely excluded from the inner city; all cars are parked in silos around the perimeter of the transportation system. Passage into the inner city is provided by "people movers."

Drawing by Roy Mason

produce more food than an acre of farmland!

Another major element determining the shape and functioning of cities is transportation. Current projections indicate that the U.S. demand for transportation services will double in the next twenty years. Will all U.S. cities go the way of Los Angeles, where 35% of the land already is devoted to highways? Alternatives now under discussion include the building of elevated highways to free the ground for other activities of man, or constructing ribbon-like apartment complexes with the roofs serving as highways.

Public transit of the near future will most likely elaborate on the best of what already exists, such as the Bay Area Rapid Transit (BART) system in San Francisco, Japan's high-speed intercity trains, and the elevated monorail systems operating at Disney World and the Montreal Expo site. In addition, personalized rapid transit systems (PRTs) may alleviate the immense future demand for mobility. Numerous demonstration PRT systems are now under study.

Personalized and mass transit systems can be integrated into a total city plan, and linear cities could develop along transportation corridors. Hubs for all transport modes can be incorporated into a single building, thus facilitating the movement of both people and goods within and among urban centers.

Greenhouse Cities?

Hints of future cities may perhaps be seen in the greenhouse-like Regency Hotels of John Portman and the plans for Battery Park, a proposed "city within a city" in Manhattan. On a larger scale, new towns like Reston, Virginia, may typify the semi-rural development that some planners see in the future, even though Reston has failed to become self-sufficient in employment and residence, as some planners hoped.

Another totally planned community, Auroville, near Pondicherry, India, may foreshadow spiritually based new communities that emphasize aesthetic and ecological concerns.

The growth of megalopolises can be controlled, to a certain extent, through land use codes and regional zoning. Satellite cities could be developed as appendages of a central city. The late planner Constantinos Doxiadis foresaw the development of a single worldwide city, which he named Ecumenopolis. A physically connected network of urban communities, Ecumenopolis could retain many of the physical and social characteristics of the small town or village.

Though new communities will be built, existing urban centers will probably undergo continued revitalization. Old buildings, instead of being

Greenhouse-interior of hotel designed by John Portman (above) shows how sunlight and green plants can be introduced into the center of a building, yet residents remain protected from rain and cold.   Photo: Regency Hyatt Hotel, Chicago

"Living-learning center" gives all residential units a view of the surrounding woods. This complex (below) is the Xerox Corporation's International Center for Training and Management, located in Loudoun County, Virginia, near Washington, D.C. Opened in June 1974, the Center has accommodations for 1,014 students.
Photo: Xerox Corporation

"House of the Century" is made of ferrocement, a material that gives architects unusual freedom to shape buildings any way they want. This structure, widely known in Texas, was created by the imaginative architectural group known as the Ant Farm.
Photo: The Ant Farm

destroyed to make way for new structures, will be recycled, that is, remodeled for new uses. Housing is another primary element of the urban system, but the problems it poses appear to be the most difficult to resolve. Man walks on the moon but builds houses by methods that have changed little since the days of the guild system. The conventional single-family dwelling uses 70,000 nails and 30,000 individual components, almost all of which are assembled on-site. The high labor costs associated with this form of construction are pricing the individual house beyond reach of the average family. Future housing needs to combine new conceptions of living space with the use of new manufactured components and construction methods.

New Materials Cause Excitement

Several recently developed materials foreshadow future construction possibilities. Among these are:

● *Plastics.* The strength, light weight, molding capability, and even light-transmitting properties of plastics make possible an almost endless variety in the design of components and entire structures.

● *New forms of steel.* Today's lighter, stronger steel permits the construction of extremely long spans.

● *Filament wound system.* Based on aerospace component technology, the filament wound system involves the wrapping of continuous strands of resin-coated glass filaments around a collapsible mold to produce on-site housing shells. In effect, a builder can "spin" a building at the site.

● *Ferrocement.* A builder working with ferrocement first creates a framework of metal reinforcing rods and chicken wire. He then coats the structure with cement. The metal supports and strengthens the cement, making it possible for the architect to sculpt buildings according to almost any design.

● *Concrete.* An old friend with new possibilities, concrete can now be manipulated in an unlimited variety of expressive and inspiring ways by using free form steel rod reinforcing systems.

● *MASC extrusion process.* Developed by the Midwest Applied Science Corporation, this process makes it possible to "spin out" or extrude buildings in one piece by using plastic foams that rise and harden very rapidly.

● *Urethane foam.* Originally developed as an insulation material with three times the insulating capacity of fiberglass, urethane foam can be sprayed on a variety of molds or forms to create exciting structures and interior spaces. After the recent earthquake disaster in Turkey, a reusable inflatable plastic mold was sprayed with urethane foam to provide instant shelter for the homeless.

New Systems Liberate Architects

But new materials are not the only technological developments that will liberate tomorrow's architects. Recent developments in building systems will also play a part. These include:

● *Kinetic structures.* Usually featuring a combination of inflatable and hydraulic components, these collapsible structures can be transported from site to site.

● *Fiberglass sandwiched component systems.* Precast sections of fiberglass can be connected by flexible corridors to permit many design variations. Lightweight and movable, the structures fold up like an umbrella for transportation, or are laid out in all sorts of shapes to meet specific needs.

● *Modular housing.* The rising costs of land, labor, and materials have made the relatively unattractive and uninspiring mobile home a potent factor in the home-building industry. One

Self-erecting multistory building, designed by students at the University of Virginia, can be prefabricated and transported to its site, where it pops up like a Jack-in-the-Box. The force needed to erect the building is provided by wrapping cables connecting the outer joints of the "scissors" frame around a shaft located on the ground.
From *Kinetic Architecture*

alternative to the mobile home is flexible modular housing. In this system, prefabricated panels are shipped to building sites for assembly on the spot. Modular housing is not yet competitive with traditional housing, because of such factors as high transport costs, the opposition of building trade unions, and the lack of high volume. But the U.S. government has attempted to stimulate the expansion of the modular industry. Several projects supported by the Department of Housing and Urban Development involve the stacking of prefab living units to form apartment complexes.

Structural Forms of the Future

The new materials and building systems help make a wide variety of structural forms both more possible and, in some instances, more desirable. These structures include the following:

Cellular Structures. Single modules, with the walls serving both as structural supports and space dividers, can be aggregated in a variety of ways to

Prefabricated cellular dwellings, exhibited in Germany in 1971, are now being used primarily for recreational purposes, but could typify the houses of the future.

Photo: *Neuf* Magazine

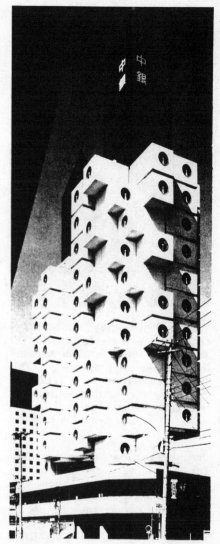

create ever larger systems. Modules can also be added onto existing conventional structures in order to increase the available area.

The most noted architect of modular or cellular structures is Moshe Safdie, the Israeli who designed the widely noted Habitat for the 1967 World's Fair in Montreal. For Habitat, Safdie stacked 160 residential units, made from 354 precast sections, into a visually striking apartment complex.

Modular or cellular construction allows architects to bring together modules in a wide variety of ways. Shown here is *Habitat*, the megastructure designed by Israeli architect Moshe Safdie for the 1967 World's Fair in Montreal.

Photo: *Progressive Architecture*

This exciting megastructure houses hundreds of people but gives them terraces where they can enjoy remarkable privacy. A subsequent project developed in Puerto Rico consisted of hexagonal units stacked in various ways to create large communities on mountain slopes.

Since modules or cells can be mass-produced in factories, cellular systems offer a way to house people that is less expensive than traditional methods.

Clip-on, Plug-in Architecture. A plug-in structure consists of two parts: A central stable core and one or more removable modules. The stable core provides the structural support for the system and houses the service facilities. The individual modules are added or removed as needs dictate.

One of the first developers of the plug-in concept was Peter Cook of the Archigram Group in London. Cook's objective was to create buildings which were so basic and adjustable that they could meet almost any future need for change. Kisho Kurokawa, a Japanese businessman, has already constructed a plug-in tower and is currently marketing individual modules through a Tokyo department store. Sale price includes the cost of installation.

Bridge Structures. Bridge structures, as the name implies, are constructed of either girder or cable systems stretching between tower supports or other combinations. Spanning long distances, these structures can function independently of local topogra-

Apartment house in Tokyo features plug-in living units, which Japanese can purchase at a local department store along with all the furnishings. A crane attaches the living unit to the central towers which contain elevators and service facilities. "Capsule living" was conceived by Japanese architect Kisho Kurokawa, who believes that people will someday buy capsules and take them from city to city as they move.

Photo: *Architecture Plus*

phy and previous development. The bridge is compatible with clip-on conceptions: individual cells can be added to girder systems or attached to the primary support towers.

Japanese architect Kenzo Tange has developed many bridge designs for the Tokyo Bay Project. The Hungarian-born French architect Yona Friedman has proposed bridge structures that would span whole cities, but such facilities would deprive earth dwellers of air and light.

Plug-in structures designed by Swiss architect Daniel Grataloup provide for separation of the units on the towers, thus permitting maximum acoustic isolation—difficult to achieve in traditional buildings.
Photo: Courtesy of Daniel Grataloup

Transit system is located in the center of the X-supports of this bridge structure, designed by the Paris architects Andre Biro and Jean-Jacques Fernier.
Photo: *Neuf* Magazine, Brussels

High-density terraced new town was designed to fit comfortably into the natural contours of the mountainous California terrain. The structure was planned for Sunset Mountain Park by Cesar Pelli and A. J. Lumsden.
Photo: *Progressive Architecture*

Bridge structure designed by Japanese architect Kenzo Tange for the Yamanashi Broadcasting Company (left) is currently being built in Tokyo. In this bridge structure, space for offices is provided between the supporting towers, which contain service facilities. Spanning a long distance, a bridge structure can function independently of local topography and earlier buildings. Photo: *Neuf* Magazine, Brussels
A container structure, such as this model (right) developed by the Institute for Lightweight Structures at the University of Stuttgart, Germany, permits the development of controlled microclimates in urban areas. The director of the Institute is Frei Otto.
Photo: Institute of Lightweight Structures

Diagonal Structures. Another innovative comprehensive approach to urban structures makes use of the diagonal. The diagonal structure is terraced either on a hillside or on level ground, permitting each living unit to have its own deck and outdoor garden. In contrast to bridges and other high rise structures, the terraces created by diagonal forms offer much natural light and spatial variety.

Diagonal structures can be erected in very different ways with the more complex forms assuming funnel and hyperbolic shapes. In the case of pyramidal forms, terraces can be constructed on all sides. One example is R. Buckminster Fuller's tetrahedonal

macrostructure which can accommodate one million people in one enclosure.
Container Structures. Container structures are very big buildings whose outer skin or shell encompasses a large unbroken interior. Current examples of container structures include the domed stadiums in Houston and New Orleans and Cape Canaveral's huge Vehicle Assembly Building, the largest unbroken contained space in the world.

One of the purest examples of container architecture is Buckminster Fuller's spherical geodesic dome, which has been erected in various forms throughout the world. Fuller has proposed enclosing sections of the Arctic and a two-mile diameter area of

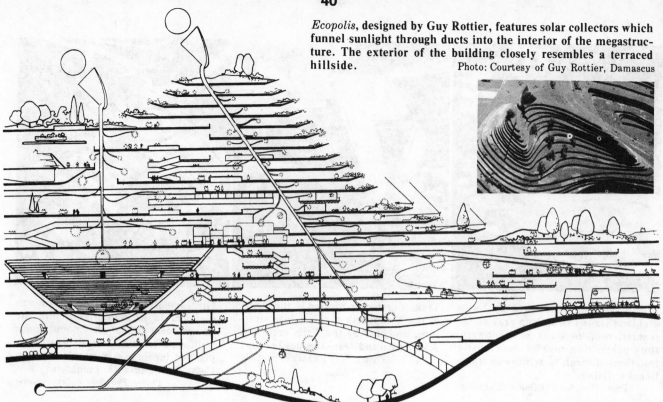

Ecopolis, designed by Guy Rottier, features solar collectors which funnel sunlight through ducts into the interior of the megastructure. The exterior of the building closely resembles a terraced hillside.

Photo: Courtesy of Guy Rottier, Damascus

Manhattan Island within dome skins which would shield people underneath from the weather and permit the creation of habitable micro-climates.

Another pioneer of container architecture is Frei Otto, whose most famous tensile structure served as the stadium for the 1972 Olympic Games in Munich.

Much of today's container research concentrates on light-weight inflatable or pneumatic structures which permit the creation of instant and mobile environments—even whole cities—within a matter of hours. The inflatable can provide an exterior skin for structures ranging in size from greenhouses to office towers to stadiums.

Biostructures. Biostructural designs may emerge in the next twenty years as the strongest single force in the architect's repertory. In seeking to emulate the biological processes of reproduction, growth, and cyclical change, the architect can help enhance man's perception of himself as a natural organism.

Biological forms and systems supply an untapped reservoir of ideas for the design of structures and cities. Fuller's geodesic dome, for example, was partly inspired by the radiolarian, a protozoan whose ribbed shape suggests a basket—or a geodesic dome.

One variant of the biostructure is the exoskeleton, or second skin, which can

serve as an extension of the human body and as a life support system. The space suit developed for extraterrestrial use may foreshadow the time when people on earth may walk around with their homes on their backs.

Marine Structures. With seven tenths of the earth's surface covered by oceans, marine structures offer one possible answer to the urban crisis. Stemming from the twin pressures of Tokyo's population explosion and scarcity of open land, the Tokyo Bay Project has developed many ways to use Tokyo Bay for residential and commercial purposes.

Marine structures may be either floating or stable. Stable structures are

Radiolaria Structure

This residence is a biostructure built of concrete sprayed into a framework shaped out of steel rods. Swiss architect Daniel Grataloup developed this home for a French client.

Photo: Courtesy of Daniel Grataloup

Underwater structures such as this village (left) designed by Jacques Rougerie and colleagues in Paris would facilitate research in marine biology as well as provide vacationers with an exciting locale. Increasing population densities on land may provide a major impetus for moving underwater in some coastal areas.
Photo: Courtesy of Jacques Rogerie

Marine structure (right) proposed by Pierre-Andre Martin of Sete, France, would permit the expansion of urban and port facilities over adjacent water areas.
Photo: Courtesy of Pierre-Andre Martin

usually built on pylons similar to those used on offshore oil drilling platforms. Floating structures generally use lightweight plastics such as fiberglass and foam to achieve buoyancy. Fuller's Triton City consists of several terraced megastructures supported by barges and connected by floating decks.

The underwater living and research environments now used by scientists, oil drilling teams, and others foreshadow the development of subsurface communities. The lure of an underwater vacation may provide the major impetus in developing these structures. Large ocean resorts located in the ocean depths are now envisioned, and construction of submarine environments for vacationers may be anticipated in the next decade.

Space Structures. The landing of men on the moon has made the future colonization of space seem inevitable. But lunar buildings will probably not be the first major extraterrestrial buildings. Large orbiting structures will probably come first. Recent space lab efforts have enabled scientists and engineers to understand how human beings can exist in space for long periods of time and cope with the problems of weightlessness.

The advent of the reusable space shuttle will substantially reduce the costs of space transportation, thereby reducing the costs of building structures in space. Service stations for space vehicles, astronomical observatories, scientific laboratories, and other manned space facilities will create a need for space housing and the eventual

creation of orbiting space cities. Space architecture will have many problems but will also be free of many of the constraints faced by architects on earth (gravity, weather, building codes, etc.). Space stations can link together like Tinker Toys to create a wide variety of strange-looking structures impossible to realize on earth.

Future lunar explorers will employ numerous vehicles and devices for improved observation and study and eventually will create permanent lunar bases. The first lunar buildings may be structures that can be erected easily on the moon's surface. But the best environment for lunar habitation will most likely lie under the surface. In one underground proposal developed by University of Houston students, a space

Floating industrial structure (below, left), made of fiberglass, shows another use of cellular architecture. Additional cells and central units can be attached as desired and easily moved later as necessary. This design is from Jacques Beufs of Paris.
Photo: Courtesy of Jacques Beufs

Counterpoint (below, right), a lunar colony developed by John Dossey and Guillermo Trotti, includes all facilities necessary for a self-sufficient research and production community. In the foreground is a low-pressure dome covering an experimental farm facility.
Photo: Courtesy of John Dossey and Guillermo Trotti

tug would transport prefabricated modules to the lunar surface. Living quarters, located below the surface, would be roofed over with solar panels. A series of hydroponic farms, set up both on and below the surface, would provide all the food.

Gerard O'Neill, a Princeton University physicist, has proposed the development of orbiting cylindrical communities. Structures up to 15 miles long and a mile in diameter would operate on solar energy and have an artificial gravity induced by rotation. (The "gravity" would actually be centrifugal force, which would press the inhabitants away from the axis of rotation.) Supporting more than 10,000 people, the community would eventually require no imports from earth except for carbon, hydrogen, and nitrogen. Other materials could be shipped from the moon at a relatively low cost. The community could support itself by exporting industrial materials that can be manufactured much more easily in a weightless environment than on earth. By constructing duplicates of itself, the community could facilitate the movement of human populations into space.

(See Space Department.)

Fantasy Structures: Today's "Impossibles"

Beyond the structures discussed so far are buildings that today are impossible but which could become feasible when currently unpredicted or unforeseen technologies are discovered and developed.

Aerotectures such as Fuller's Floating Sphere may someday float above the earth. Fuller suggests that a huge sphere could be placed in the air above the earth. The sun would heat the enclosed air, giving it such buoyancy that it could float like a balloon. On a lesser scale, a large dirigible could support hotels or apartment complexes.

"Biotecture." Architects have fantasized that increasing biological knowledge may some day make it possible to grow structures such as the octopus-like creation shown here.
Drawing by Glenn Small

Light-weight structures could also be held aloft by new, highly efficient (jet?) propulsion systems, or antigravity devices, as illustrated on the cover by the space artist Robert McCall.

Growing structures or **biotectures** of all types offer a vast field for architectural inventiveness. If, for example, biologists come to understand fully how certain animals can regenerate limbs or organs, architects may be able, by using a programmed chemical package, to grow a giant rib cage that can serve as the structure for a stadium.

Agritectural structures, as conceived by Rudolf Dornach, might be created out of green plants. Living enclosures could be shaped by nets, careful pruning, judicious use of nutrients, and so forth. With greater understanding of

plant growth processes, it might even be possible to develop varieties of plants that would develop naturally into functional enclosures.

Chemitectures might be formed by using new liquid materials which could grow like crystals into structures that are sufficiently rigid to enclose living spaces.

The "imaginary architecture," proposed by Friedrich St. Florian, who uses lasers, best epitomizes the mind-expanding and body-liberating possibilities of future structures and environments. St. Florian suggests that people will be able to switch spaces on and off by creating perceptually real, three-dimensional holographic structures on open land. People could walk

"Agrotecture." Structures could be made of living plants which would be shaped by nets, pruning, and careful fertilizing. In this drawing, a number of agrotectures appear, with the two in the foreground sliced through to show the interior. Root systems nourish the structure. Inhabitants might enjoy an unusually fine atmosphere, since the plants would convert carbon dioxide into oxygen. Courtesy of Wolf Hilbertz

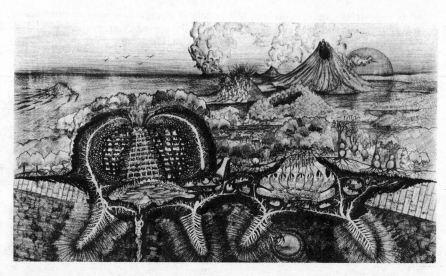

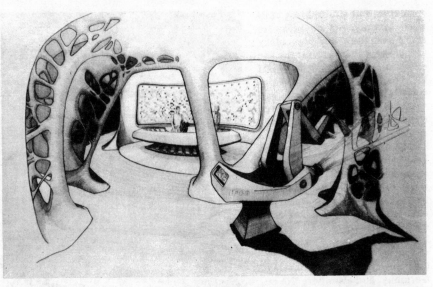

"Videotecture." (Left) Imaginary architecture is being developed by Friedrich St. Florian in his studio at the Center for Advanced Visual Studies at the Massachusetts Institute of Technology. St. Florian uses lasers to create structures that can be seen but are not made of solid substance. People can walk through the "walls" of the structures. In this conception, an imaginary museum of architecture rises from the Arizona desert. *Courtesy of Friedrich St. Florian*

"Photofabrication." (Above) Single molecules of a liquid plastic are sprayed toward a surface. Laser-created diffraction patterns force the molecules into extended chains of polymers which harden as they strike the surface. *Courtesy of Wolf Hilbertz*

through the walls of buildings as if they were mirages.

Another **videotectural** possibility is Wolf Hilbertz' Photo-Fabricated structures. Hilbertz suggests creating interference patterns among laser-projected images which could become solid shapes by introducing a polymerized plastic. In effect, the "mirage" or image would solidify into tangible reality.

Michael Jensen's Thought Forms may stretch videotecture to its limit. Jensen would have people visualize various forms and shapes and record—in an as yet unknown way—the distinctive brain wave patterns that the thoughts produced. The patterns could then be converted to sound waves which, when projected through directional antennas, form imaginary structures.

Mediatectural possibilities include covering all surfaces of a room with television screens, creating infinite possibilities for interior design. In conjunction with video cameras and recording equipment, a person could live in a total video environment. With computer access and a video synthesizer, he could play a keyboard and invent visual effects beyond imagination, or call up scenes (e.g., the Grand Canyon or the Taj Mahal). By attaching the system to biofeedback devices, one could visually experience his own biological fluctuations.

Other experimenters are using video, fiber optics, sound-sensitive light reflectors, and lasers which allow people to see the optical visions that drug users experience in altered states of consciousness. The Hans Rucker Company in New York has designed headset and body enclosure units that can shut out normal sensations and create entirely new sensory, interpersonal, and psychic experiences.

Sound architecture consists of creating perceptual space through sound equipment. Developments in the study of the relation of sound to matter and energy could permit the shaping of structure by creating a vibration matrix from which the final form is

"Cryotecture." Structures can be created by spraying a fine mist of water onto various inflatable or shaped mesh forms to produce buildings. Wolf Hilbertz of the University of Texas's Symbiotic Processes Laboratory and his colleagues created buildings like this at Fargo, North Dakota, for an "Ice City." *Photo: Fritz Dessler*

Auroville, a new town being built near Madras, India, seeks to combine nature and technology in a concept that features the use of spiral forms. Funded in part by UNESCO, the community will have an international and spiritual emphasis, as suggested by the Sanctuary of Truth at the center of this model. To become a resident of Auroville, one must be "convinced of the essential unity of mankind and have the will to collaborate in the material realization of that unity." Auroville's pioneer residents dug wells and built bamboo huts. The town now has about 400 residents, coming from India, the U.S., Britain, France, Germany, and elsewhere. No automobiles are allowed in the city. Courtesy of Shri Aurobindo Society

solidified. In effect, the sound patterns would become patterns of a solid material.

Cybertectures employ computers to create the most responsive personalized structures ever developed. On a mundane level, computers can design almost any kind of structure. At a more intimate level, the computer could be programmed to respond to human moods by varying the color, light, sound, shape, and size of structures. The computer might even be joined with man to form a man-machine, or cyborg (short for "cybernetic organism"), extending man's longevity, physical strength, and endurance.

Cryotectures are structures which use water and other liquids to form enclosed spaces. Though cheap and abundant, water might not seem to be a good building material, but Eskimos have used it for centuries to build their igloos. The appealing features of water to some architects is that it is thermoplastic; that is, it changes from a solid to a liquid when heated. In the liquid state, it can be molded into all manner of shapes; frozen, those shapes retain their form.

Water is the material that architect William Katavolos of Pratt University chose for his proposed 270-mile-high city at the North Pole. The city would

be located at the Pole so that the earth's centrifugal force would not create a problem.

Similarly, an Ice City is under study at the Symbiotic Process Laboratory of the University of Texas. In this concept, a fine mist of water would be sprayed onto various inflatable or shaped mesh forms to produce buildings.

Three Scenarios for the Future

Perhaps the best way to try to get at the basic character of tomorrow's architecture is to consider three scenarios of architectural development. These scenarios are oriented around the twin poles of nature and technology which are the two fundamental forces influencing man's design directions.

Scenario I: Nature Dominates

In the first scenario, natural forces and processes predominate, either because people have voluntarily chosen a more natural lifestyle or because technology has failed. (The energy "crisis" has suggested how dependent present technology is on dwindling supplies of fossil fuel.) Structures are built of locally derived natural materials like wood, stone, earth, animal skins, and adobe, clay or ice bricks. Yurts, teepees, hogans, and igloos exemplify this type of dwelling. The chief occupations are in agriculture and animal husbandry, with

excess production available for export. Little or no energy storage occurs; local materials, chiefly wood, are used to heat homes and cook food. In this scenario, human beings would revert to the primitive technology of the past.

Scenario II: Nature Merges with Human Technology

The second scenario involves the integration of man's tools and structures with the natural environment. Respecting but not worshiping natural forms and rhythms, man benefits from technology but maintains his contact with nature. He uses a startling variety of structures and materials: modular components, marine structures, natural and synthetic materials, etc. In general, the structures may be smaller rather than larger so as not to overwhelm the natural surroundings. But humanized megastructures, perhaps conforming to the existing terrain, are possible. In this scenario, people would use fairly sophisticated technology but would seek close harmony with natural processes.

Scenario II people might favor solar energy systems and greenhouse or hydroponic facilities because the sophisticated technology could minimize environmental damage. Current large-scale attempts to integrate nature and technology include the new towns of Reston in Virginia and Auroville in India, as well as the arcologies of Paolo Soleri.

Scenario III: Technology Dominates

In the third scenario, man creates an environment that is almost totally devoid of any connection with nature. Inhabitants of these totally synthetic environments, typified by megastructures placed in urban areas, could spend their entire lives indoors, if they so desired. Housing, offices, and shops are all located within the same structure or in nearby connected buildings. Massive production and distribution facilities provide food, energy, and other goods. Present structures such as the John Hancock Center in Chicago and city environments such as Manhattan (without Central Park) are examples of what happens when total technology becomes dominant in architectural and planning circles.

In all likelihood, none of the foregoing scenarios will be fully realized, but they suggest the broad choices which people will have.

Today when we think of future communities, many of us think of new towns like Columbia, Maryland, or Tapiola, Finland. But our options are much broader. We can also live in large megastructures housing thousands of people or we can carry our homes on our backs. Our homes can be on the sea as well as on the land, under the ground, or in the air. In a few years we will be able to live in solar-powered apartments on the moon or in space stations rotating around the earth.

What we must do now, I believe, is to explore the various options open to us and begin a general dialogue concerning the possibilities of tomorrow's built environment. Architects must work with planners, social scientists, and many other types of people to create the best sort of habitations for individual needs. From this general collaboration, which must include the people who will live, work, and play in the new structures, there will emerge, I believe, a consensus on what sort of built environment will best meet the needs of the future. We can then go about creating it.

The author, Roy Mason, was assisted in preparing this article by Scott Dankman, Director of Information Systems, Future Options Room, Washington, D.C., and Texas A&M professor Peter Jay Zweig, author of a forthcoming book entitled *Alternative Architecture #1: A History of the Future.*

Megastructure designed by Italian architects Loris Rossi and Donatella Mazzoleni integrates residential units and transportation systems. Lake is artificial. This concept, by Italian architects Loris Rossi and Donatella Mazzoleni, suggests the triumphant technology discussed as a third scenario for future architecture.
Courtesy of A. Loris Rossi and Donatella Mazzoleni

For Further Reading

Author Mason suggests the following volumes for people interested in reading more about the future of architecture:

Urban Structures for the Future by Justus Dahinden. Praeger Press, New York. 1972.

Architecture 2000 by Charles Jencks. Studio Vista, London. 1971.

Anthropodes by Jim Burn. Praeger, New York. 1972.

The City in the World of the Future by Hal Hellman. M. Evans, New York. 1970.

The Future of the City by Peter Wolf. Whitney Library of Design, New York. 1974.

Kinetic Architecture by William Zuk and Roger Clark. Van Nostrand Reinhold, New York. 1970.

The Oceans in Our Future

by Larry Booda

Live under the sea? Mine the ocean floor? Grow salt-water oysters in Kansas City? All these are real possibilities for the coming decades. In the following article, a specialist in ocean affairs reports on what is now happening in the utilization of the sea, and what can be expected in the future.

Man is a land animal, but is more closely tied to the sea than most people ever realize. Sixty percent of the world's largest cities are located within less than 30 miles of the ocean, and an estimated two-thirds of all of the world's people live within 50 miles of the coast. This heavy concentration of people in only 12% of the total land area comes from the fact that the sea has, from the earliest times, served a multitude of human needs. Down through the millennia, coastal-dwelling people have harvested bountiful crops of food from the sea, often depending almost entirely on fish and marine invertebrates for their dietary protein. In addition, the sea has provided man with an efficient means of travel, making worldwide trade very easy.

Today man is beginning to run out of resources on land, and is turning ever more to the sea, which until recently seemed an inexhaustible storehouse. But he is fast learning that the sea, though immense, also has limits. Already he has seriously overfished many of its most productive areas, so that they now produce only a fraction of their former bounty.

Offshore oil exploration began only three decades ago, but vast quantities of oil and natural gas now are being pumped from beneath the Gulf of Mexico and the North Sea. Valuable deposits of manganese and phosphates are known to exist on the ocean bottom, but are not yet being exploited. Vast renewable sources of energy exist in both the motion of the water and the temperature gradients of the sea, and engineers believe that they can tap this energy, if adequate development funds are provided.

As man's technology to exploit the resources of the sea advances, the political climate surrounding the oceans is becoming heated. Revolutionary changes came after World War II when more efficient methods of catching fish and killing whales were developed. In recent years, foreign fleets have been literally "vacuuming" the rich fishing grounds off U.S. coasts without regard to species.

However, the situation is now changing. Law of the Sea conferences have been held for the past six years in Geneva, Caracas, and New York, and one of the few points of agreement is that every coastal nation should have control over a zone along its shores extending out to 200 nautical miles. The coastal nation would have jurisdiction over the resources of that zone, though the zone of total territorial control would be only 12 miles. (Traditionally, it was only three miles.) Many countries have established such zones, and the United States joined them last year when Congress passed a law establishing a 200-mile zone. Starting last March, foreign fishermen became subject to licensing and fishing quotas. Several countries disregarded the new ruling at first, but after the well-publicized seizure of two Soviet fishing vessels by the U.S. Coast Guard, compliance improved markedly.

By the year 2000 there should be complete international agreement on fishery quotas so that a maximum sustainable yield of every species will be maintained. There are partial controls in effect now through bilateral and multilateral agreements and through organizations covering the northwest Atlantic and the northern Pacific. These agreements have brought under control such practices as the Japanese taking salmon in the deep Pacific before they could return to spawning grounds in northwestern U.S. and Canada, and in the Atlantic where the Danes have been taking salmon that would otherwise have spawned in Scottish streams. International conferences on whales have reduced the destruction of the magnificent mammals, though the Soviets and the Japanese still operate whaling fleets.

Oceanographic research scientists also have a stake in the Law of the Sea negotiations. In the past, scientific vessels were free to roam wherever they pleased. Now they find it increasingly difficult to keep from violating other countries' zones. Paul Fye, Director of the Woods Hole (Massachusetts) Oceanographic Institution, states that his research vessels spend 38% of the time within 200-mile limits, and that it is becoming increasingly difficult to make arrangements with controlling countries to conduct research in their zones.

Mineral Wealth Snags Negotiations

The potential mining of the deep sea has created an international furor, threatening to upset all other Law of the Sea negotiations. The principal reason is that vast areas of the ocean floor beyond the 200-mile limit are covered with black, potato-sized, mineral-rich nodules that may eventually be worth many fortunes to their takers, whoever they may be. The nodules carpet the ocean bottom in many places, lying within inches of each other at depths of from 15,000 to 18,000 feet. The principal component of these nodules is manganese—about 29% in the Pacific nodules. Other metals in the nodules include iron (6.3%), nickel (1.28%), copper (1.07%), and cobalt (0.25%). It is the last three metals rather than the manganese that make mining the nodules economically attractive.

Some 15 years ago, Deep Sea Ventures, Inc., of Gloucester Point, Virginia, began to investigate the nodules in the Pacific at a location about equidistant from Hawaii, Los Angeles, and Acapulco, Mexico. They invested heavily in developing methods to retrieve the nodules and refine them, and began test-mining operations early in 1977. In the meantime, three consortia headed by U.S. firms (Kennecott Copper, International Nickel, and Lockheed) plus German and French combines, have entered the field. The Japanese are active in several of these groups. The companies have now advanced to the point where they have the know-how and the technology for profitable mining of the nodules.

The realization of the full potential of the nodules dawned suddenly on the developing nations participating in the Law of the Sea Conferences. This group, the so-called "77," gathered their votes together and proposed a radically different approach for control of deep-sea mineral exploitation. The developing nations want control of deep sea mining

Left: OTEC plant proposed by Lockheed would generate 160 megawatts of power. Plant would have four power-generating modules, with warm water discharged from the upper ports and cold water from the lower. Central cold-water pipe, made of concrete, would extend 1,500 feet down into the ocean.

Lockheed Missiles and Space Co.

Submarine *Nekton Gamma* cruises into port after mission. Designed, built, and operated by General Oceanographics, of San Diego, California, she and her sister ships *Nekton Alpha* and *Nekton Beta* are commercial "workhorse" submarines. The three have made a total of about 2,000 dives on a wide variety of missions including pipeline inspections, environmental studies, fisheries research, dam inspections, and search and salvage missions. *Nekton* submarines are 15 and a half feet long, carry a crew of two, are powered by lead-acid batteries, cruise at two knots submerged, have a range of seven miles, and have a maximum operational depth of 1,000 feet.
Photo: General Oceanographics, Inc.

placed in the United Nations, with the mining operations conducted by a UN "Enterprise" which would be launched with financing and technological know-how from the developed nations but dominated by the "77" through their numbers. Some delegates fear that the Law of the Sea negotiations will polarize the industrialized and the developing nations on completely divergent and incompatible courses. One delegate has said that the developed nations will go ahead with their mining plans regardless of whether agreement is reached.

In November 1974, Deep Sea Ventures sent a lengthy legal document to the U.S. Secretary of State asking for protection of its investment if the company began mining, and to allocate a "claim" in which it would be protected. The State Department did not act on this claim, believing that it would adversely affect the Law of the Sea talks. Because of Administration inaction, bills were introduced in Congress that would protect companies that want to mine in the deep sea. Hearings were held early in 1977, and chances of passage of such laws are good whether the State Department approves or not.

Besides these jurisdictional problems, there may be serious environmental problems to be solved before large-scale undersea mining can take place. Over the past two years, the U.S. National Oceanic and Atmospheric Administration (NOAA) has been conducting a study of deep ocean mining to determine its environmental effects. NOAA officials believe that they should give guidance to industry on equipment design to meet environmental standards, and that this must be done soon, before the companies commit vast sums of money for equipment that would be difficult to change later. If these jurisdictional and environmental problems can be solved and mining companies given the signal to go ahead, undersea mining operations could be well under way by 1982 and a large-scale industry existent by the year 2000.

Other valuable mineral deposits are known to exist on the seabed, including phosphorite (calcium phosphate), which is used mainly for fertilizer. NOAA has identified valuable deposits along the coasts of California and Georgia that could be exploited without developing any new technology. Present domestic sources will be nearly exhausted by the 1990s. By that time these large marine deposits could relieve pressures on land sources and ease the necessity of

transporting the mineral over long distances.

Other hard-rock minerals that exist on the seabed include barite, copper, molybdenum, lead, zinc, and possibly uranium. Coal deposits are known to exist off Massachusetts and metallic sulfides off the U.S. Gulf Coast. California and Alaska are famous for their alluvial gold deposits; during glacial periods, when much of the world's water was frozen in glaciers, the oceans were lower and streams extended much farther out than they do now. The ancient stream beds, now submerged, are thought to contain gold and other precious metals. Other promising submerged stream bed sites exist in Lake Superior and off the Atlantic coast between Cape Henry, Virginia, and Cape Hatteras, North Carolina.

Aquaculture Promises Abundant Food

Throughout history, the sea has served man primarily as a source of food, and even though we may be about to witness a great expansion of man's uses of the sea, food production will probably remain the most important. One of the most economically promising and environmentally acceptable ways of exploiting the sea for human needs is through controlled-environment fish farming, or aquaculture. The culture of fish and shellfish is an ancient skill, practiced in the past mainly by oriental peoples. They raised many kinds of fish, clams, and oysters in primitive ponds and protected waters. Today's aquaculturist, in western countries, at least, is more likely to run a highly scientific, specialized operation. For example, "Domsea Farms" in Puget Sound, Washington, is raising pan-sized salmon that never go through the cycle of leaving the streams where they were hatched, migrating to the sea, spending their adult lives there, and returning finally to their birthplace to spawn and die. Domsea's 12-ounce beauties are raised in pens that permit circulation of the natural waters of Puget Sound, and are fed scientifically-balanced rations. After years of trial, the company has now become a profitable venture.

The outlook for a U.S. national aquaculture program, supported by legislation now before Congress, is good. A special committee of the National Research Council of the National Academy of Sciences is constructing a National Aquaculture Plan. Committee Chairman Don Walsh, Director of the Institute for Marine and Coastal Studies, University of Southern California, hopes to have the plan ready for the second session of the 95th Congress. The plan will take into account not only the role of government, but also of private industry and universities. Walsh, incidentally, is co-holder of the world's depth record of 35,800 feet, set in January 1960, in the bathyscaphe *Trieste,* in the Marianas Trench west of Guam. It is the task of the Walsh Committee to determine the extent that aquaculture can contribute to the U.S. food supply. Possible roles of government, industry, and universities in aquaculture research are being examined, and the committee will recommend ways to stimulate a program.

The United States established a National Sea Grant Program in the mid-1960s, and it is now active in the universities of all of the coastal states and one Great Lakes state. It is hoped that the Sea Grant Program, by funding research, can lead the way in marine food production, much as the Land Grant College Program that was started in 1865 helped the U.S. to become the greatest agricultural nation in the world. The Program now allocates $27 million a year, and is matched by local and state funds.

Following is a sampling of Sea Grant-supported research:

- Salmon are being cultured in pens on both the Atlantic and Pacific coasts as part of investigations now under way in the controlled growing of popular salt-water fish.
- Marine shrimp farming is developing along the Texas Gulf coast and on the east coast of Florida and Georgia.

- Very large fresh-water prawns are being grown in Hawaii, Puerto Rico, Georgia, and Florida.
- Lobsters are being grown experimentally in the northeastern states and at one location on the west coast.
- The blue, or hardshell crab, is a subject of investigation from Maryland to Miami, while other crabs are being experimented with in San Diego and Guam.

A project in Maine uses the heated effluent of a power plant to speed the growth of shellfish. In both Maine and Massachusetts, experimenters are using "raft" culture in which the oysters are grown in multiple trays suspended vertically from rafts in natural waters rich in algae, the food of the mollusks.

Oyster culture is currently of very special interest, and the Woods Hole (Massachusetts) Oceanographic Institution is a leader in the field. Under the guidance of biologist John Ryther, young oysters feed on algae fertilized with human wastes as part of a project to develop a way to convert sewage into food. The cycle begins with human wastes being mixed with sea water and held in settling ponds. During the summer, a lush growth of algae occurs in the ponds, and this water is then circulated through tanks with long trays of young oysters. Oysters are "filter feeders," siphoning tremendous quantities of water through tubes lined with microscopic projections called cilia, which extract the algal cells. In winter, the sewage-enriched

Ocean Thermal Energy Conversion: A Promising Energy Source

The sun heats surface waters in tropical seas to temperatures of about 85° F. At the same time, frigid polar water at temperatures of around 40° F. flows in beneath these warm seas. This great difference in water temperature can be put to use generating electricity by utilizing low-boiling liquids like ammonia to drive turbines in closed systems. To obtain this power from the sea, large floating power-generating plants would be moored in warm seas such as the Gulf of Mexico or the Bay of Bengal. The electricity generated by Ocean Thermal Energy Conversion (OTEC), as it is called, could be economically transmitted via submarine cable to land that is within 100 miles. Beyond that distance, the power could be put to more efficient use at the generating site, manufacturing such energy-intensive products as ammonia (used in fertilizers) or aluminum metal.

Several large corporations are now working on designs for prototype OTEC plants which may be operating by the early 1980s. The first OTEC plants will generate about 25 megawatts of power, and engineers hope to have plants in operation by 1985 that will generate 100 megawatts or more.

Capital construction costs for the first OTEC plants are expected to be around $2,000 per kilowatt generated, but for later models may be reduced to as little as $1,100 per kilowatt, making it very competi-tive with oil-fired generating plants.

Environmental impact of the power generation would be minimal, and could even enhance the growth of desirable sea life by enrichment of the surface waters with mineral nutrients brought up from the depths in the cold water.

OTEC plant proposed by TRW Systems of Redondo Beach, California, would produce 100 megawatts of power. The 340-foot diameter floating concrete structure would bring up cold water from as deep as 4,000 feet through a 50-foot diameter fiberglass pipe, to cool the working fluid, probably ammonia. Manufactured goods such as aluminum ingots are shown being loaded onto an oceangoing vessel.
Diagram: TRW Systems Group

sea water is bubbled in plastic-sided tanks where fluorescent lights take the place of the sun.

This kind of aquaculture can be carried one step further by adding sea worms, young lobsters, and juvenile flounders to the mollusk farm. The worms thrive in the sludge of solid wastes produced by the oysters, and are in turn eaten by the lobsters and bottom-feeding fish.

A similar effort is under way at the Virginia Institute of Marine Science at Gloucester Point, Virginia. The Institute has been engaged in oyster culture for several years, and is now beginning to process human wastes to grow algae nearby. Special care is being taken to prevent toxic chemicals from nearby industries from entering the waters.

The College of Marine Studies at the University of Delaware is now growing oysters under completely closed-cycle conditions in its laboratory at Lewes, Delaware. The mature oysters are placed in trays to spawn, and the juveniles—so small they look like pepper specks—siphon the algae-rich salt water and grow rapidly to marketable size. The algae are grown in a plastic-covered quonset building where sunlight rather than fluorescent lighting promotes photosynthesis. After the water flows by the oysters, it is run through a purifier. This closed-cycle system is now perfected to the point where only 10% replacement water is needed, and that need not be fresh sea water, but could be artificial sea water made by dissolving sea salt in fresh water. William Gaither, Dean of the College, predicts that future oysters may be grown far from the sea, perhaps in Kansas City, using purified stockyard wastes to feed the algae.

Another method of aquaculture—confining fish to a portion of the sea near shore where they can eat small fish but not be eaten by bigger ones—is advancing rapidly but is troubled by problems relating to the rights of boaters and sport fishermen in the area. State legislatures may have to settle this problem with new regulations.

Marine plants, such as kelp, a form of seaweed, hold promise in aquaculture. The Japanese have grown seaweed for centuries, and use large quantities for food. In the U.S., kelp beds off southern California and Maine furnish algin, an emulsifier used in many foods such as ice cream and salad dressing, and in paints. Scientists are also making progress in producing protein and biomedicals from seaweed.

One aquaculture enthusiast is Robert B. Abel, head of the Sea Grant Program for its first 10 years, and now Director of Oceanographic Education and Research at Texas A&M University. "Although most projects are not yet breaking even economically," Abel says, "the beautiful part of aquaculture is that you don't need a boat, and the demand is greater than the supply of oysters, shrimp, and salmon." The consensus of opinion among informed members of the oceanic community is that within the next 10 years, aquaculture will become attractive to private capital, and from that point onward it will grow rapidly.

Oceans Offer New Energy Sources

The past 15 years have witnessed great strides in the technology of tapping undersea oil and gas. The continental shelves off the U.S. Gulf Coast and beneath Europe's North Sea have been the sites of some of the most important new oil strikes made by western nations, and have helped greatly to save Great Britain from economic disaster. By the year 2000, however, the world's continental shelf deposits of oil and gas will have been widely tapped and seriously depleted. There are hints that deeper ocean deposits exist, but these would require tremendously expensive equipment.

With oil and gas deposits being used up rapidly, many countries are seeking alternative sources of energy, some of which exist in the ocean. Possibly the most promising of these potential sources would take advantage of the temperature differential existing between water on the ocean's surface and water at great depths, often as much as 45° F. That difference in temperature can be put to use in a way similar to the steam in a steamship. (The ship's boiler heats water to produce steam, which turns turbines and then is condensed by cool sea water for use once again.) In the case of Ocean Thermal Energy Conversion (OTEC), the difference in the temperature between water at the surface of the sea and the water some distance below would be used to boil and recondense a volatile liquid (ammonia, for example) in a closed system. The OTEC principle was demonstrated by a Frenchman, Georges Claude, who experimented with it in Cuba during 1929 and 1930. More recently, a demonstration plant was operated in the U.S. Virgin Islands, pumping cold sea water through the jacket of a vapor condenser utilizing a low-boiling liquid. As an added benefit, the deep-ocean water—rich in dissolved

Living Beneath the Se

Technology is enabling man to explore ever deeper into the sea by overcoming the long-standing problem of adjusting to changes in pressure. Changes of pressure in deep dives place great physiological strain on the human body and long periods of time are required for returning to sea-level pressure after a deep dive, in order to avoid the painful and sometimes fatal condition known as "the bends."

The new undersea technology eliminates this problem by providing the diver with diving suits and undersea chambers that are maintained at sea-level pressure (one atmosphere). Thus, the problem becomes one of engineering design, not human physiology. The development of strong new materials has made this development possible.

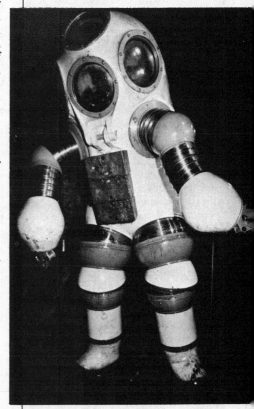

Advanced model of "Jim" diving suit has more flexible arms than earlier model. Arms are equipped with external manipulators that are hand-controlled from inside suit. Diver in suit can walk, climb ladders, and do almost any task associated with underwater construction, repair, maintenance, inspection, and salvage.

Photo: Oceaneering International, Inc.

Diver is readied for deep dive in "Jim," a rigid metal-and-fiberglass diving suit that is maintained at one atmosphere of pressure, and will take the diver down to depths of 1,500 feet. Human divers are still considered indispensable for seafloor oil drilling, and the "Jim" diving suits greatly extend the depths at which exploratory drilling can take place. "Jim" diving-suit models now on the drawing boards will take divers down to 3,000 feet.

Photo: Oceaneering International, Inc.

A modern (1976) undersea living habitat is being towed 100 miles out into the Gulf of Mexico before being sunk in 240 feet of water, where it will be used in the manned control of production from oil and gas wells on the ocean floor. It is maintained at one atmosphere of pressure and is designed for use in water down to depths of 3,000 feet.

Photo: Shell-Lockheed

An early (1972) undersea living habitat rests on the bottom beneath 50 feet of water and is maintained at the pressure of the surrounding water. Divers live in the subsea environment for days at a time while going about their work.

Drawing: NOAA Manned Undersea Science and Technology Program

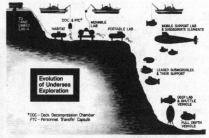

Artist's diagram shows progression from scuba-diving habitats on shallow continental shelf to manned exploration of the continental slope, and a living chamber at one atmosphere of pressure on the deep-sea bottom. Engineers are steadily increasing the depths at which man can work and live in the sea.

Drawing: NOAA Manned Undersea Science and Technology Program

Research submarine *Alvin* is loaded onto large oceangoing vessel for transport to site for Mid-Atlantic Ridge study. *Alvin* is a deep-diving vehicle designed specifically for oceanographic research and is operated by the Woods Hole (Massachusetts) Oceanographic Institution. Powered by lead-acid batteries, it has a submerged cruising speed of one and one fourth knots and a range of 15 miles. It can remain submerged for 24 hours and work at depths down to 6,000 feet. It has a mechanical arm for collecting objects from the sea bottom, and has a sonar telephone system for voice or code communication with the mother ship.

Photo: Woods Hole Oceanographic Institution

mineral nutrients—provided fertilizer for algae growing in shallow ponds and used as food for fish and shellfish. Future OTEC plants will probably be large installations moored at sea. If close enough to land, they could transmit electrical power directly to shore via undersea cable. If far from land, they could be put to such uses as providing power for manufacturing ammonia and urea (both used as fertilizer) from air and sea water.

Congress recently gave the U.S. Energy Research and Development Administration (ERDA) $25 million to prove the OTEC concept. ERDA has taken over the barge used by the submarine salvage ship *Glomar Explorer,* and is converting the barge to carry an OTEC plant which should be ready for demonstration runs sometime during 1978. Eight companies, including TRW, Inc., General Electric, and Lockheed, are experimenting with designs for possible large-scale development. By the year 2000, OTEC may be an important source of electrical power, taking indirect advantage of the sun's energy on an ever-yielding basis.

Ocean currents offer another source of energy. A conference of engineers and economists, held in Miami three years ago, declared that huge, submerged, anchored watermills (the seagoing equivalent of windmills) in

Manipulators Speed Undersea Work

Manipulators developed for space technology have entered the undersea domain. Two U.S. companies, General Electric and Oceaneering International, are building a diving capsule equipped with external arms operated by a diver sitting in comfort inside the capsule at one atmosphere of pressure. The diver looks through large viewing ports while he operates the controls to do mechanical work outside the capsule. The tethered capsule, called ARMS, for Atmospheric Roving Manipulator System, will be able to dive to 3,000 feet and promises to become extremely useful in the maintenance of offshore oil wells.

The two companies are also developing a tethered, unmanned remote-controlled manipulator vehicle, with television "eyes." Since no life-support system will be needed, the vehicle will have a much greater range, both in depth capability and in operating time duration.

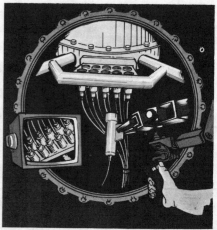

Left: Deep-diving, remote-controlled vehicle has television "eyes" and a force-feedback manipulator arm. Force-feedback "feeling" will be very important in cloudy water that blocks television viewing. Unmanned remote-controlled underwater work systems represent a new capability of infinite value to the diving industry in terms of economics, reduced personnel hazards, and increased work capability.

Right: View from inside manned ARMS capsule shows diver's hand operating "master" arm. "Slave" arm manipulator, outside capsule, duplicates motion. Manipulator holds television camera, wired to TV monitor in foreground, enabling diver to make detailed inspection of seabed installation.

Drawings: General Electric

the Gulf Stream could produce great quantities of power. So far, however, the U.S. government has not appropriated any funds to develop this source of energy.

ERDA is now paying some small attention to wave power, another possible source of energy, but the funding is very modest. Two engineers at the University of Delaware have envisioned a coastline system of moored floats that, as they moved up and down, would pump seawater to elevated reservoirs on land, which, in turn, would produce hydroelectric power.

Long-Range Weather Forecasts

The science of weather forecasting has developed rapidly since World War II. A network of automatic instruments on land, sea buoys, ships, aircraft, and satellites permits almost real-time analysis of atmospheric conditions. Forecasts of up to five days can now be made with relative accuracy. When meteorologists venture beyond that five-day period, however, their accuracy declines sharply because the longer-term atmospheric effects are regulated by the massive heat sink of the oceans. Water is 800 times as dense as air and moves commensurately slower. It stores great quantities of heat or cold. The major currents such as the Gulf Stream in

the North Atlantic, the Kuroshio Current off Japan and Alaska, and the Humboldt Current off the west coast of South America are relatively stable, but now and then aberrant eddies spin off. These eddies may last for several weeks and markedly alter the weather patterns over the continental land masses.

Little has been done as yet to plot the movements and temperatures of the deep ocean, where these eddies mainly occur. NOAA has deployed a number of big weather buoys in the Pacific, the Gulf of Mexico, and the Atlantic, but these are limited to readings of the ocean surface and the nearby atmosphere. What is needed for long-range weather forecasting is a network of buoys that will read the ocean temperatures and currents as far down as 2,000 feet and transmit this data constantly to weather computing centers.

The year 2000 should see an advanced network of automatic weather stations that will enable meteorologists to make long-period forecasts and provide valuable information for agriculture, shipping, and many other human activities.

Pollution: A Growing Problem

Scientists are becoming increasingly concerned about the oceans as the ultimate recipient of man's wastes.

The pervasiveness of pollution of the sea is well-illustrated by the pesticide DDT. DDT was developed and put in widespread use as an insecticide in the U.S. some 30 years ago. Soon the runoff from agricultural lands dispersed this relatively indestructible compound along coastal zones where traces began to be found in fish. The stately pelican became a victim, because female pelicans that ate fish contaminated with DDT laid eggs with shells so thin and fragile that most broke, killing the embryos and preventing the bird from reproducing. The bald eagle, national bird of the U.S., suffered a similar decimation of its numbers, as it, too, feeds largely on fish. But the telling evidence of widespread pollution came some years later when Antarctic penguins, also fish eaters, were found with traces of DDT in their bodies! Due to such discoveries, the use of DDT has been cut to nearly zero, but other substances just as lethal are now being used.

Pollution of the sea is an international problem, and it is being taken up at the Law of the Sea conferences. Nearly everyone agrees that controls are needed. But here again the underdeveloped nations have offered a novel plan under which pollution regulations would be followed by the developed countries but not by the emerging nations! If the sea is to be

Diver, inside ARMS capsule, installs blowout preventer component on a sea bottom oil well. External arms can duplicate motion of human arms.

Drawing: General Electric

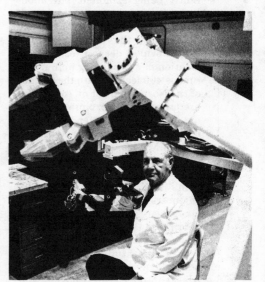

Operator demonstrates underwater manipulator in laboratory. "Slave" arm (foreground) duplicates motion and amplifies power of "master" arm, held by operator. Forces exerted by the slave arm are reflected back to the master, providing force feedback or "sense of touch."

Photo: General Electric

Man Readies Technology for Exploitation of Sea Bottom

The sea will become increasingly important as a source of energy and minerals as land deposits dwindle, according to a report from the U.S. National Academy of Sciences. Until recently, the submerged riches were unavailable because the technology did not exist for finding and exploiting them. Within the last two decades, however, the situation has changed, and man has begun, with offshore oil drilling, to tap the riches of the ocean floor.

The Academy's Committee on Seafloor Engineering, which conducted the study, had two main objectives: (1) to examine present capabilities in seafloor engineering and predict the capabilities required to meet future national needs, and (2) to identify the research necessary to extend present techniques and recommend procedures for implementing research programs. The report, entitled *Seafloor Engineering: National Needs and Research Requirements,* has identified five areas demanding expertise in seafloor engineering: energy, minerals, waste disposal, transportation and communication, and national security.

Offshore oilpools are the principal seafloor mineral deposits currently being exploited, but about two-thirds of the continental shelf off U.S. shores is still inaccessible to drilling, the Committee says. The world's deepest sea-bottom location of a producing well at this time is 400 feet beneath the surface of the North Sea, but oil companies are preparing for exploratory drilling in 850 feet of water off California and in 1,000 feet of water in the Gulf of Mexico.

Robot equipment with television camera "eyes" and mechanical arms will soon be available, engineers say. The robots will be far easier to maintain at great depths than human divers, who require complex life-support systems.

Vast, potentially oil-rich continental shelves exist off the coast of Alaska in the Bering, Chukchi, and Beaufort Seas, but the exploration of these areas awaits the development of new undersea technologies that are not subject to the destructive force of arctic ice and raging seas.

Although the sea bottom is thought to be very rich in minerals, the deposits have hardly been exploited at all so far, except for petroleum, because of the difficulties of prospecting on the ocean bottom. Effective technology for extracting non-petroleum minerals from the sea bottom is now becoming available. One unsolved problem is the clouding of the water when the seabed is disturbed. Clouding is seriously objectionable not only to environmentalists, but also to miners, for whom visibility is of great importance.

The sea has long been a dumping ground for solid waste. This practice is beginning to create major problems in some areas such as the coast of Long Island, New York, which has become heavily polluted from sludge and debris washing ashore. The Academy report states, however, that there are many places on the seafloor which are well-suited to solid waste disposal. Furthermore, solid wastes could be useful in the construction of artificial islands.

The report says that the ocean holds great advantages for renewable energy sources such as waves, tides, and currents. Two of the most promising technologies involve: (1) the use of differences in temperature between relatively warm surface waters and the colder water below to operate electric turbines, and (2) the use of photosynthesis to grow seaweed which could be processed to yield methane and other fuels. To do this, the seaweed (kelp) would be attached to a steel mesh 40 to 80 feet below the surface of the ocean. The mesh, in turn, would be anchored to the ocean bottom in waters up to 1,000 feet deep. The crop would be fertilized and the water temperature conditioned by artificial upwelling of cold water rich in nutrients from the sea bottom. Periodically, the tops of the plants would be harvested and taken to processing facilities located either on the ocean surface or along the coast. Sewage wastes could be used to fertilize the kelp beds, and these large "energy farms," with their high concentration of nutrients and limitless hiding places, might prove very productive of many forms of marine life including commercially valuable fish.

The sea bottom is already crisscrossed with many pipelines, cables, sensors, and transmitters used for oil transport, communication, navigation, and national security, and the amount of such equipment on the ocean floor is certain to grow exponentially, the report states.

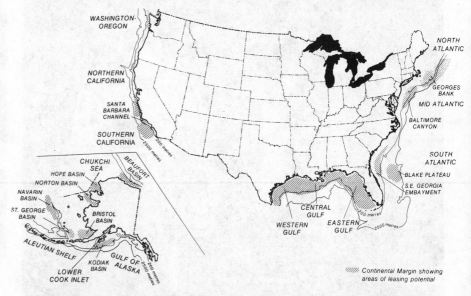

Map shows continental shelf (white) and continental slope (out to 2,500 meter contour) off continental U.S. and Alaska. Promising areas for oil exploration are cross-hatched. Most U.S. offshore oil now comes from the western and central Gulf of Mexico. Areas of high interest for exploration include the Baltimore Canyon and the Santa Barbara Channel.

Map: U.S. Geological Survey

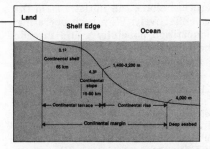

Profile of continental margin illustrates concept of continental shelf, slope, rise, and deep seabed. Continental shelf extends down to 200 meters. Although oil deposits are thought to exist beneath waters more than 2,000 meters deep, most exploration is still confined to the continental shelf zone.

Diagram: U.S. Geological Survey

The equipment is frequently damaged by heavy-duty fishing trawls, ship's anchors being dragged, and the corrosive action of sea water. Maintenance is costly and difficult, and improving the technology will be a high-priority assignment for engineers.

The Academy study predicts a proliferation of large ocean-bottom structures as well as anchoring systems for tethered floating islands. For these developments, knowledge of the character of the ocean bottom will become increasingly important. Seafloor architects will need a thorough knowledge of the terrain in order to build their structures. The importance of sea-bottom soil, sediment, and bedrock surveys will rival the importance of similar studies on land, but few such surveys have been done so far. Bottom contours have been fairly well mapped, and the stratigraphy of potential oil-bearing formations is being actively worked on, but no comprehensive surveys have been made of the bearing strength of the sea floor.

The environmental impact of man's exploitation of the sea bottom will figure heavily in any programs of seafloor development. The report cautions that seafloor development must proceed carefully so that it does not disturb nature's balance or degrade the quality of the environment.

The 81-page report, No. PB-254 171, *Seafloor Engineering: National Needs and Research Requirements,* can be purchased from the National Technical Information Service, U.S. Department of Commerce, 5285 Port Royal Road, Springfield, Virginia 22151.

North Sea oil drilling platform on a calm day. Winter gales and 350-foot depths make oil exploration here hazardous and expensive, but the rewards are high. The British economy has received a major boost from oil and gas discoveries, and the Norwegians are now sometimes called the "Arabs of the North" due to their new-found oil riches.

Photo: Exxon Corporation

saved from serious pollution, an agreement restraining all nations will have to be worked out.

Ocean transportation will probably change relatively little in the next 25 years. The oceans will continue to offer the cheapest avenue for bulk carriage of commodities. The hydrodynamic design of ships will improve, though no great breakthroughs are foreseen. Handling of cargo will also improve, with ships carrying barges, containers, and roll-on, roll-off cargo leading the way for further improvements.

The roll-on, roll-off system already is revolutionizing the world's transport system. Barges leave inland ports on the Rhine River, are towed down to Europort, loaded aboard ocean-going ships, carried to New Orleans, unloaded and towed up the Mississippi and Ohio Rivers. Truck trailer-size containers are loaded in Japan, carried by ship to Vladivostok, put on flatcars for shipment across Siberia and Europe, and reloaded on ships which ply to numerous North American ports. More and more ships are being built to allow truck tractors direct access for loading and unloading their trailers, thereby eliminating the use of huge cranes.

Shipping will benefit from more accurate weather forecasts. Vessels will be controlled much as air traffic is to-

day. International bodies such as the Intergovernmental Maritime Consultative Organization are seeking to bring the traditionally independent-minded ships' masters to accept control from central points and to be better trained.

There has been much speculation about floating cities, since land will grow increasingly crowded. Most of the current research is being done in universities, with densely-populated Japan leading the way. (Such a "city" was constructed in Japan three years ago for exhibition in a major ocean conference in Okinawa.) Floating manufacturing plants could offer an economic base for floating cities. A joint study by the Continental Oil Company and a Tokyo group of Mitsui companies is currently examining the feasibility of constructing a floating methanol plant. The concept was proposed as a means of developing natural gas in remote areas. By the year 2000, there will probably be numerous floating industrial plants moored near sources of raw materials or near markets.

Seafloor living is becoming a reality with an underwater oil-production system developed by a Lockheed subsidiary in Vancouver, Canada. The system consists of a steel "house" located over a sea-bottom oil or gas well, at depths potentially as great as

3,000 feet, and maintained at sea-level pressure. Whenever maintenance or repair work is to be done, men are lowered from the surface to the "house" in a transfer chamber. The men descend quickly at sea-level pressure, transfer to the "house," and work there in comfort, still at sea-level pressure. This isn't a "dream system," but one already in production and use. By the year 2000, oil production systems utilizing sea-level pressure chambers will probably be in common use at 3,000-foot depths.

Military Uses of the Ocean Depths

One shudders when contemplating the war-making capabilities that will exist in the oceans by the year 2000. Today, ballistic missile submarines of the U.S., the Soviet Union, Great Britain, and France are lurking beneath the waves with their deadly loads. Attack submarines, fitted from stem to stern with hydrophones, seek them out, aided by ships and aircraft. Bottom-mounted hydrophones can detect ships and submarines across an entire ocean, and in the future there will be no privacy anywhere above or beneath the seas: Every vessel, no matter whether on the surface, in the depths, or on the bottom, will be tracked in real time. Perhaps so many detection and kill systems will have been perfected that all forces will have neutralized each other!

In closing, I would like to make a few recommendations for utilization of the sea as a source of food:

Man should shift from simply harvesting the oceans' natural production of food to actually *farming* the seas. The following steps should be taken,

under some international auspices such as the United Nations Food and Agricultural Organization (FAO):

- Sponsor research on how much sea life can be harvested without harming the ability of the living things to replenish themselves.
- Provide funds for experiments on the domestication of sea creatures. Could the porpoise, for example, be domesticated?
- Encourage intensive aquaculture in bays, estuaries, and close-in shores.
- Offer incentives to private industry to invest in aquaculture.

Neither public nor private enterprise, alone, can initially farm the seas effectively. With both operating, competition hopefully would provide the incentive for developing efficient management techniques.

Larry L. Booda has been Editor of *Sea Technology* magazine (*Undersea Technology* before 1974) since 1964, with the exception of three years, 1969-1972, when he published the newsletter *Seas,* now merged with the *Washington Letter of Oceanography.* Booda's address is c/o *Sea Technology,* Compass Publications, Inc., Suite 1000, 1117 N. 19th Street, Arlington, Virginia 22209.

Larry L. Booda is the Editor of *Sea Technology.* He was an aviator with the U.S. Navy for 23 years, during and after World War II, and is a former Editor of *Naval Aviation News* and a past Military Editor of *Aviation Week and Space Technology.*

Ocean Miners Prepare to Harvest Seabed Nodules

Vast expanses of the deep ocean bottom are covered with potato-sized nodules rich in manganese, nickel, copper, cobalt, and iron. This treasure of the deep has accumulated for eons of time and man has not yet exploited it. Several companies, however, plan to begin seabed mining operations to recover the valuable nodules later this year. The richest known deposits are in the eastern Pacific at depths of 15,000 to 20,000 feet, and this is the area where most of the companies plan to start mining.

Tomorrow's Aviation: The Sky Won't Be the Only Limit

by Jerry Richardson

The U.S. Federal Aviation Administration has developed five scenarios which describe what the United States might be like in the next 25 years and how the evolution of aviation might be affected. By identifying events which are common to most of the scenarios, the FAA has been able to make a number of conclusions about such concerns as the need for new airports and new types of airplanes, safety, and increased noise levels over the next few decades.

In the past, growth in air transportation was largely determined by the capabilities of available technology. But recent developments have indicated that, in the future, the aviation system will be significantly influenced also by concern for environmental impacts, social legislation, economic developments, and life-styles, both in the United States and abroad.

Such recent developments as hijacking and bombing, air-system congestion, and the vehement opposition from noise-impacted neighborhoods near airports have convinced aviation officials that they no longer can plan in terms of simple "projections of demand," nor base their forecasts on new technological developments. Indeed, events of recent years suggest that socioeconomic change may, for the foreseeable future, be more dynamic than technological change.

Recognizing that they frequently were being caught off guard by galloping technology, life-style changes, and new developments in the economy and the ecology, the U.S. Federal Aviation Administration (FAA) created a multidisciplinary task force a few years ago to peer into the future and help the agency anticipate some of the changes that may take place in commercial aviation by the year 2000. The agency is now hopeful that anticipatory planning can save a great deal of money and discomfort in the years ahead.

"It's impossible to predict with precision the number of planes, the volume of passengers, the types of aircraft, and the frequency of flights

we'll have to cope with 23 years from now," says Duane Freer, FAA's Acting Associate Administrator for Policy Development and Review. "But we can measure how aviation has reacted historically to variations in socioeconomic variables such as the gross national product, birthrates, disposable income, personal spending—and this is the basis of FAA's Future Program."

The FAA commissioned The Futures Group of Glastonbury, Connecticut, to do a study of potential future environments facing the U.S. aviation system. The study was directed at constructing five alternative scenarios describing various conditions which may exist in the U.S. from now to the year 2000 and would be important in shaping demand for air transportation. Each scenario describes the potential evolution of various socioeconomic conditions, along with a projection of the amount and type of air transportation likely to exist under those conditions.

The FAA emphasizes that these scenarios should not be viewed as forecasts of what will happen. Their purpose is merely to describe a range of plausible conditions "so that those involved with designing and assessing aviation system policies might have a framework for policy analysis and synthesis."

The Limited-Growth Scenario

In the first scenario, both the U.S. population and gross national product (GNP) show only a slow increase. Following the energy crisis of the early

1970s, a series of related problems develop: There are shortages of critical materials. Prices increase. Capital is limited. The problems lead to general economic instability. The gathering ills seem to validate the philosophy that growth is intrinsically wrong and that the economies of all developed countries must ultimately stabilize. General acceptance of the need to limit growth leads to the adoption of government and industrial policies and personal life-styles characterized by a degree of constraint that would have seemed unthinkable only a few years before.

Limitations placed on economic growth and the concentration of population in large urban areas result in a slowing in the growth in demand for all forms of transportation. Mass transit is encouraged by government subsidy; intercity rail service improves in the largest high-density corridors. Telecommunications are used extensively for business conferences and

Aviation Scenarios at a Glance

The five scenarios prepared for the FAA are based on the following basic assumptions:

Limited-Growth Scenario—low population growth, low economic growth

Muddling-Through Scenario—high population growth, low economic growth

Resource-Allocation Scenario—low population growth, moderate economic growth

Individual-Affluence Scenario—low population growth, high economic growth

Expansive-Growth Scenario—high population growth, high economic growth

Short takeoff and landing (STOL) aircraft, using propulsive lift concepts like the augmentor (extendible) wing shown here, could operate from short runways, increasing capacity of existing airports and bringing into use smaller community airports to reduce terminal congestion. In the FAA's Resource-Allocation, Individual-Affluence, and Expansive-Growth scenarios, 150-passenger STOL aircraft begin service in the 1990s.
Illustration: NASA

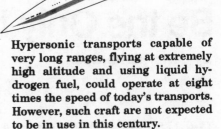

Hypersonic transports capable of very long ranges, flying at extremely high altitude and using liquid hydrogen fuel, could operate at eight times the speed of today's transports. However, such craft are not expected to be in use in this century.
Illustration: NASA

visiting with friends, as well as leisure-time diversion in the home. By the year 2000, nearly 7% of the white-collar labor force can work largely at home, using terminals to communicate with central offices.

Airlines curtail their flight frequencies to increase seat occupancy rates and postpone modernization of fleets as fares are forced upward by as much as 50% by rising energy-conservation taxes between 1975 and 2000. General aviation (non-commercial), air taxi, and cargo flights expand gingerly. A new third-generation air traffic control (ATC) system is installed nationwide. The accident rate declines, but the number of air carrier fatalities does not decline significantly because larger planes are in service and there are fewer empty seats on the average flight because the airlines have adjusted their routes and schedules to cut costs.

The Muddling-Through Scenario

In the second scenario, the U.S. population grows at a high rate, despite low GNP growth, and the state of the economy declines. The United States never seems to be able to "get it all together." When it tries to halt inflation, recession follows; when recession is the target, inflation accelerates. Muddling Through is the norm: Cohesive policies which last beyond one presidential term are rare. A

1930s type depression does not occur because conditions are different, but the *feeling* of depression is inescapable. This is a modern depression—and it is long lasting. By the end of the century, 90% of the population resides in urbanized areas and signs of crowding are evident in almost every aspect of urban life. Real disposable income

shows little growth. The threat of an OPEC oil embargo leads to a system of energy and resource rationing. As conditions worsen, the petroleum industry is nationalized in 1990. Recreational activities tend to be low cost and to use less energy.

Air transportation demand climbs but then declines. Airlines accommodate new passengers with somewhat larger aircraft and increased occupancy rates. User and fuel taxes increase; fares go up by about 50%, despite government subsidies. All public interstate transportation is nationalized, and a new independent regulatory agency sets service standards for all forms of transportation. Multi-state regional authorities assume responsibility for coordinating inter-modal (train to air to bus, etc.) transportation. The quality of airline service is cut back to avoid further

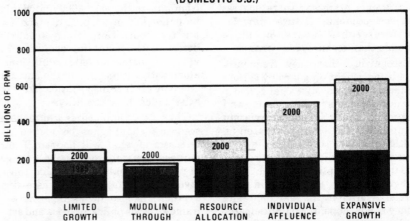

The total number of revenue passenger miles flown in the United States would exceed 600 billion annually by the year 2000 under the Expansive-Growth scenario, which assumes a plentiful supply of fuel at reasonable prices will be available. At the other extreme, the number of passenger miles would decrease to less than 200 billion under the Muddling-Through scenario, which assumes deteriorating economic conditions and rising oil prices.
Source: FAA

fare increases. The only significant technological advances are energy-saving aircraft engines. Decreased flight activity forces the National Air Transportation Corporation to take over bankrupt airports and purchase marginal operations. Many general aviation airports are closed and converted to other uses. Decreased traffic volume leads to a decline in congestion delays and accident rates. Modernization of the air traffic control system ends around 1985, basically for the same reason.

The Resource-Allocation Scenario

The third scenario offers a "middle of the road" view of the future. This scenario assumes a moderate growth of the GNP and low growth of the U.S. population. Resources—particularly energy resources—are in short supply. Groups of nations, functioning essentially as cartels, unilaterally establish resource prices and continually threaten to withhold supplies unless consuming nations meet their demands. Once a year, one of the cartels withholds supplies for several weeks, forcing the importing countries to cope as best they can. Prices fluctuate. Inevitably, the response is a determined move toward self-sufficiency to reduce the demand for critical imports. The United States decides that the way to continue growth is to develop indigenous resources, to allocate stringently, to recycle, and to plan. Urban mass transit grows, supported by increased gasoline taxes. Urban centers are revitalized, and intercity automobile travel decreases because of the high degree of economic and cultural self-sufficiency within the cities. Ninety percent of the population lives in urban areas.

Increasing urbanization and energy conservation lead to an emphasis on energy-efficient ground transportation systems. But increased purchasing power encourages a substantial growth of air travel, which increases 150% by the end of the century. General aviation grows because businessmen elect that means of travel, though rising costs discourage pleasure flying. All-cargo service more than doubles by the year 2000.

Technological advances in aviation aim at improving fuel efficiency, lowering costs, and reducing noise. A new 150-passenger short takeoff and landing (STOL) aircraft begins operating in 1990 and a long-range extra-large passenger/cargo transport begins service in 1995. Supersonic transports are not used domestically due to environmental and energy conservation concerns.

A few new regional airports are constructed or converted from military use in the 1990s, but most of the increased capacity in the system is achieved by making internal improvements at existing fields and by the development of new special-purpose general aviation airports.

An increasingly automated ATC system and improved instrumentation in general aviation aircraft reduce the number of aircraft accidents, but fatalities increase due to larger aircraft and fewer empty seats.

The federal government increases its involvement in the coordination

Aviation Authorities View Future Trends

FAA officials say that none of the scenarios mentioned here is viewed as the most likely to become reality. But aviation experts have identified a number of general trends that they believe may be important in the future.

First of all, they appear very confident that growth will continue, at least in the general aviation sector, which includes all non-commercial aircraft—from recreational and small business aircraft to Lear jets and DC-9s for large corporations. Business aviation currently is growing rapidly, because corporation managements feel that the value of their executives' time justifies the cost of flying.

Aviation experts are concerned, however, about what a future energy crisis could do to aviation. During the 1973 energy crisis, the airlines were faced with both a shortage of fuel and higher prices for the amount they were able to obtain. In a future energy crisis, the fuel simply may not be available for aviation at any cost. This concern has sparked increased interest in alternative aviation fuels. The growth of fiber optics and other new telecommunications technologies may substitute for some aviation growth, too, the experts say, but with much less impact.

Short takeoff and landing (STOL) aircraft are likely to enjoy great popularity in the future. Their main function will be to provide feeder service from small towns to major airport terminals. They can handle commuter traffic in places where it is not economically feasible for larger carriers to operate. Superwide-body planes carrying 1,000 passengers are another likely development during the next few decades.

The air traffic control (ATC) system will probably become more sophisticated, the experts say, but the extent of the improvements will depend on how much extra money the user is willing to pay. It is also possible that computer control and satellite navigation systems may return more direct control to the pilot. Sophisticated electronic equipment on board may tell the pilot where he is and where other craft are, and to a high degree of reliability. There may be less voice contact between pilot and controller; instead, the pilot will get an alpha-numeric readout through his computer. Alternatively, it is still possible that the emphasis will be on adding more people to the ATC system rather than more technology.

In recent years, the FAA has had to be responsive to segments of the public that it did not have to take into consideration before, a trend which is expected to continue. Public concern about the noise, smells, and highway congestion caused by airports, along with more general concerns about the effect of aviation on the environment (the ozone layer vs. the SST, for example), will mean more consultative planning in the future with a broader segment of the public.

Land banking may become a widespread practice. By setting aside desirable undeveloped land for an airport before the need for the airport arises, many of the problems encountered today in obtaining land for new airports or airport expansion can be avoided— and the cost of the land will almost surely be lower, too.

Even though the aviation accident *rate* is not expected to increase, there is speculation that aviation safety will be perceived as a growing problem because there will be so many more planes in the air, many of them carrying more passengers than today's planes.

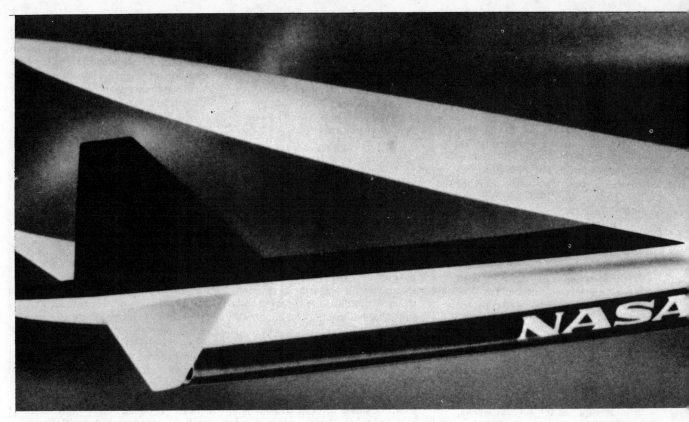

and financing of aviation and all other forms of transportation.

The Individual-Affluence Scenario

In the fourth scenario, low population growth combined with high economic growth leads to a phenomenal rise in disposable personal income per capita. Government, which is highly centralized, puts great emphasis on the planning and achievement of explicit goals. Government policies are anticipatory, not reactive. New technology solves energy supply problems. Business productivity reaches an unprecedented high by the year 2000. Nearly 90% of the population lives in metropolitan areas; central cities are revived by effective federal and state aid programs. The work week drops to 36 hours and many workers get almost two months of vacation time per year. Spending on leisure activities in the year 2000 is more than three times what it was in 1973, and much of this money is spent on luxuries and cultural pursuits.

The demand for transportation is greatly stimulated by the rapid increases in business activity and personal income. However, there is a great deal of environmental consciousness and regulation. Such environmental concerns and the growth of high-speed ground transportation systems temper the demand for air transportation somewhat, but aviation growth still continues at a rapid

pace. Commercial airline operations double between 1975 and 2000, and general aviation operations grow by 225%. Airline passenger miles grow at an average rate of over 5% annually. Air cargo tonnage increases tremendously, with much of it being carried on all-cargo flights. The length of the average commercial-airline trip increases because high-speed ground transportation systems compete strongly on short-distance runs.

The increased demand leads to the introduction of extra-large transports and 150-passenger jet STOL aircraft; the average aircraft size grows from 120 to 160 seats. To accommodate the increasing air traffic, several large regional airports are built to serve major hubs, and existing facilities in those areas are converted to feeder service and general aviation. A number of new feeder airports also are constructed. The government begins advance "land banking" to insure that satisfactory land will be available for future airport construction when it is needed. New airports are designed to include all possible noise-impacted areas within their boundaries.

Fares are kept down by improved technology and by regulatory action to increase operating efficiency. Federal regulations eliminate competing flights to the same cities at close time intervals and encourage airlines to reduce the number of unoccupied seats.

A fully automated "fourth generation" ATC system is phased in, begin-

ning in 1990. Aircraft operators are forced to make large investments in new avionic equipment in order to enter most parts of the airspace, but the effect on the growth of aviation is minimal due to the strong economic situation.

The Expansive-Growth Scenario

The last scenario combines high GNP growth with high population growth. The United States makes technological advances that solve the resource-availability problem, resulting in rapid economic growth and a national mood of vitality. The nation finds it possible to create images of what might be and then to adopt policies to achieve its end. There is renewed faith in the free enterprise system, which is given most of the credit for solving the country's problems. The federal government subsidizes research and development, but otherwise cuts back sharply its intervention in the private sector. The emphasis is on individualism and on corporate achievement.

The U.S. population grows to 297 million by the year 2000. The urban centers do not attain the dominance found in most of the other scenarios, mainly due to industrial decentralization. As a result of this decentralization pattern, population density is held down and people are able to maintain a high degree of community identity.

The increasing abundance of domestic energy supplies allows a

This advanced swing-wing aircraft could be the commercial jet transport of the future, NASA researchers believe. The angle of the wing can be changed to obtain maximum performance at different flight speeds. At lower speeds, for example, the wing would be fixed at right angles to the fuselage, allowing landings and takeoffs with a minimum of power and noise. Illustration: NASA

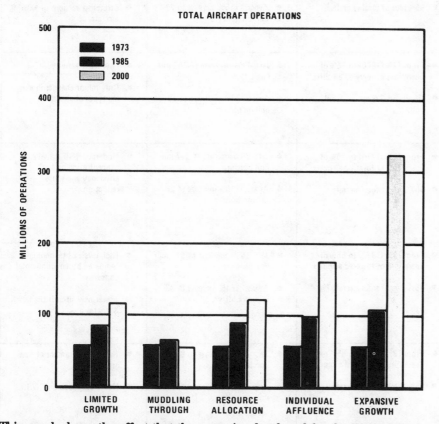

This graph shows the effect that the scenarios developed for the FAA's futures study might have on the number of airplane flights. Only in the Muddling-Through scenario does the number of flights actually decrease. Source: FAA

highly mobile society to develop. People move frequently to find better job opportunities. Workers have much more leisure time as a result of a 38-hour work week and month-long vacations, and they have much more money to spend on leisure activities. Consequently, the demand for transportation grows tremendously.

With energy no longer a concern, automobiles and small personal aircraft are very popular because of the independence they offer. The highway system expands extensively. Growth of mass transit is inhibited because the decentralization of industry and commerce requires continued reliance on the flexibility offered by the automobile. Within highly populated urban corridors, however, high-speed ground transportation becomes competitive.

Air passenger traffic increases strongly, both in long- and short-haul markets. The development of an STOL airport system stimulates the growth of short airline trips. General aviation increases, too, both for business and pleasure. Increased air cargo shipments, spurred by rapidly growing domestic and foreign trade, lead to the development of all-cargo airports in the 1990s. New airports of all types proliferate after the government allays citizens' complaints by controlling adjacent land use, by improving road and rail links to the airports, and by careful planning to reduce environmental impacts. Airport congestion causes authorities to charge higher landing fees during peak periods in an effort to redistribute the traffic.

New aircraft introduced during this period of prosperity include a 150-passenger jet STOL, a 1000-passenger jumbo jet, and an advanced supersonic transport. The jumbo jet is used for mass, long-range, low-cost charter flights, while the SST serves a limited but lucrative high-speed, high-fare international market. Noise levels are down and fuel efficiency is up.

The ATC system, now highly automated but highly costly, is operated by a COMSAT-like quasi-governmental authority. The FAA's activities concentrate increasingly on safety regulation and on safety-related research and development.

Scenarios Contain Uncertainties

The FAA has not identified any one of the scenarios as the most likely; in fact, the FAA believes that elements of each scenario can and probably will coexist during the years ahead. In addition, there are a number of uncertainties. Though most current life-style trends seem conducive to more travel by air, the trends could change:

"Increased sophistication of telecommunications might provide an acceptable substitute for some travel. The 'new ruralism'—the movement of a relatively small number of middle-class young people to the country in recent years—may accelerate, resulting in strong value being placed on staying at home. Moreover, larger families could again become an American

Summary of Major Findings* by Scenario

This table briefly notes the most important findings of the Federal Aviation Administration's recently completed study, *Aviation Futures to the Year 2000*. Most of the scenarios show continuing growth in air carrier operations, air cargo flights, and general (non-commercial) aviation. Most of the scenarios also allow for competition by high-speed ground intercity transit, while several suggest a decline in the use of automobiles for intercity travel.

In the high-growth scenarios, new airplanes such as short takeoff and landing (STOL) craft and 1,000-passenger transports are put into service; in the other scenarios, the emphasis is on improving existing aircraft. Aviation safety improves in most of the scenarios, but the number of accidents increases in some because of the great increase in the number of people flying.

Source: FAA

	AIR CARRIER TRENDS	GENERAL AVIATION TRENDS	FUEL CONSUMPTION	AIRCRAFT TECHNOLOGY
LIMITED GROWTH	• Small increase in operations. • No new aircraft introduced. • Enplaned passengers increased from 208 million (1975) to 406 million.	• From 72% (1970) to 84% of operations at towered airports. • 95% plus of total aircraft.	• Jet: 65% increase to 317 million bbls/yr. • Avgas: 115% increase to 27 million bbls/yr.	• Low R&D activity except for fuel efficiency. • Stretched versions of existing aircraft.
MUDDLING THROUGH	• Decline in operations. • High load factors. • Enplaned passengers increased from 208 million (1975) to 272 million.	• From 72% (1970) to 75% of operations at towered airports. • Decline in GA ops by 4 million.	• Jet: 17% *decrease* to 158 million bbls/yr. • Avgas: 23% *decrease* to 10 million bbls/yr.	• Low R&D activity. • Only minor changes in existing types of aircraft.
RESOURCE ALLOCATION	• Small increase in operations. • Enplaned passengers increased from 208 million (1975) to one-half billion.	• From 72% (1970) to 84% of operations at towered airports. • 95% plus of total aircraft.	• Jet: 65% increase to 317 million bbls/yr. • Avgas: 115% increase to 28 million bbls/yr.	• Moderate R&D activity, concentrating on fuel efficiency and noise reduction.
INDIVIDUAL AFFLUENCE	• 100% increase in operations. • Enplaned passengers increased from 208 million (1975) to 800 million. • STOL and Super turbojets.	• From 72% (1970) to 85% of operations at towered airports. • 95% plus of total aircraft.	• Jet: 169% increase to 517 million bbls/yr. • Avgas: 154% increase to 33 million bbls/yr.	• High levels of technology tempered by environmental concerns. • Fewer new aircraft than Scenario 5
EXPANSIVE GROWTH	• 300% increase in operations. • Enplaned passengers increased from 208 million (1975) to 1 billion. • Jet STOL, Super large, and SST aircraft.	• From 72% (1970) to 85% of operations at towered airports. • 95% plus of total aircraft.	• Jet: 342% increase to 850 million bbls/yr. • Avgas: 423% increase to 68 million bbls/yr.	• Rapid development of new aircraft. • Heavy emphasis on R&D.

*Unless otherwise stated all figures shown are for the year 2000.

norm, especially if anti-abortion legislation passes and/or nursing home care of the elderly is no longer available at acceptable prices. Family enlargement could sharply reduce demand for air pleasure travel because of the reduction it would bring in discretionary income.''

The availability of fuel and other materials in the years ahead is also uncertain.

Other uncertainties which will have an effect on the future of aviation include the availability of capital funds, the role that "special interest" groups will play in public decisions affecting transportation, and the degree of government regulation and economic influence in the transportation field.

Aviation Trends Identified

The FAA says it had two objectives in undertaking the aviation futures study—to see what might be in store for itself and for the aviation community in the next 25 years and "to develop a systematic, repeatable method of conducting this broad planning function.'' The agency believes that the study was a success on both counts.

Although not committing itself to the likelihood of any particular scenario becoming reality, the FAA has drawn some tentative conclusions from its study. Since almost all of the scenarios foresee some growth in aviation, the FAA is generally basing its thinking about the future on the assumption that growth will continue, although it may be very modest under some conditions.

The number of airline passengers will range from 272 million to over one billion by the year 2000 (compared to 208 million in 1975), depending upon the state of the economy and other factors. The amount of cargo shipped by air is expected to grow at least 3% per year for the rest of this century. General aviation, which currently accounts for 98% of the aircraft in use and 75% of total operations at

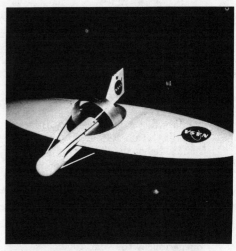

Wind-tunnel model of an advanced technology Remotely Piloted Vehicle (RPV) designed for NASA's Ames Research Center, Mountain View, California. The RPV, whose wing can be yawed at various angles to the flight path, is thought to have potential for a wide variety of civil and military uses. Photo: NASA

AIR TRAFFIC CONTROL TECHNOLOGY	COMPLEMENTARY AND COMPETING MODES	AIR CARGO	AVIATION SAFETY
• UG3rd installation began in 1985. • NAS rate of growth reduced.	• Auto intercity travel declines. • Shift from auto divided between air, rail and mass transit.	• Low growth (less than 3%) due to weak economic conditions.	• Relatively low demand. • Decline in rates and number of accidents.
• Little change in NAS from 1970's.	• Increased telecommunications substituted for travel.	• Low growth (+2%) then decline due to economic conditions.	• Demand less than system capacity, resulting in • Fewer accidents.
• UG3rd in 1985. • 4th generation ground-based ATCS by 2000.	• Auto intercity travel declines. • High speed ground intercity transit.	• Moderate growth (+4%).	• Relatively low rate of increase in demand, and • Increased use of technology in NAS, results in, • Decline in rates and number of accidents.
• UG3rd by 1980. • 4th generation ground-based ATCS by 1990.	• Auto retains major role. • High speed ground intercity transit.	• High growth (+9%). • All-cargo flights increased.	• Technological and procedural advances, but • No decline in numbers of accidents, because of • Heavy increase in aviation activity.
• Automated air-based ATCS by 1990.	• Auto retains major role. • High speed ground intercity transit.	• Very high growth (+12%). • All cargo airports in 1990's.	• Improved technology and operating procedures. • Number of accidents and fatalities do not decline because of high demand.

FAA-towered airports, is expected to remain at approximately that level, even under the more pessimistic conditions, and could account for an even greater percentage of aircraft operations if economic growth is strong. General aviation is expected to be the major FAA workload factor and the primary factor in expansion of the national aviation system throughout the remainder of the 20th century.

The FAA foresees few difficulties in terms of airspace capacity, but the impact of increasing air cargo operations on airports could be a problem. With very high real economic growth, a few large all-cargo airports could be in operation by the year 2000.

These all-cargo airports would be comparable in size to today's large airports. They would have "truck terminal and access facilities of unprecedented scale and sophistication, including access highways built at least to present interstate standards, a sophisticated truck dispatching system, a complex truck routing system within the airport perimeter, and advanced means of maintaining security."

Airport access is very likely to be enhanced with further development of urban transit systems or as an offshoot of new high-speed ground transportation systems.

Unconventional aircraft such as lighter-than-air aircraft probably will not be introduced for passenger service between now and the year 2000, the FAA study concludes. However, with moderate to high economic growth, new conventional aircraft such as a 1,000-passenger transport and a 150-passenger jet STOL will form a small percentage of the air carrier fleet by the end of the century. Only with high growth is a domestic SST expected to enter international service.

People will still rely heavily on airlines for long-distance travel, but various forms of high-speed ground transportation are expected to compete with the airlines over shorter distances. Consequently, the average length of airplane trips is going to increase.

For the next 25 years, all aircraft are expected to continue to burn petroleum-based jet fuel and aviation gasoline; no substitute fuels such as hydrogen are likely to be in use. Due to environmental concerns and energy-saving efforts, existing aircraft engines will probably be improved for fuel efficiency and noise reduction. Airlines likely will operate more economically by serving specific market areas with especially suited and cost-efficient aircraft.

FAA Looks at Its Own Future

The FAA describes its main responsibilities as "the regulation of air commerce to promote its development and safety, and the operation of the air traffic control system in a manner consistent with those objectives."

One of the key questions facing the FAA in the future is how the aviation system should respond to increased demand. Two basic responses are possible: (1) attempting to meet all demand and (2) meeting demand within a selected benefit/cost or cost-effective range. Outside that range, limits could be set by imposing absolute quotas or by excluding certain classes of aircraft or categories of aviation.

The public's response to increasing noise levels near airports as air traffic intensifies has already resulted in airport curfews in some areas, reducing overall airport capacity. In acquiring land for new airports or expansion of existing airports, additional acreage will be required to serve as a noise buffer, adding to the expense. One possible solution to the land problem that the FAA is taking a close look at is "land banking," which involves setting aside land for future airport sites well ahead of the time when they may be needed. Many complications can be avoided by land banking, the FAA

How the Scenarios Were Prepared

The FAA based its study on the assumption that the future of aviation will be based on the interrelationships between new technology and socioeconomic conditions. The study group first identified a set of key variables in the National Aviation System (NAS)—aviation operations, flight lengths, enplaned passengers, FAA employees, trust fund revenues, business productivity, etc. The study group then identified the socioeconomic variables that bear the closest relationship to conditions in the National Air System, including population, GNP per capita, wellhead price of crude oil, price of ferrous and nonferrous metal, etc.

After the major relationships between the two sets of variables had been identified, the group constructed five scenarios based on various rates of growth of population and gross national product. The group then tried to identify the changes that each scenario would bring in FAA policies, air transportation network structure, competition from other modes, etc. For each scenario, projections were then made for the key NAS variables (operating costs, cargo tonnage, general aviation operations, etc.), based on past performance, but adjusted to reflect the new conditions.

All of the data amassed by the preceding steps was then used to project the values of internal aviation system variables such as average seats per aircraft and aircraft speed.

The final step was calculation of revenue passenger miles, aircraft operations, commercial miles flown, air carrier fleet mix and size, fuel consumption, accidents, noise, etc. This was accomplished with the aid of a series of submodels, or algorithms.

The entire process was repeated until internal consistency was achieved. The validity of the forecasts made by this method was checked with the aid of a computerized feedback model.

> "The FAA foresees few difficulties in terms of airspace capacity, but the impact of increasing air-cargo operations on airports could be a problem."

believes. Waiting until the demand exists for an airport means running the risk that the most desirable land may be developed in ways incompatible with airport needs. Also, people living nearby may oppose the building of an airport; with land banking, the property could be purchased in isolated areas where there is little inconvenience to residents and where sufficient land for a noise buffer exists.

In Atlanta, in the early days of aviation, planes began to land on a race track in the surrounding countryside; the property eventually developed into Atlanta's present airport. Atlanta's air traffic has grown and the airport has no room to expand. If futuristic planning and land banking had been used in Atlanta in choosing a site, the problems might have been avoided.

In terms of safety, the FAA says that fatality and accident rates will remain low, but the growth in activity could force up the absolute levels of fatalities and accidents unless stronger or additional safety programs are instituted. To keep up with the increasing numbers and variety of aircraft that will have to be handled, the FAA is implementing a sophisticated semiautomated air traffic control system at all large and medium airports and, near the end of the century, a more fully automated system may be essential as well.

Believing that the challenges of growth in the aviation system over the next 25 years will be increasingly complex and require careful planning, the FAA considers the study described here to be only a first step in its efforts to insure as smooth an adjustment to changing realities as is possible. FAA officials say that the study has already pinpointed some important issues for them. One of the first outgrowths from the study was an issue paper pointing out the potential importance of air cargo in the future—and the accompanying problems. The FAA's futures material is also being used in congressionally requested studies on airport land banking and the need for new airports. The agency is updating the study and expanding it to cover international aviation. FAA officials say that they are very interested in getting feedback from both the aviation community and the public.

With the help of the ideas and methodology developed for this study, the FAA believes that it can reduce the chances of again being caught unprepared for new developments in the aviation field—or in the world at large.

Author Jerry Richardson is Assistant Editor of THE FUTURIST.

Copies of the FAA's study report, Aviation Futures to the Year 2000, may be obtained by writing to: Federal Aviation Administration, Aviation Futures (AVP-110), 800 Independence Avenue, S.W., Washington, D.C. 20591.

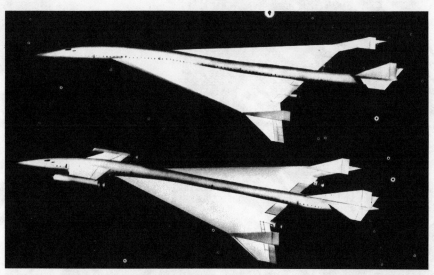

Two proposed designs for advanced supersonic transports. SSTs will be added to the U.S. domestic fleet only as part of an expansive-growth scenario, according to a new Federal Aviation Administration report. Illustration: NASA

Commuter Airlines Enjoy Rapid Growth

Commuter airlines, which provide air service between small communities and large urban airports, have expanded rapidly during the past decade.

The key reasons for this growth are identified by Jonathan D. Mayer in the April issue of Traffic Quarterly. Only one of the four main factors was a technological improvement; the others were favorable changes in the socioeconomic area. The growth factors are:

- Since 1965, the commuter airlines have been allowed to carry U.S. mail, an operation that has been very profitable for them.
- The Civil Aeronautics Board (CAB), in 1964, began to allow the larger airlines to discontinue service to some small communities because "small aircraft in the hands of a commuter carrier could provide better service to the public at the small city involved, primarily by making additional frequencies possible" and because "the commuter could operate at significantly lower cost than could the certificated carrier with its larger equipment."
- Small turbo-prop airplanes have been developed which can carry more passengers than the planes previously used by commuter airlines, yet can still be landed at small airports.
- Some major airlines, such as Allegheny Airlines, have contracted with commuter airlines to provide service to small communities. In describing the advantages of such an arrangement, the CAB says that "While relieving Allegheny of the expenses normally involved in its obligation to provide service to a small community at which it is certificated, the Allegheny Commuter service nonetheless preserves for Allegheny much of the advantage of providing the service. The tie-in between the Allegheny Commuters and Allegheny itself provides Allegheny with a guaranteed source of feeder traffic for its long haul routes, just as if it served the small points itself."

Mayer also notes that 80% of the commuter air traffic consists of people who "take commuter flights to connect with some form of long-haul air transport service."

See "Local and Commuter Airlines in the United States" by Jonathan D. Mayer, Traffic Quarterly, April 1977.

Space Colonies:
THE HIGH FRONTIER

by Gerard K. O'Neill

Photo: NASA

An earth-like space colony could be orbiting our world by 1990, says a Princeton University physicist. The colony's 10,000 inhabitants would enjoy green plants, animals, plains, valleys, hills, and streams. The colonists would pay off the cost of building their extraterrestrial home by manufacturing satellite solar power stations, which would supply cheap, virtually inexhaustable power to the earth.

During the past decade, a number of premises about the basic problems of the world have become very widely accepted. The more important of these accepted ideas are:

1. For the foreseeable future, every significant human activity must be confined to the surface of the earth.

2. The material and energy resources of the human race are just those of our planet.

3. Any realistic solutions to our problems of food, population, energy, and materials must be based on a kind of zero-sum game, in which no resources can be obtained by one nation or group without being taken from another.

Given those premises, logic has driven most observers to the conclusion that long-term peace and stability can only be reached by some kind of systematic global arrangement, with tight constraints to insure the sharing—equable or otherwise—of the limited resources available. I find it personally shocking that many such observers, even those who profess a deep concern for humankind, accept with equanimity the need for massive starvation, war, or disease as necessary precursors to the achievement of such a systematic global arrangement.

In my opinion, based on studies carried out at Princeton University, these three basic premises on which most discussions of the future have been based are simply wrong. The human race stands now on the threshold of a new frontier whose richness is a thousand times greater than that of the new western world of 500 years ago.

That frontier can be exploited for all humanity, and its ultimate extent is a land area many thousands of times that of the entire earth. As little as 10 years ago we lacked the technical capability to exploit that frontier. Now we have that capability, and if we have the willpower to use it, we can not only benefit all humanity, but also spare our threatened planet and permit its recovery from the ravages of the industrial revolution.

The high frontier which I will describe is space, but not in the sense of the Apollo program, a massive effort whose main *lasting* results were scientific. Nor is it space in the sense of the communications and observation satellites, useful as they are. Least of all is it space in the sense of science-fiction, in which harsh planetary surfaces were tamed by space-suited daredevils. Rather, it is a frontier of new lands, located only a few days travel time away from the earth, and built from materials and energy available in space.

Space Colonies: The Basic Plan

The central ideas of space colonization are:

1. To establish a highly-industrialized, self-maintaining human community in free space, at a location along the orbit of the moon called L5, where free solar energy is available full time.

2. To construct that community on a short time scale, without depending on rocket engines any more advanced than those of the space shuttle.

3. To reduce the costs greatly by obtaining nearly all of the construction materials from the surface of the moon.

4. At the space community, to process lunar surface raw materials into metals, ceramics, glass, and oxygen for the construction of additional communities and of products such as satellite solar power stations. The power stations would be relocated in synchronous orbit about the earth, to supply the earth with electrical energy by low-density microwave beams.

5. Throughout the program, to rely only on those technologies which are available at the time, while recognizing and supporting the development of more advanced technologies if their benefits are clear.

The two key factors that make space colonization an economically sound idea are solar energy and lunar

The wheel-like design shown above (and also on the cover) might be used for the first space colony. The mirror floating above the colony reflects sunlight into the ring mirrors below, which reflect it through 100-foot strip windows into the colony's interior for light and agriculture. Above the core sphere are communications and spacecraft docking facilities. Long rectangle in foreground is a heat radiator. The facility below the colony is the manufacturing area where lunar ore is melted with solar power. Lower central sphere is the original "construction shack" for the colony.

Drawing: NASA

materials. As everyone knows, the sun is a virtually inexhaustible source of clean energy. On earth, solar energy use is hampered by nighttime, by seasonal variation in the day-length, and by clouds; in space, solar energy is always available, and also much more intense. The amount of solar energy which flows unused, in a year, through each square meter of free space is 10 times as much as falls on an equal area in even the most cloud-free portions of Arizona or New Mexico. A solar-energy installation in space, therefore, is potentially able to operate at a tenth the cost at which it could operate on earth.

The cost of space colonization could be reduced further by obtaining construction materials from the moon. On earth, we are the "gravitationally disadvantaged." We are at the bottom of a gravitational well 4000 miles deep, from which materials can be lifted into space only at great cost. The energy required to bring materials from the moon to free space is only one twentieth as much as from the earth, and Apollo samples indicate that the moon is a rich source of metals, glass, oxygen, and soil. The moon's lack of an atmosphere reduces further the cost of transporting lunar materials to orbiting space colonies.

Lunar surface raw materials would be transported by a launching device called a mass driver; it exists now only on paper, but it can be designed and built with complete assurance of success because it requires no high-strength materials, no high accelerations or temperatures, and its principles are fully understood. The mass driver would be a linear electric motor, forming a thin line several miles long, which would accelerate small 10-pound vehicles called buckets to lunar escape velocity, at which time they would release their payloads and then return on a side track for reuse. The mass driver would be an efficient machine, driven by a solar-powered or nuclear electric plant.

Building the First Colony

If we were to start now, with determination and drive, I believe that the first space colony (Island One) could be in place, with its productive capacity benefiting the earth, before 1990. This is possible, I must emphasize, within the limits of present-day, conventional materials and technology.

A modified space shuttle and a chemical space tug would be used to transport basic construction equip-

ment, supplies, and 2,000 workmen to a point in space called L5. (L5 is a point in the moon's orbit equidistant from the earth and the moon at which objects will remain in a stable orbit, stationary with respect to the moon.) A smaller work force of about 200 people would establish a lunar outpost which would provide 98% of the raw materials needed for the construction of Island One.

The mass driver, operating only 25% of the time, could lift 500,000 tons of material to L5 in the six-year construction time of Island One. An identical machine, located in space, could be a very effective reaction motor for the shifting of heavy payloads in the 100,000-ton range.

Lunar soil is 40% oxygen, 19.2% silicon, 14.3% iron, 8% calcium, 5.9% titanium, 5.6% aluminum, and 4.5% magnesium. The aluminum would be the primary building material and the oxygen would be used as atmosphere and to fuel rocket engines. Lunar surface materials are poor in carbon, nitrogen, and hydrogen, which would have to be brought from earth. For every ton of hydrogen brought from earth, nine tons of water could be made at the colony site, using oxygen from the processing of lunar oxides.

The removal of half a million tons of material from the surface of the moon sounds like a large-scale mining operation, but it is not. The excavation left on the moon would be only five meters deep and 200 meters long and wide, not even enough to keep one small bulldozer occupied for a five-year period.

In the long run, we can use the fact that the asteroids are also a source of materials. The three largest asteroids alone contain enough materials for the construction of new lands with a total area many thousands of times as large as that of the earth. Once the asteroidal resources are tapped, we should have not only metals, glass, and ceramics, but also carbon, nitrogen, and hydrogen. These three elements, scarce on the moon, are believed to be abundant in the type of asteroid known as carbonaceous chondritic.

Island One

Within the materials limits of ordinary civil engineering practice and within an overall mass budget of 500,000 tons (about the same as the mass of a super-tanker), several designs for the first "island in space" have evolved. All are pressure

Below is an artist's conception of a segment of the wheel-shaped space colony during final stages of construction. Shown is an agricultural area with a lake and a river. These farming sections are interspersed with three more-populated areas, all protected by a shield of lunar slag attached to the outside of the colony shell.

Drawing: NASA

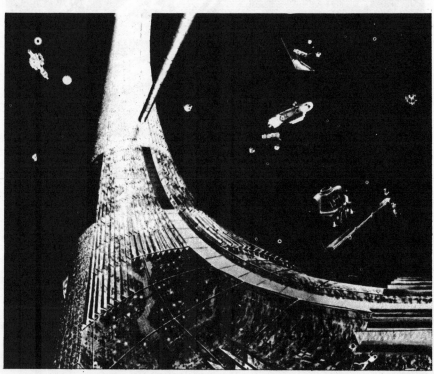

vessels—spherical, cylindrical, or toroidal—containing atmospheres with the same oxygen content as at sea level on earth and rotating slowly to provide a gravity as strong as that of the earth. The axis of the structure would always point toward the sun, the source of all the energy used by the colony.

The first space community would house 10,000 people; 4,000 would be employed building additional colonies, while 6,000 would be producing satellite solar power stations. The interior of the colony will be as earth-like as possible—rich in green plants, trees, animals, birds, and the other desirable features of attractive regions on earth. The design would allow a line of sight of at least a half mile, giving the residents a feeling of spaciousness. The landscape would feature plains, valleys, hills, streams, and lakes. The residential areas might consist of small apartment buildings with big rooms and wide terraces overlooking fields and groves. Near the axis of the structure, gravity would be much reduced and, consequently, human-powered flight would be easy, sports and ballet could take on a new dimension, and weight would almost disappear. It seems almost a certainty that at such a level a person with a serious heart condition could live far longer than on earth, and that low gravity could greatly ease many of the health problems of advancing age.

The space colony would have separate residential, agricultural, and industrial areas, each with its optimal gravity, temperature, climate, sunlight, and atmosphere. Intensive agriculture would be possible, since the day-length and seasonal cycle would be controllable independently for each crop and care would be taken not to introduce into the agricultural areas the insect pests which hamper earth agriculture. Agriculture could be efficient and predictable, free of the extremes of crop failure and glut which the terrestrial environment forces on our farmers. Only 111 acres would be needed to feed all 10,000 residents.

Energy Without Guilt

Energy for agriculture would be used directly in the form of sunlight, interrupted at will by large, aluminum shades located in zero gravity in space near the farming areas. An advanced sewage system would quickly and efficiently turn wastes into pure water and agricultural chemicals. The air, constantly filtered, would be cleaner than in any city on earth.

Non-polluting light industry would probably be carried on within the living-habitat, convenient to homes and shops. Heavy industry, though, could be located in nearby external non-rotating factories because of the advantages of zero gravity. The combination of zero gravity and breathable atmospheres would permit the easy assembly—without cranes, lift-trucks, or other handling equipment—of very large, massive products. These products could be the components of new colonies, radio and optical telescopes, large ships for the further exploration of the solar system, and power plants to supply energy for the earth. Within a century, other industries might be shifted to space colonies because of the abundant, free, pollutionless energy supply and the greater efficiency made possible by zero gravity and the vacuum of space.

Process heat for industry, at temperatures of up to several thousand degrees, would be obtainable at low cost, simply by the use of aluminum-foil mirrors to concentrate the ever-present sunlight. In space, a passive aluminum mirror with a mass of less than a ton and a dimension of about 100 meters, could collect and concentrate, in the course of a year, an amount of solar energy which on earth would cost over a million dollars at standard electricity rates.

Electrical energy for a space community could be obtained at low cost, within the limits of present technology, by a system consisting of a concentrating mirror, a boiler, a conventional turbogenerator, and a radiator, discarding waste heat to the cold of outer space. It appears that, in the environment of a space community, residents could enjoy a per capita usage of energy many times larger even than what is now common in the United States, but could do so with none of the guilt which is now connected with the depletion of an exhaustible resource.

Shape of Future Colonies

While the first space colony will probably be a torus (a wheel-shaped structure), later colonies will be cylinder-shaped. The main reason for the change is that the first colony will be by far the most expensive to produce and the torus will cost less to construct. Once the first colony is in place, the initial investment in equipment and materials from earth will not need to be repeated; consequently, the cost of colony construction will drop drastically. The cylindrical design, considered the most efficient,

---

Why Not a Moon Colony?

Gerard O'Neill offers the following reasons why a colony in space is more practical than one on the surface of the moon:

1. **The availability of energy.** The moon has a 14-day night; therefore, there is a serious problem of obtaining energy. Convenient, low-cost solar power is cut off because of the fact that energy storage over a 14-day period is extremely difficult. On the moon one is probably forced to rely on nuclear power, so one loses one of the principal advantages of working in space.

2. **The moon is more expensive to get to.** To reach the moon, you first have to go into free space, and then go down again.

The analogy that I use is that in our old-fashioned talk about colonizing planetary surfaces, we were rather like a small animal which was deep down in a hole in the ground. The animal climbs at great cost up to the top of the hole and looks out and sees all the grass and flowers and sunshine, and walks across the grass. Then he finds another hole and climbs down to the bottom of that hole again. And in gravitational terms that is exactly what we are doing if we go into free space and then climb down again to the surface of the moon.

The transport costs to get to the moon are about twice as high as they are to go out into free space; that means that the capitalization for productive equipment is up by the same factor of 2.

3. **Control over gravity.** The moon has one-sixth the earth's gravity, you have to take it as it comes, and you can never cut it off. Even to get higher gravity than that is a lot more complicated and expensive on the surface of the moon than it is in free space, where you can simply rotate a vessel to get any gravity that you want. □

will then be as easy to build as the torus.

Each colony would consist of a pair of cylinders, connected by cables and spinning in opposite directions so that the total system would have almost no spin. Alternating stripes of land and window areas would run the length of the cylinders; the cylinder walls would be made of aluminum and glass. Agriculture would be housed in auxiliary capsules connected to the cylinders.

The smallest cylindrical colony, like the torus, would support 10,000 people. Each cylinder would be 3,280 feet long and 328 feet wide. A Model II colony would have three times more area and as many as 100,000 people, and would be less dependent on earth for resources. Model III, which might be built early in the next century, would be so large that a portion of the island of Bermuda or a section of the California coast like Carmel could fit easily within one of its "valleys." Model III residents would begin mining the asteroid belt for resources and would no longer need to import any materials from earth.

A Model IV colony consisting of two cylinders, each 19 miles long and four miles in diameter, could house several million people comfortably. Its atmosphere would be deep enough to include blue skies and clouds. The endcaps of the cylinders could be modeled into duplicates of a mountain range such as the Grand Tetons, with 8,000-foot peaks. A reflected image of the ordinary disc of the sun would be visible in the sky, and the sun's image would move across the sky from dawn to dusk as it does on earth. The land area of one cylinder could be as large as 100 square miles.

Eventually, it may be possible to build even larger spherical structures with diameters of up to 12 miles and a total habitable land area of 250 square miles.

The date of realization of Model IV colonies does not depend on materials or engineering—those we have already. Rather, it depends on a balance between productivity, a rising living standard, and the economies possible with automation. Under the space colony conditions of virtually unlimited energy and materials resources, a continually rising real income for all colonists is possible—a continuation rather than the arrest of the industrial revolution. Reasonable estimates of 3% per year for the real income rise, 8% for interest costs, and 10% for automation advances put the crossover date (the date when large

The largest (Model IV) space colonies, which could be functioning by 2025, will probably consist of two connected cylinders, each 19 miles long, four miles in diameter, and containing as much as 100 square miles in total land area. The most beautiful living areas on earth could be duplicated in the colonies. The bridge shown here, to give an idea of the dimensions involved, is similar in size to the San Francisco Bay Bridge. A Model IV colony could hold up to several million people comfortably, but the interior design pictured here is intended for only about 200,000 people.

Drawing: NASA

Night is approaching in this Model IV space colony cylinder, which is 19 miles long and four miles in diameter. The atmosphere in the large colonies is deep enough to include blue skies and clouds. A reflected image of the sun moves across the sky from dawn to dusk. The amount of light entering the cylinder is controlled by mirrors outside the stripes of window areas which alternate with the land areas in the colony. The earth-like atmospheric effects make the colony seem more spacious and natural.

Drawing: NASA

colonies become economically feasible) about 40 to 50 years from now—well within the lifetimes of most of the people who are now alive.

First Colony Could Cost $100 Billion

The best estimate currently available is that the establishment of Island One would cost $100 billion, with a possible variation of $50 billion in either direction. That figure is 2.5 times the cost of Project Apollo and 5-15% of the estimated cost of Project Independence, the U.S. energy self-sufficiency plan. To put the cost of the first space colony in perspective, a list of approximate costs for other large-scale engineering projects (in 1975 dollars) follows:

a) Panama Canal $2 billion
b) Space Shuttle Development $5-8 billion
c) Alaska Pipeline $6 billion
d) Advanced Lift Vehicle
   Development $8-25 billion
e) Apollo $39 billion
f) Super Shuttle Development $45 billion
g) Manned Mission to Mars $100 billion
h) Project Independence $600-2000 billion

The Apollo project provided trips to the moon for a total of 12 men, at a cost of about three billion dollars per man. In space colonization we are considering, for Island One, a thousand times as many people for a long duration rather than for only a few days. With the cost savings outlined earlier, it appears that we can accomplish this thousand-fold increase at a cost of at most a few times that of the Apollo project.

The eventual cost of building the first colony will be affected significantly by the following variables:

1. Frequency and efficiency of crew rotation between the earth and L5, and between the earth and the moon, during the construction period.

2. Extent of resupply needed during construction. This item can vary over a wide range, depending on the atmospheric composition needed at the construction station, and whether food is shipped in water-loaded or dry form.

3. Atmospheric composition. The structural mass of Island One is proportional to the internal atmospheric pressure, but independent of the strength of artificial gravity produced by rotation. Nitrogen constitutes 79% of earth's atmosphere, but we do not use it in breathing. To provide an earth-normal amount of nitrogen would cost us two ways in space colony construction, because structure masses would have to be increased to

contain the higher pressure, and because nitrogen would have to be imported from the earth. A final choice of atmospheric mix would be based on a more complete understanding of fire protection.

With these factors in mind, three different preliminary cost estimates have been made for construction of Island One. My own spartan estimate, $33 billion, would allow for no crew rotation, an oxygen atmosphere, little resupply, and small power plants (10Kg/Kw) on the moon and at L5. The NASA Marshall Space Flight Center made two independent cost estimates for the project last year. The initial estimate, $200 billion, includes chemical and nuclear tugs, super shuttle development, orbital bases, an oxygen/nitrogen atmosphere, extensive crew rotation, resupply at 10 pounds per man/day, and power plants at 100 Kg/Kw. A later re-estimate, carrying a $140 billion price tag, eliminates unnecessary lift systems, but still includes the oxygen/nitrogen atmosphere, crew rotation, resupply at

10 pounds per man/day, and power plants at 100 Kg/Kw. The two NASA estimates also appear to include a contingency factor for problems not yet identified.

Energy for the Earth

Island One will pay for itself mainly by manufacturing satellite solar power stations which would supply the earth with an inexhaustible energy supply. At present, both the industrial nations and the underdeveloped third world nations are vulnerable to the threat of supply cutoff by the Middle East oil-producing nations. The only permanent escape from that threat lies in developing an inexhaustible energy source with a cost low enough to make synthetic fuel production economically feasible.

Nuclear power is moderately expensive (1.5 cents/KWH) and is accompanied by the problems of nuclear proliferation and radioactive waste disposal. Fossil fuels are scarcer now, and intensive strip-mining for coal will almost inevitably further damage the environment. Solar energy on the

Asimov Supports Space Colonization

Noted science writer Isaac Asimov, in a written statement submitted to the House Subcommittee on Space Science and Applications in August 1975, said, "It is my opinion that the important goal for space exploration over the next century is the establishment of an ecologically independent human colony on the Moon, or on artificial space colonies that use the Moon as a quarry for raw materials. The reasons for this follow:

(1) Observatories beyond Earth's atmosphere can lead to a better knowledge of the Universe and the laws of nature governing it—with unpredictable but surely great applications to the human way of life.

(2) The presence of infinite amounts of hard vacuum, of low temperatures, of high solar radiation, should make possible industrial activities of types not practical on Earth, leading to unpredictable but surely great advances in technology.

(3) The establishment of a working colony, ecologically independent, on either the Moon or in an artificial structure in space will require a society fundamentally different from our own—a society that can live in an engineered environment under conditions of

strict recycling and mineral waste. Since this is precisely the sort of condition toward which Terrestrial life is tending (barring a catastrophe that destroys our technology altogether), the colonies will serve as schools to Earth, as experiments in living from which we may profit immensely.

(4) The establishment of a colony will be difficult enough and expensive enough to require a global—rather than a national—effort. The effort will be great enough to supply mankind with a common goal and a common sense of pride that may transcend local chauvinisms, and thus encourage the growth of a global political community—and indeed serve as a substitute for the emotional catharsis of war.

(5) Lunar or space colonists, living in engineered worlds, on the inside, would be more psychologically adapted to life in a spaceship undertaking long voyages, so it will be they rather than Earthmen by whom the rest of the Solar system (and eventually the stars perhaps) will be explored.

(6) Colonies in space generally will supply a chance for growth and adventure after Earth itself has, perforce, adopted a no-growth philosophy." □

Interest in Space Colonies Rises

During the past year, Gerard O'Neill's space colonization concept has captured the imagination of a rapidly increasing number of people. He reports that he gets more mail than he can answer, and 99% of the letters are favorable.

Last July, O'Neill's testimony also impressed the Subcommittee on Space Science and Applications of the U.S. House of Representatives. Near the end of the testimony, Subcommittee Chairman Don Fuqua (a Florida Democrat) said of the space colonization project, "It's something that will happen, and even though it kind of boggles the mind at the present time, it is not beyond the realm of possibility. I hope I live to see it." The Subcommittee concluded, in its official report, that orbital colonies were "potentially feasible" and deserving of close examination. It also stated that "concepts and methods for the space-based generation of electricity, using energy from the sun, should be developed and demonstrated as

a significant contribution to solution of the fossil fuel dilemma." Finally, the Subcommittee gave its support to "an expanded space program in FY 1977-1978, at least 25% greater than current funding, to undertake new space initiatives." Fuqua later said that " ... bold new space programs, such as the possibility of space colonization, based on realistic appraisals of potential space progress, deserve serious consideration. It is apparent that the imagination, skill, and technology exists to expand the utilization and exploration of space."

Astronomer Carl Sagan, testifying before the subcommittee, declared that "our technology is capable of extraordinary new ventures in space, one of which is the space city idea, which Gerard O'Neill has described to you. That's an extremely expensive undertaking, but it seems to me historically of the greatest significance. The engineering aspects of it as far as I can tell are perfectly well worked out by O'Neill's study

group. It is practical." O'Neill says that Wernher von Braun has also expressed interest in his project.

The space colony idea also was examined last year by 28 physical and social scientists participating in the NASA/ASEE/Stanford University 1975 Summer Study at the Ames Research Center in Mountain View, California. The 10-week study was sponsored by NASA's Ames Research Center, Stanford University, and the American Society for Engineering Education (ASEE). The group found no insurmountable problems that would prevent successful space colonization and recommended "that the United States, possibly in cooperation with other nations, take specific steps toward the goal of space-colonization."

A Princeton Conference on Space Manufacturing Facilities was hosted by O'Neill last May. The Proceedings will be published later this year.

A number of technical papers supporting the space colony idea have appeared recently, including "R & D Requirements for Initial Space Colonization" by T. A. Heppenheimer and Mark Hopkins

earth is an unreliable source, suitable for daytime peak loads in the American southwest, but not clearly competitive in most applications at the present time.

For several years, design groups at Boeing Aircraft and at Arthur D. Little, Inc., have studied the concept of locating large solar power stations in geosynchronous orbit—where sunlight is available 99% of the time—to convert solar energy to electricity and beam it by microwaves to earth, where it would be reconverted to ordinary electricity. Already, an overall transmission efficiency of 54% has been demonstrated in tests. The main stumbling block has been the problem of lift costs. Construction of the satellite solar power station (SSPS) units at the space colony, using lunar materials to avoid the high lift costs from earth, would make solar energy competitive with other energy sources even from the start, according to my calculations. Eventually, solar electric power rates would be much lower than those of coal-fired or nuclear power plants. No thermal, chemical, or radioactive pollution would be created, and the microwave intensity would not exceed official exposure limits.

"The human race stands now on the threshold of a new frontier whose richness is a thousand times greater than that of the new western world of 500 years ago."

If development of the space colonies proceeds on the fastest possible time-scale (with intensive design beginning this year and major construction of the first colony beginning in 1982), the program could pay back all of the total investment (plus 10% interest) in 24 years. The total investment cost includes the development and construction cost of the first colony; the cost of lifting the materials needed from the earth for subsequent colonies and for non-colony-built SSPS components; a payment in dollars on earth of $10,000 per person/year to every colonist, representing that portion of salaries convertible to goods and services on earth (for subsequent use on visits or, if desired, on retirement); and a carrying charge of 10% interest on the total investment (outstanding principal) in every year of the program. The economic output of the program is measured in the sale of solar power at initial rates of 1.5 cents per Kilowatt-hour, gradually dropping to one cent per Kilowatt-hour.

To produce the necessary number of power satellites within this time-scale, a total work force of 100,000-200,000 people would be required. In our calculations, we assumed that the construction of the first colony would take

(both of the Summer Study) and "Space Production of Satellite Solar Power Stations," an analysis by William Agosto, a project engineer with the Microwave Semiconductor Corporation, Somerset, New Jersey.

University courses are beginning to be offered dealing with various aspects of space colonization. Magoroh Maruyama of Portland State University is teaching a course on Extraterrestrial Community Systems, which explores new cultural options; possible psychological and social problems; and alternative physical, architectural, environmental, and social designs. Massachusetts Institute of Technology now has an undergraduate course in space systems engineering, emphasizing space colonies. Beginning this May, futurist Dennis Livingston will teach a course at Rensselaer Polytechnic Institute in Troy, New York, called "Space Colonies: A Technology Assessment." The course will cover technical, economic, moral, political, and social aspects of space colonies.

The American Institute of Aeronautics and Astronautics is lobbying for more congressional support for O'Neill's project, and he was a keynote speaker during the Institute's Annual Meeting in Washington, D.C., on January 30.

For those interested in keeping informed about the latest developments in O'Neill's space colonization efforts, several newsletters are now available.

Gerard O'Neill puts out his own *Newsletter on Space Colonization* periodically. The newsletter summarizes recent work, lists the latest magazine articles and books dealing with space colonies, lists lectures scheduled on the subject, reports on the status of the space colony group at Princeton University, and advises of future plans. The newsletter is free. Simply write to Professor Gerard K. O'Neill, Physics Department, Princeton University, P.O. Box 708, Princeton, New Jersey 08540.

L-5 News is a monthly newsletter produced by the L-5 Society, a group formed recently "to educate the public about the benefits of space communities and manufacturing facilities, to serve as a clearing house for information and news in this fast developing area, and to raise funds to support work on these concepts where public money is not available or is inappropriate." *L-5 News* contains news articles; listings of courses, lectures, publications, and conferences; and letters. Membership in the L-5 Society costs $20 (regular) or $10 (student), which should be sent to L-5 Society, 1620 North Park Avenue, Tucson, Arizona 85719.

Another newsletter which reports on O'Neill's ideas occasionally (as well as other space concepts) is the *EARTH/SPACE* Newsletter. EARTH/SPACE describes itself as a commercial space venture dedicated to free space enterprise and "focusing on market development and methods of making space profitable to the commercial user." The *EARTH/SPACE* Newsletter is available for $5 per year from EARTH/SPACE, 2319 Sierra, Palo Alto, California 94303.

O'Neill received a small grant from NASA in 1975, but he believes that additional funding this year of between 0.5 and 1.0 million dollars is needed for basic research if the project is to continue to develop at the fastest possible rate. ☐

six years; thereafter, each colony could replicate itself in two years. Each colony would produce two SSPS units per year. The productivity implied, 13-25 tons/person-year, is similar to that of heavy industry on earth. New colony construction would be halted after the 16th colony, due to market saturation. In this scenario, the benefit/cost ratio would be 2.7.

By the 11th year of the program (1993 on the fastest possible timescale), the energy flowing to the power grids on earth from L5-built SSPS units could exceed the peak flow rate of the Alaska pipeline. By the 13th year, the SSPS plants could fill the entire market for new generator capacity in the U.S. By year 17, the total energy provided could exceed the total estimated capacity of the entire Alaska North Slope oil field. Given the rapid growth of the manufacturing capacity and the possibility of power cost reductions, true "energy independence" for the nations taking part in the L5 project could occur before the year 2000, with a shift to production of synthetic fuels.

Cooperative Multinational Program Is Desirable

There are, in my opinion, at least five or six nations or groups of nations

"By 2150, there could be more people living in space than on earth ... Earth might serve mainly as a tourist attraction—a carefully preserved monument to man's origin."

which possess the technical and economic ability to carry out the construction of Island One on their own. In my own view, I would like to see a cooperative multinational program formed, based on participation by all interested nations. It would be in the interest not only of the energy-consuming industrial nations, but also of the oil-producing nations to take part in the program, since it would result in a drastic drop in the market value of Middle Eastern oil before the end of this century. A cooperative international program could have a real stabilizing effect on world tensions.

It would be naive to assume that the benefits of space colonization will be initially shared equitably among all of humanity, but the resources of space are so great that those who are first to exploit them can well afford to provide the initial boost that will allow their less advantaged fellow humans to share the wealth. Suddenly given a new world market of several hundred billion dollars per year, the first group of nations to build space manufacturing facilities could easily divert some fraction of the new profits to providing low-cost energy to nations poor in mineral resources, and to assisting underdeveloped nations by providing them with initial space colonies of

Author Gerard O'Neill, Professor of Physics at Princeton University, hopes that space colonization will be a cooperative international program, bringing world peace a step closer.

their own. The resources of space are so great that even those nations which achieve the ability to use them only after a long delay will still find an abundance remaining. It should also be emphasized that the provision of unlimited low-cost energy to the developing nations will probably be the most effective contribution we could make to solving the world's food problem, because the cost of chemicals for high-yield agriculture is almost entirely the cost of energy for their production.

If we use our intelligence and our concern for our fellow human beings in this way, we can, without any sacrifice on our own part, make the next decades a time not of despair, but of fulfilled hope, of excitement, and of new opportunity.

Public Response Is Favorable

The evidence of the past year indicates that, in terms of public response, space colonization may become a phenomenon at least as powerful as the environmental movement. Since the first small, informal conference in May, 1974, a rapidly increasing number of articles about it have appeared in newspapers and magazines, and all have been quite favorable. Radio and television coverage has also increased rapidly.

A volunteer organization in Tucson, Arizona, recently spent an intensive week trying to get information to people about the space project, and two weeks later carried out a random sampling telephone survey. They report that 45% of the people in that city now

know about this project, and of those who know about it, two-thirds of them are already in favor of it.

The mail that I get—from many nations around the world, as well as the United States—runs 100-to-1 in favor of the project. Also, encouragingly, less than 1% of all mail is in any way irrational. Many of the correspondents have offered volunteer help, and are actively working at the present time in support of the space colonization concept. The letters express the following reasons why this concept, in contrast to all other space options now extant, is receiving such broad support:

1. It is a right-now possibility. It could be realized within the immediate future.

2. In contrast to the elitism of the Apollo project or a manned mission to Mars, it offers the possibility of direct personal participation by large numbers of ordinary people. Many of the correspondents, from hard-hat construction workers to highly-educated

> **"The evidence of the past year indicates that, in terms of public response, space colonization may become a phenomenon at least as powerful as the environmental movement."**

professional people, see themselves as prospective colonists.

3. In contrast to such technical options as the supersonic transport, nuclear power, or the strip-mining of coal, it is seen as offering the possibility of satisfying real needs while preserving rather than further burdening the environment.

4. It is seen as opening a new frontier, challenging the best that is in us in terms of technical ability, personal motivation and the desire for human freedom. Many correspondents refer to space colonization by analogy to the discovery of the New World or to the settlement a century ago of the American frontier.

Colonies Offer Freedom and Diversity

By about the year 2018, emigration to better land, better living conditions, better job opportunities, greater freedom of choice and opportunity in small-scale, eventually independent communities could become a viable option for more people than the population increase rate. The cultural diversity will be enormous (in exact contrast, I think, to the way things are going on earth at the present time). By 2150, there could be more people living in space than on earth. The reduction of population pressures on earth, left possibly with only a few billion people, would allow the planet to recover from the ravages of the industrial revolution. Earth might serve mainly as a tourist attraction—a carefully preserved monument to man's origin. At the same time, tourism and trade among the colonies would be practical and desirable, insuring the survival and growth of the colonies.

From the vantage point of several decades in the future, I believe that our children will judge the most important benefits of space colonization to have been not physical or economic, but the opening of new human options, the possibility of a new degree of freedom, not only for the human body, but much more important, for the human spirit and sense of aspiration. □

Gerard O'Neill, Professor of Physics at Princeton University, is noted for his work in high-energy experimental particle physics. He is the leading proponent of the space colonization concept, which he originated in 1969. His address is Physics Department, Box 708, Princeton University, Princeton, New Jersey 08540. The foregoing article is based on the author's presentation to the World Future Society's Second General Assembly in June, 1975, and on his testimony before Congress on July 23, 1975.

THE PREVENTIVE PSYCHIATRY OF THE FUTURE

by Stanley Lesse

Psychiatry and psychotherapy may be replaced in the years ahead by a future-oriented health science discipline whose practitioners would stress prevention of health problems. Cybernated health science systems would handle many tasks now performed by skilled medical personnel.

Since the end of World War II, the rate of technological and social change has accelerated to a degree never before experienced in all of recorded history. Because of this rapid rate of change, many traditional institutions accustomed to today-oriented planning are being forced to modify their structure and goals in order to survive. Psychiatry and psychotherapy are no exceptions. Many of our psychiatric and psychotherapeutic theories and techniques are now anachronisms in that they reflect late Victorian sociocultural patterns and early 20th century needs rather than current realities.

The constantly changing state of society in many ways has made obsolete much of the today-oriented planning in psychiatry and psychotherapy. Psychiatric institutions, concepts, and treatment techniques must take into account not just present situations, but also the circumstances that are likely to occur in 10, 20, or even 30 years. What we do today must be seen as a logical step along a flexibly planned path leading to optimum application at a tentative period in the future. Psychiatrists and psychotherapists, in order to be prepared for their changing roles, should be students of futures forecasting.

In the next few decades, I see three basic factors that are likely to have the major impact on the structure of civilization (They will not, of course, be the only forces): (1) socioeconomic and sociopolitical forces; (2) a decrease in available living space due to population growth; and (3) the widespread use of automation and cybernation. These forces will mold the societal climate that will determine the types of psychodynamic and psychosocial disturbances that will prevail in the future, as well as the techniques that will be required to effectively treat them.

1. **Socioeconomic and sociopolitical forces:** Our future society will probably become increasingly group-oriented and more highly organized. Group orientation is evolving gradually but with growing momentum in the form of big government, big business, and big labor. Psychosocial studies indicate that the progressive growth of large hierarchically-ordered institutions leads employees to become more inclined toward group goals, *we*-oriented rather than *I*-oriented. In group-oriented environments, unanimity is stressed and great individual expectations become diluted. In large organizations, persons stressing individual expectations are often rejected as anti-group trouble-makers.

Psychosocial stress in the future will have different sources from those of today, in great measure because the group ego will supersede the individual ego in importance. The individual, rather than being preoccupied by his personal self, will probably find it increasingly necessary to change his orientations to fit in as a part of the integrated group in order to be accepted by his society—or indeed to survive.

Future man may very likely experience illness as being detached from the group and health as being integrated into the group, with one of future man's great concerns being the threat of physical and psychological separation from the group. Indeed, psychiatrists are beginning to observe such separation anxiety with increasing frequency among persons working in large institutions.

2. Population growth and scarcity of space: Despite efforts to retard population growth, the world will likely have more than six billion people by the year 2000, two billion more than now. One crucial factor that will shape our future society is the fixed and limited amount of land available for living and working. The finiteness of available space, combined with the accelerating trend toward urbanization, will make horizontal expansion difficult, if not impossible. It is important to recognize, in this connection, that with increased complexity and tightness of organization, the number of interrelationships between individuals increases geometrically. Thus, when two people occupy a limited space, there are two relationships possible. With six people, the number of relationships increases to a hundred. To cope with a situation in which millions will be living in a relatively tightly defined area, new regulatory devices will almost surely have to be instituted.

Massive population expansion and urbanization may necessitate increased structuralization of society. When individuals are integrated into any organized group, less space is needed for effective interpersonal functioning than when the same number of persons are free to act without restrictions. For example, one can imagine the chaos that would occur in a crowded army camp in which 75,000 troops were confined in an area of 25 or even 50 square miles, if there were no regulatory guidelines. If everyone in this congested situation were a grand individualist, free to follow the dictates of his impulses, destructive anarchy would result. The same rule would also hold for megalopolises saturated with tens of millions of inhabitants. The overpopulation problem will invite new efforts to determine how we can preserve individual prerogatives in the face of these anticipated restrictions.

3. Automation and cybernation: Cybernation is often confused with very sophisticated mechanization, but there is an important difference: The most sophisticated mechanical system is "open"; that is, a human being is needed to operate it by closing what is called a "controlling loop" (the on-off, go-no-go signals to the machine). In contrast, a fully cybernated system is closed; the human component is supplanted by a computing machine. The increasingly cybernated world of the future will necessitate radical changes in technological, political, and social thinking.

The cybercultural revolution, whose early rumblings are heard in the upheavals we are experiencing today, differs radically from previous innovations because man now has devices which will largely supplant certain activities of his mind as well as his body. In the age of cyberculture, enormous segments of the population are likely to live in leisure. Fewer and fewer will produce more and more. Drudgery will become increasingly unnecessary.

Heretofore, the unemployment that has occurred as the result of automation has principally affected unskilled labor. Cybernation, in all likelihood, will also replace those whom we now consider to be highly skilled technicians, including many health science specialists. Because of this equalizing effect alone, cybernation will have a profound impact not only upon the economic but also upon the philosophical aspects of this new revolution.

Cybernation, social and economic change, and population growth *must* be viewed, however, as an indivisible, interreacting group of forces. To consider them separately would inevitably lead to tragic error.

Medicine Will Be Health-Oriented

Medicine, in general, and psychiatry and psychotherapy in particular, have traditionally been disease-oriented. We wait for the patient to become ill before we institute treatment. Then, for the most part, we apply "blowout-patch treatment," with the therapeutic processes usually being directed at abnormal behavior or syndromes.

Such an approach is inefficient and anachronistic. It is like permitting an infection to become an epidemic before taking any action. In the world of the not-too-distant future, it will probably be socially and economically unthinkable to relegate psychiatric techniques purely to the repair of psychologically disturbed persons rather than to the prevention of psychic disturbances.

The disease orientation of the medical sciences is a continuation of primitive concepts concerning the causes of illness, especially psychological illness. Hopefully, the disease orienta-tion will disappear when the health sciences—which by definition will be "health-oriented"—supersede the medical sciences, including psychiatry.

Health Sciences in the Year 2000

Several current trends point to the development of cybernated systems in the health sciences and the consequent displacement of skilled personnel who are now considered indispensable. The trends include:

1. Marked acceleration in the development of sophisticated measuring equipment and computers that can readily be adapted to medical diagnostics.

2. Pressure from a mushrooming population for more extensive medical care facilities. Projected demands far exceed the projected capacities to train medical and paramedical personnel of the type with which we are now familiar.

3. Current educational trends encouraging medical students to specialize in the early years of their training, thus eliminating the traditional practice of educating the young physician to be a generalist before he becomes a specialist.

4. The crowded, group-oriented, highly automated world that seems destined to become a reality in the not-too-distant future. In this environment, patients will probably not object to a more impersonal type of health-science care.

Two New Types of Health Scientists

In 1966, I first described the apparent necessity for two general types of professionally trained individuals who would be required to care for health needs in a highly structured, integrated and automated society. Tentatively, these two types of health scientists can be labeled as *medical academicians* (MA's) and *medical-technical experts* (MTE's).

The medical academician would be trained primarily in the comprehension, expansion, and pragmatic application of the dynamic interrelationships between physiodynamics, psychodynamics, and sociodynamics. These three terms may be defined as follows:

• **Physiodynamics** refers to the state or changing state of the individual's anatomic structures and physiological and biochemical functions, and their mutual interdependence in relationship to one another and in relationship to psychodynamic and sociodynamic factors.

- **Psychodynamics** refers to the state or changing state of the individual with regard to all psychic functions, conscious and unconscious, and their mutual interdependence in relation to physiodynamic and sociodynamic factors.

- **Sociodynamics** refers to the state or changing state of an individual's external environment and its mutual interdependence in relation to physiodynamic and psychodynamic factors.

The central theme to be stressed here is that whenever there is an alteration in one area of human function, there is inevitably an alteration in other areas or aspects of the same function and all other functions both internal and external, until a state of relative equilibrium is reached. This concept differs fundamentally from the widely followed "team" approach, in which a group of specialists under a single leader expresses opinions concerning a specific patient or problem. The sum of many parts does not necessarily make for a unified, functional whole. The encouragement of expressions of creativity must be one of the cornerstones of a medical academician's training. The medical academician—as teacher, leader, and programmer in our future society—would require basic qualities different from those trained to be medical-technical experts.

The medical-technical expert working with sophisticated automated devices would take over many tasks now performed by today's highly skilled physicians. Most routine diagnoses and therapies would undoubtedly be performed by the MTE-computer combination. Automated devices would take histories, perform specialized biochemical, physiological, and psychological tests and then record and analyze the results. ("Computest" language in the form of "yes" and "no" answers can be used to sharply define specific symptoms and syndromes.) The data would then be automatically correlated. The testing and analysis of the data would probably be done far more accurately and intensively than most of today's diagnosticians can accomplish. The machines very likely would indicate not only the nature of the problem but also the appropriate types of therapy.

The medical-technical expert would be highly trained for very specific, limited jobs. Since his field of operation would be sharply circumscribed, his education would require far less time than that of today's medical specialist. He would learn to interpret and apply, in combination with automated systems, the program methods developed by the medical academicians.

District Clinics Might Replace Most Physicians

The two types of health scientists would function in an entirely new physical structure. Health science institutions would likely become hierarchically structured so as to guarantee a maximum of efficiency and a minimum of duplication. For health-science purposes, a "district general medical clinic" (DGMC) might supplant the general practitioner and, in most instances, the current types of medical specialists. These clinics, structured around the MTE-computer team, would be constructed at locations determined by area and population.

Patients whose illnesses are too obscure or refractory to treatment to be managed by the MTE-computer team would be referred to "regional specialty centers" (RSC's) equipped with more sophisticated diagnostic devices and more specifically programmed computers. Each RSC, operating under the supervision of a medical academician, would be capable of treating a limited number of in-patients on a short-term basis.

Finally, there would be "zone specialty hospitals" (ZSH's) which would manage patients who require long-term treatment entailing more intricate equipment or facilities. The zone specialty hospital, which would also serve as a research and training institute, would be headed by a medical academician who would supervise the programming of the cybernated systems and act as the coordinator of the specialized MTE-computer teams.

Enormous strides will be made in the development of newer physiological and psychopharmacological techniques that will be effective in the active treatment of individuals with psychological problems. Entirely new psychotherapeutic procedures will be necessary to accommodate patients whose clinical problems may result from types of stress different from those commonly encountered today.

"For health science purposes, a district general medical clinic (DGMC) might supplant the general practitioner and, in most instances, the current types of medical specialists."

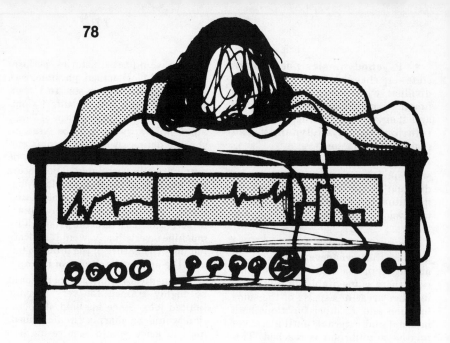

Prophylactic Psycho-Bio-Sociology

Psychiatrists and psychotherapists now spend a considerable part of their time as diagnosticians. The automated systems will take histories infinitely more detailed than those obtained today and will indicate appropriate diagnoses and treatment.

Preserving mental health is likely to be the psychiatrist's and psychotherapist's main concern in the future. Prophylactic measures of a psychological nature should become part and parcel of the socio-political structure. In the future, the psychotherapist and indeed the political scientist must be profoundly concerned with the influence of economic and political institutions on the psychological well-being of the individual. For example, the new breed of mental health scientist will seek to have positive supports to the individual's ego structure automatically built into the political system and attempt to eliminate or modify economic or political systems that may place one's adaptive mechanisms under stress.

My studies of psychological problems in different countries have demonstrated that certain types of psychological illnesses inevitably develop as nations become industrialized. For example, agitated depressions occurring in middle-aged persons are not common among those living in the agricultural, rural portions of Japan or India, whereas they are noted with increased frequency in the industrialized-metropolitan communities. In the same fashion, a variety of clinical syndromes may result from psychosocial incompatibilities due to stresses that will be unique for the developing post-industrial state.

All economic, political, and philosophical systems have some aspects that are compatible with modern man's ego structure and other aspects that are incompatible. For example, our current industrial societies have large numbers of persons who become psychologically disturbed, in part due to their inability to tolerate the stress associated with the competitive economic structure. On the other hand, the restrictions placed upon upward mobility associated with highly structured, socialistic economies also have been a source of psychic difficulty. A serious effort should be made to determine which aspects of different economic and political systems are innately more beneficial or more stressful to the psychic existence of the individual.

All those whom we now designate as psychiatrists, psychologists, social scientists, and political scientists should in the future become "psycho-bio-sociologists." Because they must understand the dynamic interrelationships between sociodynamics (the function of social groupings) and individual psychodynamics, this new breed of humanistic scientist will have to be prepared by a new concept of education. Our traditional educational system emphasizes the encyclopedic method of learning, which is anachronistic in view of the massive accumulation of new data and man's inability to memorize information beyond certain limits. This mushrooming plethora of facts can and will be recorded by automated memory banks that will have far greater retentive capabilities than the human brain. In addition, the machines have the capacity for immediate and total recall whenever required.

The emphasis on the encyclopedic method of learning should be replaced by a system that emphasizes the need to interrelate information that will be immediately available from various memory banks. The emphasis upon intelligence quotients (I.Q.'s) would be relegated to an educational museum, since they reflect a memory-bank psychology. I.Q. tests measure only the child's capacity to recapitulate or "play back" the information to which he was exposed by very verbal parents.

We must develop methods of detecting early in life those persons who have the propensity to interrelate information. In addition, we must develop theories and methodologies aimed at encouraging the development of the capacity to interrelate knowledge.

The maturation of the psychological sciences and social sciences will be signalled by their disappearance in their present form, to be replaced by an entirely new science—psycho-bio-sociology. The new science will not be a summation of psychodynamic, biodynamic, and sociodynamic factors, but will reflect the indivisible interrelationships between the individual and his society. The future psycho-bio-sociologists will be actively involved in the development and evaluation of sociopolitical systems that could be optimally compatible with human adaptation.

Treatment of Latent Illness

The concept of prophylaxis may take on another form. For example, active therapy, in some instances, very likely will be instituted *before* illnesses become overt, while they are in a latent form. This prophylactic type of therapy is likely to be made possible through *health science memory banks*. In coming decades, all individuals in the United States and certain other countries are likely to have automated medical records. Every contact that a patient has with the health system will be electronically recorded in a regional memory bank.

The records will be available for immediate recall whenever the patient has a medical examination. In addition, they will be screened periodically by computers, and those individuals whose records are interpreted by the computer-analyst as demonstrating adverse psycho-physio-sociological problems will be automatically called up for early therapy. If a person moves from one portion of the country to another, his medical records can be simultaneously transferred electronically to another memory bank in the area where the individual now resides. In keeping with this administrative-technological likelihood, most psychophysiological, psychosocial or psychosociological problems are likely to be diagnosed and treated in a subliminal or barely discernable phase. Consequently, new conceptualizations of psychiatric and psychotherapeutic techniques will be necessary.

Future-Oriented Psychotherapy

Future-oriented psychotherapy is a prophylactic therapeutic procedure that is radically new in both theory and practice. As such, it cannot be understood in terms of older theories and procedures.

Viewed in terms of future-oriented psychotherapy, psychoanalytic psychotherapy is largely past-oriented and focused upon habit patterns, frustrations, and identifications related to the early development of the individual. Similarly, the theoretical concepts that evolved from any today-oriented therapy—such as ego psychology, behavior therapy, hypnotism, or existential psychology—have no direct relationship to future-oriented theory or technique.

One obstacle to effective dealing with the future is prejudicial or mood-dominated thinking. For example, most persons project into the future in a wishful-thinking pattern. In some instances, the thinking is utopian in character. In other instances, individuals project into the future in an anti-utopian manner which might be labeled as negative or pessimistic projection. The patient should be helped to view the world of the future as it is likely to be rather than as he wishes it to be. At times, it is theoretically possible to blend wishful thinking with pragmatic projection.

In future-oriented psychotherapy, the primary goal is to help a person plan for his or her own destiny. The therapy proceeds by helping individuals to visualize how their roles will appear to be at a certain time in the future, whether five, 10, 20, or even 30 years from the present. The purpose is to motivate them to take steps in the present that will prepare them for that future reality.

The point in therapy at which futuristic considerations are introduced depends upon a number of factors, some of which include the patient's age, the nature and severity of the psychosocial problem, the patient's intelligence and social awareness, the degree of psychic maturity attained in therapy, the ability to manage current stresses and discern other symptoms and signs of mounting anxiety, and the rigidity of the personality structure. A final factor is

"The medical-technical expert working with sophisticated, automated devices would take over many tasks now performed by today's highly skilled physicians."

how urgently the patient must formulate a plan for the future due to the need for a professional or vocational decision, preparation for retirement, or plans for changes in family relationships.

During the past ten years I have utilized this procedure with approximately 150 patients. I have found that the challenge of the future is readily introduceable, since there are so many decisions in each phase of the patient's life that require futures projection. The patient is encouraged to consider the various vocational and social possibilities that are likely to be available to him in terms of the foreseeable future and to formulate a flexible plan by means of which these tentative futures may be approached. He is also encouraged to contemplate the various stresses or supports that are likely to be encountered.

Effective future-oriented psychotherapeutic techniques require that the therapists be "futurists," namely, persons dedicated to the study of factors likely to determine both individual and societal futures, and to develop the methodologies by means of which man may logically anticipate and plan for a better tomorrow.

The health sciences, including psychiatry and health science education, are faced with radical alterations in scope and quality. The health scientist whom we train today will be responsible for prevention and treatment in a society dramatically different from today. If we are to create a health science that will be optimally applicable to our anticipated societies, we

must avoid as much as possible the errors and prejudices of the past and present. We must be wary of employing ideas and techniques that will be anachronistic by the time they are applied.

Author Stanley Lesse, a neurologist, says that preserving mental health is likely to be the psychiatrist's and psychotherapist's prime concern in the 21st century.

I anticipate that the general health plan proposed here will also stop the spiraling of health-care costs. For example, in 1964 a total of $35 billion was spent for health care in the United States, with $9 billion or about 25% coming from government agencies at all levels. In 1975, the total health care cost was estimated at $110 billion with $40 billion, or approximately 36%, coming from governmental agencies and $70 billion from all other sources. The total cost represents about 9% of the gross national product. Without careful futures planning, health care could cost more than a half trillion dollars per year in another decade. I believe that the overall plan suggested here would be more thorough and efficient and in step with future needs.

Stanley Lesse is Editor-in-Chief of the *American Journal of Psychotherapy*, 114 East 78th Street, New York, New York 10021. He is also an attending neurologist at the Neurological Institute of the Presbyterian Hospital of New York, a member of the faculty of neurology of the College of Physicians and Surgeons of Columbia University, President of the Association for the Advancement of Psychotherapy, and a member of the Scientific Council of the World Future Studies Federation.

Computer Dispenses Mental Health Diagnoses

Some futurists, including Stanley Lesse, predict that computers will play a major role in diagnosing psychiatric problems by the year 2000. For patients at the Salt Lake City Veterans Administration Hospital in Utah, the future is now.

A receptionist greets each incoming patient and feeds his name, social security number, and other relevant data into the computer terminal on her desk. The patient then is sent to a testing room where he sits before a computer terminal and takes a series of six automated diagnostic tests.

The first test, lasting only five minutes, is a simple true-false test designed to determine if the patient understands the testing procedure and is likely to tell the truth. The computer then administers a personality inventory test and quickly provides both a set of raw scores and an interpretation of the findings. After a short I.Q. test, the computer goes on to a special test which measures depression level and suicidal intent in the patient. Again, the computer prints out a raw score, an analysis of the score, and a list of critical items.

The final two tests are actually conducted by paraprofessionals (human) who feed the data into the computer and receive guidance on what further questions to ask. (The computer is programmed to branch, which means that specific responses from the patient will trigger a preprogrammed series of additional questions.) One such test attempts to identify the patient's history of psychopathological symptoms, moods, hallucinations, and delusions; the other is a physical examination. The computer is also programmed to administer 11 other more specialized diagnostic tests if the initial test results indicate they are needed.

The computerized diagnostic assessment takes only five hours, compared to the three to five days taken by conventional procedures. The results of the tests are printed out only 20 seconds after the last test is completed, making it possible for a decision to be made very quickly as to whether the patient has a serious mental problem and, if so, whether he should be hospitalized or assigned to an outpatient program.

In addition to saving time, the computer testing also saves money, according to clinical psychologist James H. Johnson, a coinvestigator on the project. The computerized diagnostic assessment costs an average of $120 per patient; conventional testing costs up to $500 per patient.

Because of the short time needed for the computer to arrive at a diagnosis, fewer people are being hospitalized for mental illness, according to Johnson. Before the computer was used, 75% of the people who came to the hospital for mental health help were hospitalized. Now only 45% are admitted. The computer analysis quickly determines which people have nothing seriously wrong with them and which ones can benefit more from various types of outpatient care. Under the old system, many people who were admitted for testing became labeled as mental patients by society, even though no serious mental problem was found and they were released after the diagnosis was made.

Johnson sees little danger of the computer inaccurately labeling a person as mentally ill. In fact, says Johnson, the computer "is proving itself more accurate and definitive in its patient assessments" than previous methods used. In one study involving two groups of institutionalized patients, the computer was found to have made the correct diagnosis in 96% of its cases, while physicians diagnosed only 83% of their patients correctly.

The computer has frequently identified problems that had not been detected by physicians. In one case, the computer led doctors to discover organic brain damage in a man who had been treated unsuccessfully for years for depression and extreme anxiety. Another man who had been hospitalized repeatedly for alcoholism was scheduled for confrontive group therapy before being given the computer diagnostic tests. The computer identified him as a paranoid schizophrenic, possibly saving his life, according to clinical psychologist Ronald A. Giannetti. If he had experienced the confrontive group therapy in that state, declared Giannetti, "It could have broken the guy up. He would have gotten depressed and possibly suicidal." A 46-year-old woman, another chronic alcoholic, showed no progress until computer testing uncovered a severe depressive disorder. Now being treated for depression rather than alcoholism, the woman is given a good chance of being cured.

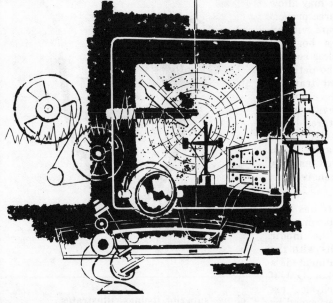

Most patients who were tested by the computer expressed a preference for it over conventional diagnostic procedures, according to a study done by psychologist Daniel Klingler. When 132 patients who had been processed both ways were surveyed, 89% preferred the computer and 56% said that they answered the computer's questions more truthfully. Seventy-eight percent agreed that the computer was not too impersonal.

Johnson theorizes that patients find the computer testing to be stimulating and gratifying, with questions flashing rapidly on the screen and the patient given the responsibility of keyboarding an immediate response. "I don't think it's as threatening to some people as sitting down with a shrink," Johnson adds. "There is no social stigma attached. There is more feedback. The extent of the testing,

all concentrated into a relatively brief period of time, seems to say to a patient that somebody really cares. They don't get this impersonal feeling of "Call me next week."

In some cases, the computer questioning even seems to have a therapeutic effect upon the patient. One patient reported that the computer's questions helped him to remember important events in his past that he had long forgotten. Another patient liked the computer so much that he wanted to have one installed in his home so that he could consult it when feeling depressed.

The program, which is supported by $500,000 in grants from the Veterans Administration and the National Institute of Mental Health, with the computer hardware donated by the University of Utah Medical Center, handles about 300 new patients a month at the hospital and is expanding to several new locations. Two new terminals have been installed, one at the nearby University of Utah Medical Center and another at the Community Mental Health Center in Salt Lake City. Thomas A. Williams and James H. Johnson, coinvestigators on the project, hope to extend the service soon to the isolated Indian reservations of southern Utah and northern Arizona.

For more information, see "Computer Crazy" by Eric Shuman, *Human Behavior*, August 1976.

Medicine in the Post-Physician Era

Doctors will be obsolete in 50 years, replaced by computers and a new type of health care professional called "the medic," predicts physician Jerrold Maxmen in his book *The Post-Physician Era*.

"Three major capabilities are required for logical medical decisions—*objectivity, probability, and memory*," says Maxmen. And the computer can outperform the doctor in every one of them. Computers are always rational, while doctors "can be unduly influenced by their feelings and can make serious errors in judgment." While a physician, in assessing the probability that a patient's symptoms mean that he has a particular disease, can rely only on his own knowledge and experience, a computer of the future, because of its gigantic storage capacity, could have access to "the collective wisdom of all physicians." The doctor's memory is limited; the computer *never* forgets.

Maxmen goes on to dispose of the criticism that a physician, by making "intuitive leaps," has an advantage in diagnosing a new patient from "scratch." "A study was conducted in which the Cornell Medical Index, a 195-item questionnaire, was administered to 5,929 consecutively hospitalized patients. A machine analyzed the questionnaires to yield a diagnosis from among 60 possibilities. The result of this investigation revealed that the derived diagnoses were slightly more accurate than those rendered by physicians," Maxmen reveals.

The biggest unsolved problem in making computer diagnoses fully reliable, Maxmen asserts, is to have an accurate program to feed into the computer. "When the logical pathways needed to make a diagnosis are delineated, they readily can be and have been programmed into the computer. Unfortunately, at present the logical pathways required to diagnose many ailments have not been identified." Improvements will also be required in storage capacity, treatment programs, precise medical terminology, and accessible hardware, but Maxmen believes that all of these problems can be overcome in the 21st century, based on the current rate of development of computer technology. He adds that, if all clinical observations were automated and stored in the computer's memory banks, researchers would be better able to "advance our medical knowledge and significantly improve patient care."

With computers taking over the technical functions of the present-day physician, a new breed of health-care professionals will be trained to assume the supportive and psychotherapeutic functions. Because of this reduced burden, Maxmen says, "the medic will not have to possess a basic understanding of health and disease concepts." The medic's training will take only 12-18 months, compared to eight years for modern doctors. "Interpersonal talents will replace scientific sophistication as the major admission criterion." Medics will be selected on the basis of their capacity to "empathize with, be sensitive to and be tolerant of people with physical and emotional disorders."

"The overall objective of the student's medical school education," Maxmen elaborates, "would be to prepare him to function within a medic-computer model. To accomplish this goal, the curriculum would have to focus upon the following areas: the psychology of illness, family dynamics, group processes, medical sociology, medical terminology, medical ethics, patient administration, and the technology of supportive care."

The evidence suggests that patients will be willing to accept medical care from nonphysicians, Maxmen claims. He notes that "Without any *major* difficulties, nonphysicians have assumed primary clinical responsibilities in other nations for centuries." Paraprofessionals have also seen widespread use in the U.S. armed forces, with generally good results. "The public's experience with nurse-practitioners, nurse-clinicians, and physician's assistants will influence the likelihood of future patients accepting the medic," Maxmen adds. The medic will gain the patient's confidence and respect because of his personality and sensitivity rather than because of his academic credentials. Maxmen

adds: "Like the shaman and physician who preceded him, the medic will perform rituals, such as utilizing complicated machines, practicing in uniquely designed settings, conversing in a strange clinical vocabulary, and wearing a futuristic medical uniform." All of these, along with licensing and certification procedures, will enhance his prestige.

The communications revolution will play a major role in the provision of medical services in the future, Maxmen predicts. "The widespread availability of videotelephones, IATV [interactive television] and computer terminals within the home may allow patients to receive a large proportion of their medical care without having to travel to a hospital, clinic, or office." Wireless sensing devices may monitor the patient's physiological state and transmit the data instantly to the clinician. (A battery-powered device which can monitor temperature, blood pressure, pulse, and electrocardiogram has already been developed by the Boeing Company, but is still too expensive for widespread use.)

After the medical data has been analyzed by a central computer, Maxmen suggests, "the medic could discuss the results with the patient and suggest treatment via a telecommunications linkup. Only if certain aspects of the physical examination cannot be performed by remote control or if selected ancillary tests are needed, would the patient have to go to a regional health center." Group therapy might be conducted via conference videophone. Outpatient psychiatric clinics might be replaced by advanced communications technology. The use of sophisticated telecommunications technology to monitor and supervise patient behavior at home might greatly reduce the need for psychiatric hospitals, as well as nursing homes.

Maxmen also devotes several chapters to speculation about future breakthroughs in biomedicine. "Just as medical computers underscore the limits of physicians," he predicts, "so too will future biomedical innovations highlight humanity's biological deficiences. The anticipated ability to manipulate genetic material, create an artificial placenta, and

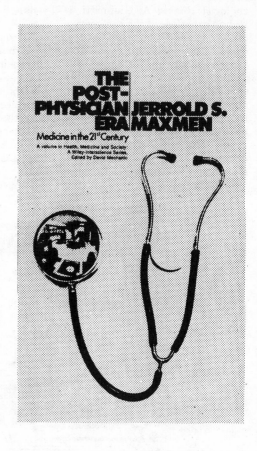

clone superior beings illustrates that technology could improve upon man's reproductive processes. In the future, synthetic organs will be able to outperform natural ones. Eventually, human-machine chimeras may be able to exceed man's physical powers, emotional functions, and intellectual capacities. These innovations may seem frightening because of their potential dehumanizing effect and impact upon man's evolutionary future. Condemning these innovations, however, can neither sweep away the fact of their possible development nor allow us to avoid recognizing the biological limitations of our species."

The Post-Physician Era: Medicine in the 21st Century by Jerrold S. Maxmen. John Wiley and Sons, New York, 1976. 300 pages. $15.95. (Available from the World Future Society's Book Service.)

Projected Developments Related to Medicine

The following forecasts are excerpted from *The Post-Physician Era: Medicine in the 21st Century* (Wiley-Interscience, New York, 1976). Author Jerrold Maxmen believes that there is at least a 50% probability that each of these developments will occur by the dates indicated.

Year	Communication and Computer Technology	Biomedicine and Therapeutics	Education and Occupations	Miscellaneous
By 1980	Establishment of TV network for MDs Wide use of computers for hospital record storage and data retrieval Routine use of cable TV for medical conferences	Development of useful tissue adhesives to replace sutures Development of tests for rapid diagnosis of viral diseases General availability of home diagnostic kits for urine and fecal examinations	Pharmacist's education stressing his consultant role Unrestricted medical license granted only after completion of residency Ombudsmen widely used in hospitals and clinics	Laboratory creation of protein for food by *in vitro* cellular processes Enactment of national health insurance covering 75 percent of medical costs Noncarcinogenic cigarette
By 1985	Wide use of videophones in hospitals Wide use of computers for medical history taking Portable telephone widely available	Artificial heart implantation Chemical synthesis of specific antibodies Laboratory solution of immunologic rejection problem Development of reliable chemical tests for psychotic disorders	Use of teaching machines that respond to a student's answers and to his physiologic state (tension) Virtual obsolescence of the general practitioner The "classical" lecture system ended in 40 percent of medical schools by teaching machines, closed circuit TV, interactive TV, and audio-visual aids	Decriminalization of marijuana Red Cross a semi-public agency in most nations Government-established standards for medical computers
By 1990	Frequent use of "telemedicine" Wide use of computers to prescribe medications Some people able to have daily checkups of body	Development of artificial colon Development of safe chemical means to reverse effects of arteriosclerosis Chemical cure for schizophrenias Development of anti-cancer vaccines Wide use of tests in children that will reliably predict their developing some major mental illnesses in adulthood	Wide use of professional nurses to deliver primary care	Failure to consult a computer considered grounds for malpractice suit Water and air pollution problems largely diminished Chemical synthesis of cheap nutritious food
By 1995	General availability of computers to conduct psychotherapy Frequent use of conference videophones for group psychotherapy Extensive use of interactive TV to monitor aged within their homes	Development of drugs that alter memory and learning *In vitro* fertilization of human ovum with implantation into host mothers Development of synthetic blood substitute General availability of physical and chemical means to modify some forms of criminal behavior First human clone	85 percent of pharmacists working in hospitals and clinics rather than in drugstores	Techniques that permit useful exploitation of ocean through aquaculture farming, with the effect of producing 20 percent of the world's caloric intake

continued on next page

Year	Communication and Computer Technology	Biomedicine and Therapeutics	Education and Occupations	Miscellaneous
By 2000	Wrist watch TV commonly available Wide availability of computers that "learn" from experience	Moderate chemical control of senility Effective transplantation of all organ systems except for CNS Development of electronic sensors enabling blind people to "see"	Robots with sensory feedback performing routine household chores in hospitals	First clinic or hospital on the moon
By 2005		Demonstration of way to decrease time between birth and maturity		
By 2010		Wide use of artificial insemination to produce genetically superior offspring Use of highly complex chemical simulation models of the human body for use in drug experimentation		
By 2015	Demonstration of man-machine symbiosis, enabling people to extend their intelligence by direct electromechanical interaction between his brain and a computer "Telemedicine" services widely delivered in homes	Use of drugs or altered prenatal conditions to raise IQ of normal individuals by 10 to 20 points Laboratory demonstration of biochemical processes that stimulate growth of new organs and limbs Extrauterine development of human fetus Replacement of human organs with those derived from specially bred animals	Virtual cessation of MDs providing clinical services except for surgery	Average US life expectancy 95 years old with commensurate prolongation of vigor
By 2020		Electrical control of mood disorders available Demonstration of long-duration human hibernation; allows for prolonged space travel Moderate use of genetic engineering in humans by chemical substitution of DNA chains		Wide use of self-contained dwellings using life support systems that recycle water and air to provide independence from external environment
By 2025		*In utero* genetic modification		

Part 3

THE FUTURE AS CHALLENGE

If we face emerging problems squarely, we
may be able to solve them or at least soften
their impact.

The Coming Energy Transition

by Denis Hayes

The world will experience a historic change in its patterns of energy use during the years ahead. This change in energy use is dictated by the rapid exhaustion of easily exploited deposits of petroleum and natural gas. However, there is now a wide area of choice about how to reshape our approach to energy in order to have a prosperous world in the future. A researcher at the Worldwatch Institute in Washington, D.C., recently reviewed the energy options and here reports his conclusions.

During the last 25 years, world fuel consumption tripled, oil and gas consumption quintupled, and electricity use grew almost sevenfold. Clearly, such trends cannot be sustained indefinitely—nature abhors exponential curves as well as vacuums.

The world has begun another great energy transition. In the past, such transformations have always produced far-reaching social change. For example, the substitution of coal for wood and wind in Europe accelerated and refashioned the industrial revolution. Later, the shift to petroleum altered the nature of travel, shrinking the planet and completely restructuring its cities. The coming energy transition can be counted upon to reshape tomorrow's world. Moreover, the quantity of energy available may, in the long run, prove much less important than where and how this energy is obtained.

Most energy policy analyses do not encompass the social consequences of energy choices. Most energy decisions are based instead on the naive assumption that competing sources are neutral and interchangeable. As defined by most energy experts, the task at hand is simply to obtain enough energy to meet the projected demands at as low a cost as possible. Choices generally swing on small differences in the marginal costs of competing potential sources.

But energy sources are not neutral and interchangeable. Some energy sources are necessarily centralized; others are necessarily dispersed. Some are exceedingly vulnerable; others will reduce the number of people employed. Some will tend to diminish the gap between rich and poor; others will accentuate it. Some inherently dangerous sources can be permitted unchecked growth only under totalitarian regimes; others can lead to nothing more dangerous than a leaky roof. Some sources can be comprehended only by the world's most elite technicians; others can be assembled in remote villages using local labor and indigenous materials. In the long run, such considerations are likely to prove more important than the financial criteria that dominate and limit current energy thinking.

Appropriate energy sources are necessary, though not sufficient, for the realization of important social and political goals. Inappropriate energy sources could make attaining such goals impossible. Decisions made today about energy sources will, to a far greater extent than is commonly realized, determine how the world will look a few decades hence. Although energy policy has been dominated by the thinking of economists and scientists, the most important consequences may be political.

After consideration is paid to the myriad constraints facing energy growth, and to the sweeping social consequences produced by energy choices, few attractive options remain. For a variety of reasons, the long-term roles of fossil fuels and nuclear fission are likely to be modest. Geothermal power is already proving useful in Italy, Iceland, New Zealand, and the United States as a means of generating electricity and as a source of space heating. However, the exploitable global geothermal potential appears to be rather small, and the environmental impact of geothermal operations is larger than most people assume.

Nuclear fusion is popularly envisioned as a clean source of virtually limitless power. But the reality belies the ideal. William Metz has noted "a gap . . . between what the fusion program appears to promise and what [it] is most likely to deliver."

When scientists speak of building a commercial nuclear fusion reactor within 25 years, they are referring to a deuterium-tritium reactor, a reactor that does not share all the idealized characteristics associated with nuclear fusion. The D-T reactor's fuel supply would not be limitless; tritium is derived from lithium, an element not much more abundant than uranium. The D-T fusion power plant might well be even larger (and hence more centralized) than current conventional facilities, and the energy produced could be much more expensive than that derived from current sources. The reactor would certainly require maintenance, but the intense radioactivity of the equipment would make maintenance almost impossible. Although cleaner than nuclear fission, a large fusion reactor might nonetheless produce as much as 250 tons of radioactive waste annually.

Renewable energy sources—wind, water, biomass, and direct sunlight—hold substantial advantages over the above alternatives. They add no heat to the global environment and produce no radioactive or weapons-grade materials. The carbon dioxide emitted by biomass systems in equilibrium will make no net contribution to atmospheric concentrations, since green plants will capture CO_2 at the same rate that it is being produced. Renewable energy sources can provide energy as heat, liquid or gaseous fuels, or electricity. And they lend themselves well to production and use in decentralized, autonomous facilities. However, such sources are not the indefatigable genies sought by advocates of limitless energy growth. While renewable sources do expand the limits to energy growth, especially the physical limits, the fact that energy development has a ceiling cannot ultimately be denied.

Power tower: an artist's concept of how the sun's energy could be used for large-scale production of electricity. Movable mirrors reflect solar heat and focus it on a boiler at the top of the tower. Water in the boiler is converted to high-pressure steam, which is pumped to a conventional steam-turbine generator at the tower's base. This concept is now under study by the Honeywell Corporation, which hopes to have a test "power tower" able to generate electricity for 5,000 homes by 1980. Photo: U.S. Energy Research and Development Administration

The highest energy priority in all lands today should be conservation. Investments in saving energy, whether to double the efficiency of an Indian villager's cookstove or to eliminate energy waste in a steel mill, will often save far more energy than similar investments in new power facilities can produce. The cheapest and best energy option for the entire world today is to harness the major portion of all commercial energy that is currently being wasted.

A transition to an efficient, sustainable energy system is both technically possible and socially desirable. But 150 countries of widely different physical and social circumstances are unlikely to undergo such a transition smoothly and painlessly. Every potential energy source will be championed by vested interests and fought by diehard opponents. Bureaucratic inertia, political timidity, conflicting corporate designs, and the simple, understandable reluctance of people to face up to far-reaching change will all discourage a transition from taking place spontaneously. Even when clear goals are widely shared, they are not easily pursued. Policies tend to provoke opposition; unanticipated side effects almost always occur.

If the path is not easy, it is nonetheless the only road worth taking. For 20 years, global energy policy has been headed down a blind alley. It is not too late to retrace our steps before we collide with inevitable boundaries. But the longer we wait, the more tumultuous the eventual turnaround will be.

Dawn of a New Era

We are *not* running out of energy. However, we *are* running out of cheap oil and gas. We are running out of money to pay for doubling and redoubling an already vast energy supply system. We are running out of political willingness to accept the social costs of continued rapid energy expansion. We are running out of the environmental capacity needed to handle the waste generated in energy production. And we are running out of time to adjust to these new realities.

For two decades, we have pursued a chimerical dream of safe, cheap nuclear energy. That dream has nearly vanished. Nuclear fission now appears to be inextricably bound to weapons proliferation and to a broad range of other intractable problems. Every week new evidence buttressing the case against nuclear power is uncovered; every week worldwide opposition to nuclear power grows stronger. Nuclear fission now appears unlikely ever to contribute a large fraction of the world's energy budget.

We are consequently no closer today than we were two decades ago to finding a replacement for oil. Yet the rhetoric that public officials in the world's capitals lavish upon the energy "crisis" is not being translated into action. Most energy policy is still framed as though it were addressing a problem that our

Author Denis Hayes is an energy specialist with the Worldwatch Institute in Washington, D.C. He stresses conservation as the best approach to the world's energy problems in the near future.

grandchildren will inherit. But the energy crisis is *our* crisis. Oil and natural gas are our principal means of bridging today and tomorrow, and we are burning our bridges.

Twenty years ago, we had some flexibility; today the options are more constrained. All our possible choices have long lead times. All new sources will require new factories to produce new equipment and large numbers of workers with new skills. Energy conservation programs will similarly require decades to implement fully, as existing inventories of energy-using devices are slowly replaced. Inefficient buildings constructed today will still be wasting energy fifty years from now; oversized cars sold today will still be wasting fuel ten years down the road.

If the energy crisis has no "quick fix," neither is there any long-term *deus ex machina*. Great progress has been made on coal conversion technologies in recent years, but environmental and resource constraints necessarily limit coal to a transitional role. Coal can and should be substituted for oil and gas in many instances, but coal cannot replace the 75% of all commercial energy these fuels now provide.

Nuclear fusion, if feasible at all, would be expensive, incredibly complex, and highly centralized. For technical reasons, the first generation of fusion reactors would probably consist of fusion-fission hybrids designed to breed plutonium. Such devices would lead the world into an unconscionable "plutonium economy" and will therefore be vigorously fought by a formidable array of opponents. While "pure" fusion deserves continued research support, it holds no immediate potential, and even over the long term there is no assurance that it will become a commercially viable source of power.

A Lesson from Spain

In 1492, the monarchs of Spain financed the explorations of Christopher Columbus to the New World. In the following century, mineral wealth from these newly found lands catapulted Spain to the height of its glory. Beginning in the 1520s, the flow of precious metals to the Iberian Peninsula grew more or less regularly for seventy-five years, making Spain one of the dominant states of Europe.

In 1598, King Philip II died after a reign of forty years. Although the nation had a heavy burden of debt, resulting from stalemated wars with England and Holland, the debt was not onerous in the face of Spain's rapidly increasing prosperity. When Philip III assumed the throne, Spain's prospects seemed bright. Unbeknownst to the Spanish rulers, however, the flow of gold and silver had already peaked: the next seventy-five years were years of rather steady falloff in production. However, traditional Spanish agriculture and small industry had languished during the nation's years of aggressive ascendancy, and were not successfully restored. The flow of precious metals had given Spain a golden moment in the sun, but the unanticipated decline in looted treasures brought the country to its knees.

The Spanish experience may hold special meaning for the contemporary world. The industrial nations have been shaped by the availability of cheap, plentiful oil at least as much as Spain was by the flow of gold. Unlike Spain, we can see the end ahead, and can choose to begin a voluntary transition, but failure to do so will lead to a fate much like Spain's.

—From *Rays of Hope*

Although no easy answers exist, some solutions clearly outshine others. Of the supply technologies in hand today, solar, wind, water, and biomass sources appear most attractive. And for years to come, the world's greatest opportunities will lie in energy conservation.

Priorities for a Post-Petroleum World

The energy crisis demands rapid decisions, but policies must nevertheless be formulated with an eye to their long-term implications. In making each of hundreds of discrete decisions, we would be well advised to apply a few basic criteria. Thrift, renewability, decentralization, simplicity, and safety should be the touchstones. Using these, we might judge whether a given action will move us closer to, or further from, the type of energy system we ultimately seek.

Both rich industrial countries and poor agrarian ones can cull far more benefits in the immediate future from investments in increased efficiency than from investments in new energy sources. In fact, because they are unable to afford to make the necessary initial investments that conservation sometimes requires, the poor frequently waste a higher fraction of the energy they use than the well-to-do. By eliminating waste and by matching energy sources carefully with appropriate uses, people can wring far more work from every unit of energy than is now the case. A sensible energy strategy will help accomplish this sensible goal.

Energy is a means, not an end. Its worth derives entirely from its capacity to perform work. No one wants a kilowatt-hour; the objective is to light a room. No one wants a gallon of gasoline; the object is to travel from one place to another. If our objectives can be met using a half, or even a quarter, as much energy as we now use, no benefit is lost.

Investments in conservation must mesh with plans for a rapid switch from fossil fuels to sustainable energy sources. An intelligent strategy will lead to dependence upon energy derived solely from perpetually reliable sources. Solar technologies alone can provide us with as much energy as can be safely employed on our fragile planet.

In establishing priorities for the post-petroleum period, foremost attention should be given to basic human needs — to food, shelter, clothing, health care, and education. Fortunately, such needs either require comparatively little energy or have energy requirements that can be met with renewable energy sources. Indeed for most of history *Homo sapiens* has been entirely dependent upon renewable energy sources and could not have survived if renewable

sources had not met the most basic needs.

The industrial world, powered mostly by renewable energy sources a mere hundred years ago, now runs almost entirely on fossil fuels. The agrarian nations still obtain more than two-thirds of their fuel from sustainable sources— mostly firewood and forage for draft animals. These two worlds consequently face different problems and may honor different priorities during the coming transition.

In the Third World, enormous strides can be made with relatively modest investments if those investments are made wisely. For example, 2% of the world military budget for just one year could provide every rural Third World family with an efficient stove—doubling overnight the amount of useful work obtained from fuel wood, and reducing the pressure on the world's forests accordingly. If, in addition, armies were mobilized in major tree-planting campaigns, the firewood crisis could eventually be alleviated.

In the industrial world, the situation is arguably more precarious, and dramatic steps are in order. However, such steps are not being taken. For example, a responsible energy policy reflecting the urgency of the necessary transition would require that all new automobiles average at least 35 miles per gallon

within three years, and that the transition to non-petroleum vehicles be well under way within a decade. If the energy transition were proceeding on a reasonable timetable, tens of millions of solar water heaters would be produced annually; current production, by contrast, is in the thousands. While the generation of electricity from high-temperature industrial steam is the cheapest and most attractive new power source in many countries, institutional factors have caused this technology to be slighted all over the world.

It is virtually impossible to develop a list of global energy priorities. Each country must pursue those options most compatible with its conditions and its aspirations. But in general, conservation investments will prove more immediately productive than new source development, and genuine necessities, such as food, must always take precedence over frivolous trimmings.

Suitable Energy Technologies

Historically, many important inventions have consisted of no more than ingenious new applications of existing knowledge. In recent decades, however, large teams of specialists wielding complex and expensive research tools have been increasingly rubbing against the boundaries of knowledge. Nowhere is

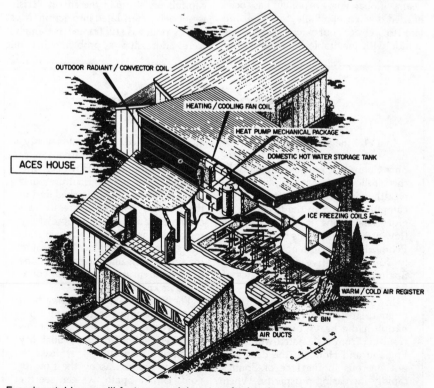

Experimental home will feature special system for heating and cooling. The first demonstration of the Annual Cycle Energy System outside the laboratory will be this three-bedroom house built on University of Tennessee property outside Knoxville. The principal component of the system is an insulated tank of water which serves as an energy storage bin. Designed to save at least 50% of the electrical energy now used to heat and cool a home, the system is being developed at the Oak Ridge National Laboratory.

Photo: Oak Ridge National Laboratory

this phenomenon more clear than in the industrial world's response to the energy crisis. Research is currently focused on the liquid metal fast breeder reactor, with fusion reactors and coal conversion technologies vying for the remaining funds. Sources that don't cost billions of dollars to develop seem almost unworthy of serious consideration. The "hard" technologies obtain the most funds, attract the brightest researchers, kindle the greatest public interest, and accrue the most glamour. They do not, however, necessarily represent the wisest choices. Nuclear fusion research may well yield a Nobel Prize someday; no plausible line of research on biogas plants seems likely to win a trip to Stockholm. Nevertheless, biogas plants will almost certainly provide more energy to those who need it most then fusion reactors ever will.

Energy funding continues to be apportioned as though big were beautiful, and the reasons for this are understandable. "Those in power always want big accomplishments—scientific breakthroughs and politically visible facilities," explains M. C. Gupta, director of the Thermodynamic Laboratory at the Indian Institute of Technology. "But those things aren't what India needs most. The needs of our neediest can only be met by small, inexpensive devices that use indigenous materials and are easily maintained."

Even research on direct and indirect solar sources will not necessarily produce devices that meet the diverse needs of the world's peoples. Most significant research on sustainable energy sources has been performed in industrialized countries. Technological advances have therefore reflected the needs of societies with temperate climates, high per capita incomes, abundant material resources, sophisticated technical infrastructures, expensive labor, good communication and transportation systems, and well-trained maintenance personnel. Such societies are wired for electricity—indeed, two-thirds of the U.S. solar energy research budget is devoted to the generation of electricity.

Clearly, some of the findings of this research are not easily or wisely transferred to societies with tropical climates, low per capita incomes, few material resources, stunted technical infrastructures, cheap labor, poor communications, and only fledgling maintenance forces. Most people in the world do not have electrical outlets or anything to plug into them. What they need are cheap solar cookers, inexpensive irrigation pumps, simple crop dryers, small solar furnaces to fire bricks, and other basic tools.

With the traps of technology transfer in mind, some argue that a major solar research and development effort on the part of the industrialized world is irrele-

vant to the true needs of the poorer countries. This argument contains a kernel of truth in a husk of misunderstanding. Countries can choose to learn from each other's experience, but each country must view borrowed knowledge through the lens of its own unique culture, resources, geography, and institutions. The United States and China can trade knowledge to good purpose, but little of what they trade can be transplanted intact.

The differences between such industrialized lands as Japan and France merit note, but the differences between two Third World countries may be more striking than the similarities. Surinam (with an annual per capita income of $810) has energy problems and potential solutions to those problems that bear little resemblance to those of Rwanda (with an annual per capita income of about $60). And national wealth is not the only feature in an energy profile. The tasks for which energy is needed vary from country to country. In some, the most pressing need may be for pumps to bring water from a deep water table to the parched surface. In lands with more abundant water supplies, cooking fuel may be in desperately short supply. The availability of sustainable resources may also differ. One region may have ample hydropower potential, another strong winds, and a third profuse direct sunlight. Successful technology transfers require a keen sensitivity to such differences.

Some disillusioned solar researchers in both industrialized and agrarian countries contend that the major impediment to solar development has been neither technical nor economic. The devices *do* work and many simple devices can be cheaply made. Instead, they claim, the problems have social and cultural roots. Many Third World leaders do not want to settle for "second-rate" renewable energy sources while the industrial world has flourished on oil and nuclear power. Often, officials who found themselves in charge of new technologies, such as windmills, were unable to find technicians who could maintain and repair them. Occasionally, people who were given solar equipment refused to use it because the rigid time requirements of solar technology disrupted their daily routines or because the direct use of sunlight had no precedent in their cultural traditions.

Many of these attitudinal impediments may now be vanishing as the global south begins developing its own research and development capacity. Indigenous technologies born of this new capability may prove to be more compatible with Third World needs than borrowed machines and methods. Brazil's large methanol program, India's gobar gas plants, and the Middle East's growing fascination with solar electric

Nuclear Terrorism

Researcher Denis Hayes argues strongly against nuclear power as an answer to the world's energy problems. His chief reason is the impossibility of assuring that the technology will not be diverted to terrorists and aggressive nations. Even today, nuclear technology is widely disseminated and within the capabilities of many individuals and groups.

Hayes writes:

Once assembled, nuclear weapons could be rather convenient to use. The dimensions of the Davy Crockett, a small fission bomb in the U.S. arsenal, are 2 feet by 1 foot (0.6 meters by 0.3) The smallest U.S. bomb is under 6 inches (0.15 meters) in diameter. Such bomb miniaturization is well beyond the technical skill of any terrorist group, but no wizardry is required to build an atom bomb that would fit comfortably in the trunk of an automobile. Left in a car just outside the exclusion zone around the U.S. Capitol during the State of the Union address, such a device could eliminate the Congress, the Supreme Court, and the entire line of succession to the presidency. With careful planning and tight discipline, armed groups could interrupt the fuel cycle at several vulnerable points and

escape with fissile material. The high price likely to be charged for black market plutonium also makes it attractive to organized crime: sophisticated yet ruthless, modern criminals have close links with transport industries in many parts of the world. Perhaps most frightening is the inside thief—the terrorist sympathizer or the person with gambling debts or the victim of blackmail. A high official of the U.S. Atomic Energy Commission had, it was discovered in 1973, borrowed almost a quarter of a million dollars and spent much of it on racing wagers.

Quiet diversion of bomb-grade material may have taken place already. Plutonium has often been found where it should not have been, and, worse, not been found where it should have been. Determining whether or not weapons-grade material has already fallen into the wrong hands is impossible. . . .

Theodore Taylor, formerly the leading American atom bomb designer, has described at length where the detailed instructions for building atomic bombs can be found in unclassified literature and how the necessary equipment can be mail-ordered. An undergraduate at MIT, working alone and using only public information, produced a plausible bomb design in only five weeks.

The Art of Retrofitting

At the National Bureau of Standards in Gaithersburg, Maryland, scientists and engineers are conducting studies on how to install a solar heating and cooling system in an existing house. Since it is impractical to try to build a new house to meet the new requirements for energy efficiency, retrofitting is developing into a new science—and art.

Engineer inspects solar collector atop experimental townhouse.

Townhouse before retrofitting with solar heating and cooling system.

Townhouse after retrofitting. The system is intended to supply three-fourths of the heating, cooling, and domestic hot water needs for a four-bedroom townhouse.

Photos: National Bureau of Standards

technologies can all be read as signs of an interest in renewable energy resources that bodes well for the future. At the same time, the Third World, stunned by a simultaneous shortage of firewood and petroleum, may be more willing than it was a few years ago to adopt solar solutions.

In much of the global north as well, solar technologies are being embraced as important future options. In Japan, the Soviet Union, France, and the United States, renewable resources are increasingly being viewed as major components of future energy planning. Some of the innovative research in these countries could well be of global significance.

Energy and International Equity

Decisions on energy sources can dramatically affect the international distribution of wealth. High-priced oil, for example, has brought a flood of dollars —mostly from the rich industrial countries—to what had previously been some of the world's poorest lands. The rest of the Third World, although itself hard hit by rising oil prices, has rather steadfastly maintained its solidarity with the oil exporting countries; rising prices for raw materials are viewed as crucial components of a far-reaching new economic order, and oil is currently the world's most important raw material. Other countries that export natural resources hope that OPEC's successful price hikes will blaze a trail they can follow.

Although the new economic order is generally defined in terms of commodity prices and monetary reforms, its success may hinge on the choice of a postpetroleum energy source. Whereas complex technologies would divert a major stream of scarce capital to the industrial world, the development of safe sustainable sources could cause investment dollars to flow in the other direction. Direct and indirect solar sources thus appear to hold a double economic promise for the Third World.

Investment funds tend to become available where energy is available. Industries compete vigorously for the right to build plants in the Middle East, less to penetrate the region's small markets than to be assured of a supply of fuel. As renewable sources attract more adherents, hard currencies can be expected to flow to the world's richest sources of sunlight, wind, water, and biomass, and most of these are located in the Third World.

If resource exporting countries are to enter fully into a new economic order, they must be able to process much of the material they produce, tapping locally available flows of energy. In an era of diffuse energy resources, the enormous use of energy that now characterizes the industrial world would be spread out over the entire globe. Instead of shipping ore to Europe for refining, the producing country would ship refined metal. Containing "embodied" energy derived from natural sources, the refined metal is worth much more than ore, so the exporting country would achieve a more favorable balance of trade. As an industrial infrastructure takes shape, the exporting country would also be able to produce and sell more manufactured products.

Waste heat from power plant heats greenhouses in Minnesota. Minnesota's Northern States Power Company's Sherburn County power plant produces waste heat along with electricity. The waste heat can be used to grow top quality vegetables and flowers during the harsh Minnesota winter. The Energy Research and Development Administration in Washington says that this is the largest experimental greenhouse using waste heat from a power plant. If the demonstration proves economically feasible, private commercial growers could begin operating their own facilities at this and other plant sites. In addition to selling electricity, the power company would sell heat from water warmed during power generation.   Photo: ERDA

Poverty is, of course, a matter of people as much as of countries. Almost all poor countries have some rich people, and all rich countries have poor people. Increases in national income do not necessarily mean that the new wealth will be shared. In some oil producing countries, rising revenues have left the rich richer and the poor untouched.

If vigorous conservation is to lead eventually to an energy ceiling, population growth must be constrained as energy is equalized. The alternative is to divide a constant amount of energy among an ever-increasing pool of people. Population stabilization is imperative both in the industrial world, where non-renewable fuel consumption per person is twenty to thirty times higher than in the Third World, and in the Third World, where burgeoning population growth is outstripping traditional energy sources such as firewood. Like energy itself, population is a global problem, and it requires a worldwide solution.

The development of renewable energy sources cannot itself abolish poverty— only widespread social and political change can. But decentralized sources of energy are compatible with a development strategy that grows from the bottom up, rather than one that merely permits a few benefits to trickle down to the masses from the elite in control of centralized high technologies. The use of appropriate energy sources will facilitate a more equitable distribution of wealth and power both within and among nations, by transferring control from distant corporations and bureaucracies to more responsive local units.

Energy and the Human Prospect

For 20 years, the world has pursued a dead-end path. This energy route can-

not be changed without fundamentally altering society. Some alternatives are better than others because the changes they dictate are relatively attractive, but there is no way of avoiding some form of pervasive change. If, for example, the world were to opt for harmonious, small-scale, decentralized, renewable energy technologies, few aspects of modern life would go unaffected.

Farms would begin to supply large fractions of their own energy through wind power, solar heaters, and technologies for harnessing the energy in agricultural wastes. Such self-sufficient farms would tend to be smaller and to provide more employment than those

that prevailed in the oil era. Food storage and preparation would slowly be shifted to solar-powered technologies. Meat consumption in the industrial world would drop and the food processing industry would become more energy-efficient and less pervasive in its impact on diets.

In the new energy era, transportation would be weaned from its petroleum base even as improved communications and intelligent city planning began to eliminate pointless travel. Energy efficiency and load factors would become important criteria in evaluating transport modes and would be reflected in the costs of travel. Bicycles would begin to account for an important fraction of commuter traffic as well as of other short trips. And freight transport would be transferred wherever possible to more energy-efficient modes, especially trains and ships.

If we were to opt for the best renewable energy technologies, buildings could be engineered to take full advantage of their environments. More and more of the energy needed for heating and cooling would be derived directly from the sun. Using low-cost photovoltaics that convert sunlight directly into electricity, many buildings could eventually become energy self-sufficient. New jobs and professions would develop around the effort to exploit sunlight, and courts would be forced to consider the "right" of building owners not to have their sunshine blocked by neighboring structures.

While industry would doubtless turn to coal for much of its energy during the

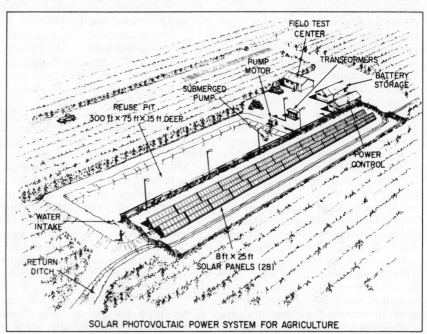

SOLAR PHOTOVOLTAIC POWER SYSTEM FOR AGRICULTURE

Largest array of solar cells ever constructed will power a crop irrigation system on an experimental farm near Mead, Nebraska. The project is being conducted for the U.S. Energy Research and Development Administration by the University of Nebraska-Lincoln and the Lincoln Laboratory of the Massachusetts Institute of Technology.   Photo: ERDA

transition period, eventually it would also draw its primary energy from natural flows. Thus, energy availability would play an important role in determining the locations of future factories. The sunshine-rich nations of the Third World, where raw materials and renewable energy sources are most plentiful, could become new centers of economic productivity. The across-the-board substitution of cheap fuel for human labor would be halted. Recycled metals, fibers, and other materials would become principal sources of raw materials. Seen as energy repositories, manufactured products would necessarily become more durable and would be designed to be easily repaired and recycled.

Using small, decentralized, and safe technologies makes sense from a systems management point of view. Small units could be added incrementally if rising demands required them, and they would be much easier than large new facilities to integrate smoothly into an energy system. Small, simple sources could be installed in a matter of weeks or months; large, complex facilities often require years and even decades to erect. If gigantic power plants were displaced by thousands of smaller units dispersed near the points of end use, economies of size would become relatively less important vis-a-vis economies of mass production. Technology would again concern itself with simplicity and elegance, and vast systems would become extinct as more appropriately scaled facilities evolved.

To decentralize power sources is in a sense to act upon the principle of "safety in numbers." When large amounts of power are produced at individual facilities or clusters of plants, the continued operation of these plants becomes crucial to society. Where energy production is centralized, those seeking to coerce or simply to disrupt the community can easily acquire considerable leverage: for example, a leader of the British electrical workers recently noted that "the miners brought the country to its knees in eight weeks," but that his co-workers "could do it in eight minutes." Disruption need not be intentional, either. Human error or natural phenomena can easily upset fragile energy networks that serve wide areas, while use of diverse decentralized sources could practically eliminate such problems.

The societies that will develop around efficient, renewable, decentralized, simple, safe energy sources cannot be fully visualized from our present vantage point. Indeed, one of the most attractive promises of such sources is a far greater flexibility in social design than is afforded by their alternatives. Though energy sources may not dictate the shape of society, they do limit its range of possi-

bilities, and diverse, dispersed energy sources are more compatible than centralized technologies with social equity, freedom, and political participation.

Societies based upon natural flows of energy will have to wrestle with the concept of limits. Endless and mindless growth is not possible for nations living on energy income instead of capital. Such societies will need public policies and ethics that disparage rather than whet the appetite for frivolous consumption. Materialism, which gives sanction to what Voltaire saw as humanity's perpetual enemies—poverty, vice, and boredom—will need to be replaced by a new source of social vitality that is less corrosive to the human spirit and less destructive to the collective environment.

The attractions of sunlight, wind, running water, and green plants as energy sources are self-evident. They are especially appealing in their stark contrast to a world of nuclear garrison states. Scarce resources would be conserved, environmental quality would be maintained, and employment would be spurred. Decentralized facilities would lead to a more local autonomy and control. Social and financial equity would be increased, within and among nations.

Had industrial civilization been built upon such forms of energy "income" instead of on the energy stored in fossil fuels, any proposal to convert to coal or uranium for the world's future energy would doubtless be viewed with incredulous horror. The current prospect, however, is the reverse—a shift from trouble-ridden sources to more attractive ones. Of the possible worlds we might choose to build, an efficient solar-powered one appears most inviting. ❧

From *Rays of Hope: The Transition to a Post-Petroleum World* by Denis Hayes. W. W. Norton, New York. 240 pages. Paperback. $3.95. Available from the World Future Society's Book Service.

Strategies for Conserving Energy

Ways to save energy include "leak-plugging" and "machine-switching," says Denis Hayes in his book *Rays of Hope*. If all else fails, there is "belt-tightening."

Americans waste more fuel each year than is used by two-thirds of the world's population, energy researcher Denis Hayes reports in his new book *Rays of Hope*. Overall, fully 50% of all the energy generated in the United States is lost through inefficient consumption practices.

Most energy waste is a direct result of entrenched policies that have encouraged energy extravagance, Hayes says, but there is still much that individuals can do to conserve.

He divides strategies for conservation into two types: (1) technical solutions, which require changes in the types of machinery we use or in the way that we use them and (2) social solutions, which require changes in the way we live and act. Adoption of either type does not exclude the other, but Hayes feels that it might be advantageous to start with the possible technical alternatives since they involve essentially no behavioral alterations, and consequently could be utilized by a larger segment of the population.

Hayes characterizes technical conservation strategies as either "leak-plugging," which eliminates waste in existing technologies, or "machine-switching," which involves the replacement of existing energy-consuming devices with ones with a higher efficiency.

Leak-plugging on an individual level includes tuning up your automobile, insulating your house, and putting on a blanket when your feet get cold. Machine-switching includes purchasing a smaller car, installing a heat pump in a building, and wearing warmer socks.

Social solutions in energy conservation include "belt-tightening" tactics like turning off unnecessary lights, driving cars more slowly, and using heating and cooling systems more sparingly. More vigorous endeavors of a cooperative nature include car pools, public transit, apartment buildings, and joint ownership or rental of infrequently used items.

"A comprehensive program of energy conservation initiated today will allow the earth's limited resource base of high-quality fuel to be stretched," Hayes says. "It will enable our descendants to share in the earth's finite stock of fossil fuels. It will make an especially critical difference to those living in underdeveloped lands where the marginal benefit per unit of fuel used is far greater than it is in highly industrialized countries."

Population and Education: How Demographic Trends Will Shape the U.S.

by Joseph F. Coates

Changing life-styles are transforming U.S. schools. More women are entering the work force and marrying later, and fewer babies are being born. Unless population trends are better understood, education planners may be increasingly baffled by changes in school enrollment.

Birthrates in the United States have declined significantly over the past 18 years, with 28% fewer children being born now than were born in 1959. This "baby bust," which has followed the post-war baby boom, has already reduced the number of children enrolled in elementary school by about 10%, and a drop of another 7 or 8% by the mid-1980s is certain. As the children born during the baby bust become older, their numbers will affect high school enrollments. During the 1980s, enrollments may drop as much as 25%. These statistics represent a basic, nationwide trend, but other demographic factors—those which most concern planners on the regional, state and local levels—make school planning much more complex and uncertain than simple aggregate fertility rates suggest.

Other trends that will affect education:

• Women are increasingly entering the work force and staying longer. This will create more demands to change curriculum and add new school-centered services.

• Continued immigration will place special burdens on school systems in major cities, where immigrants tend to settle.

• Local mobility—the ease with which populations move within this country—will create increasing uncertainty among education planners.

The principal impact of these demographic trends occurs at the state and local levels. Since this is where most education planning is done, improved demographic study must begin at these levels. To see just what problems arise from these trends, it is useful to examine them in detail.

Left: Crowds can be fun, but they may not be beneficial to mental development. Children placed together with other children for extended periods of time—as in daycare—may experience slower intellectual growth.

Photo: Joe Di Dio, National Education Association

The Changing Family

The traditional image of the family—mother, father, and children, around which public policy has been framed—is increasingly at odds with reality. The growth of the single-parent family is one of the major demographic trends affecting schools. Approximately 45% of children born in 1976 will have lived with a single parent for some time before reaching 18 years of age. Between 1970 and 1976, the number of children living with a divorced mother increased by two-thirds, and the number living with a single mother increased by about 40%. The number of female-headed families with children has increased by over 250% since 1950. These families comprise 41% of all poverty-level families; the limited income of these families creates new demands and stresses on all public services, including schools.

Another factor relating to marriage and the family which can influence the school is the tendency of women to defer marriage. In 1970, 12% fewer 20-year-old women had been married than in 1960. The decline in the number of married 24-year-olds was only 7%. This suggests that women are not turning away from marriage in any great number; they are merely delaying it. During that period of deferral, women tend to enter the work force or to continue their education in order to prepare for work.

The entry of women into the work force is perhaps the demographic trend that most profoundly influences curriculum, services, the child's environment and the whole family structure. The shifting roles that women assume as they enter the work force create a demand for curriculum changes to prepare women for their entry. And working mothers need services to take care of their children.

The effects on schools of women in the work force will be great. First, there will be a decline in volunteerism. At a time when the school system is experiencing greater demand for volunteers to meet the pressures for more services, fewer women will be available. An example of this has been experienced by the League of Women Voters. Much of the envelope-licking and stuffing that once was done with free labor now must be done on a fee-for-service basis because so many of the League's members have moved into the work force. Similar effects will soon be felt by schools.

Demographers associate increasing female participation in the work force with a decline in the number of children a family will bear. And education encourages participation in the work force. In the future there will be a cycle in which education promotes work, work promotes a decline in fertility, and declining fertility increases the problems of elementary and secondary schools. The increasing number of dual-income families, especially among middle-class managerial and professional households, provides more discretionary money, money which may lead such families to send their children to private schools or to relocate their residences outside of central cities. The exodus of middle-class families may bring about a big-city public school system whose sole purpose is to educate the underclass.

Female participation in the work force may lead to changes in the purposes and structures of public schools. Schools will face an increased demand to overcome stylized gender roles associated with occupational choices. Career counselling may change to meet new work-sex roles. The new role models for girls will probably increase the number of students desiring vocationally-oriented curricula and counselling. Deferred marriage and earlier entry into the work force may create a demand for curricula that focus upon independent living, and training in financial management and personal affairs. Those who live in the lowest economic strata and are burdened by small children or single parenthood need education that focuses on improving one's economic status through continuation course certification and specially-tailored high-school programs.

The increased demand for day care and nursery care for preschool and young school children of working mothers may be met by the school systems. For children roughly aged 7 to 13, the school day is not quite long enough to accommodate the needs of single-parent working households. There are efforts in some communities to extend the length of afternoon care, not by extending the school day, but by extending the use of school buildings. Some 15% of children in this age group can be usefully served by extending the use of facilities from 3 p.m. to 6 p.m.

The family is becoming less of a dominant factor in the socialization of

Working Women— and Men

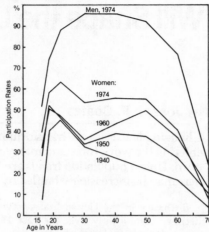

Labor force participation rates for men in 1974—and for women in 1974, 1960, 1950, and 1940. More women are entering the work force, and fewer are dropping out during the childbearing years. This trend is increasing demand for child care.

Chart: Juanita Kreps, ed., *Women and the American Economy*, 1976.

How Many Will Be Born?

Much of the future will be influenced by present age distributions and birth and death rates that prevail now and in the coming years. The age composition of the population is in a state of continuous flux. As the post-World War II baby boom age group matures, it will create "waves" of expanding and contracting age groups.

Babies produced by the post-World War II "baby boom" generation will create a second-wave effect which is likely to create an upswing in school populations by the mid-1980s. Yet it appears that the long-range trend in the United States is toward fewer children. Recent survey data collected by the Bureau of the Census on the birth expectations of young wives aged 18 to 24 show that nearly 75% expected two or fewer children. If these young wives achieve their expectations—and other fertility surveys have shown a fairly close correlation between the number of children that women say they want and the number that they actually have—then they will experience an average 2.17 births per woman. This works out almost exactly to replacement fertility.

the child. A child now entering the first grade may have been exposed to nursery school or day care. He may have been involved with Head Start or related programs, or have had extensive exposure to television. The size of his family is different from what it was for children born 10 years ago. Organized religious groups, grandparents and other members of the family, and adult neighbors seem to be playing a declining role in the socialization of children.

The reduced amount of time available for parenting in families where females work may create a demand for new school services that deal with functions traditionally learned at home. Schools may need to teach the skills of eating, drinking, dressing, social behavior, deportment, manners, self-control, and other functions to compensate for reduced parental care. In view of the underuse of schools and of surplus teacher capacity, the possibility of extending school functions into these areas may seem quite attractive to teachers' unions. However, a word of caution is necessary: Data from social psychological literature indicate that children put together with large numbers of other children for extended periods of time may suffer a reduced mental development.

Immigration and Non-English Speaking Students

Immigration accounts for one-fourth of net population growth in the United States. Since immigrants tend to settle in metropolitan areas, continuing immigration will create a chronic source of stress for big-city school systems.

There is an interesting relationship between high school dropout rates and the language spoken at home. Where English is the language spoken, or where English is spoken along with some other non-English language, the dropout rate is between 8 and 10%. But where a language other than English is the only language spoken at home, the dropout rate rises to 38%.

Among the specific population of those of Spanish origin, the situation is even worse. The principal non-English language spoken in the United States by people four years old and over is Spanish, spoken by almost 10 million people. Among school-age children, about five million speak Spanish as their primary language. Where English is spoken among families of Spanish descent, the dropout rate of their children is 14 to 15%. Where only Spanish is spoken, the dropout rate is 45%.

Among students who do not measure up to standard performance, non-English speaking students represent the biggest problem. Only 10% of English-speaking students are two or more grades below their peers. In grades one through four, approximately 17% of the non-English speaking students are two grades below mode; at the high school level, some 35% are two or more grades below mode.

The implication of these statistics is significant when they are coupled with the long-term movement of American society toward that of an information society. Approximately 55% of the work force is now in the information business. This situation raises questions about the value of bilingual education, and whether it denies students the chance for an economically useful education. The data suggest that, as now taught, students of foreign origin may be precluded from getting their first foot up on the economic ladder.

If the higher cost of bilingual education of students whose primary language is not English precludes other priorities, the level of education of English-speaking students may be reduced, further accelerating the decline of the urban school systems. Whether or not bilingual education continues, the steady stream of foreign-born students will renew the kinds of cross-cultural stresses associated with students who are hard to acculturate. This often results in delinquency and poor school performance, particularly for urban school systems. And proposed changes in the status of new illegal immigrants might encourage them to make greater use of the school system for their children. This will especially affect big-city schools

Preschooler "reads" to himself. The increasing entry of mothers into the workforce will increase the demand for daycare.
Photo: Joe Di Dio, National Education Association

About the Author

Joe Coates is Assistant to the Director of the Office of Technology Assessment for the U.S. Congress. Before joining OTA, he served on the staff of the National Science Foundation and the Institute for Defense Analyses. He has also worked as a research chemist and as a lecturer in philosophy and chemistry, technology assessment, and futurism.

His previous articles in THE FUTURIST include: "Technology Assessment: The Benefits .... the Costs ... the Consequences" (December 1971) and "The Future of the U.S. Government" (June 1972). His address is Office of Technology Assessment, U.S. Congress, Washington, D.C. 20510.

This article is adapted from testimony before the Subcommittee on Elementary, Secondary, and Vocational Education of the Committee on Education and Labor of the U.S. House of Representatives, May 10, 1977, and is based on an analysis he made for the Office of Technology Assessment.

and the smaller communities in the Southwest and in California.

Local Mobility and Internal Migration

Internal mobility and migration are perhaps the demographic factors that most perturb education planners at the state and local level. Between 16 and 18% of the U.S. population moves annually. The data reveal some evidence that people seem to be attracted to the city for work and other opportunities; but as they enter the childbearing years, people have a tendency to move out of central cities.

The overall effect of internal migration is a trend of movement out of the city and into suburban and rural areas. From 1970 to 1974, cities experienced a net exodus of 1.8 million people. The eight largest cities saw a net out-migration of 1.2%. Population growth in rural areas during this same period was 5.6%, contrasting with a growth of 4% for the nation as a whole. Educational management in these nonmetropolitan and small-community growth centers may run into special problems, because such growth was unexpected. The tax base may be inadequate to meet the demands caused by the influx of people, and the social values of the new migrants may be substantially at odds with those of the local people. The redistribution of population will create an acute problem for education planning in boom towns. In order to come to grips

with the energy crisis, we will open up coal resources in Wyoming, the Dakotas, Colorado and other areas in the West, and Kentucky and southern Illinois in the east. One can reasonably anticipate surges in population for which the local communities in these areas will be totally unprepared.

There is a long-term trend toward the equalization of regional incomes. Once the nation's economic backwater, the sun belt areas of the South, the Southwest and southern regions east of the Rockies are all currently undergoing economic growth. In the early 1930s, regional income varied from 50% below average to 50% above the national average. In 1974 this range had narrowed to about 15% to 20%. Equalization may reduce regional differences in cost and quality of education, undercutting regional disparities of funds available per child on a statewide basis.

Migration in and out of metropolitan areas is having the effect of concentrating minority students within the big cities and non-minority students outside of those big cities. This phenomenon, along with concern about the quality of schools, and about the curricula, are increasing white and middle-class dissatisfaction. There are only a small number of options open to middle-class parents who do not wish to have their children experience the effects of the decline in metropolitan school systems. One alternative is to withdraw the pupil to a private or parochial school. The data suggest that families that have the financial option of sending their children to private schools tend to exercise it. Even families with incomes in the $10,000-$15,000 range often send children to private schools.

For families without the income to send their children to private schools, the alternative may be a change of residence. Other options include early graduation and entry into college—a process that may stimulate programs of graduation based on credentials—and tracking, or grouping students by ability. In any case the net effect of all these alternatives open to a white or middle-class population—those dissatisfied with school systems in urban areas—is resegregation.

Teenage Childbearing

The only group in the United States now undergoing significant expansion in birthrates is that of females under age 15. Of the 3,144,198 live births in the United States in 1975, 12,642 were born to girls under 15 years of age. This situation has several implications for the educational system. Young motherhood interferes with the ability of the mother to continue her education. Children who are born to young mothers are far more likely to suffer a variety of congenital defects. These children born to adolescent mothers are themselves more likely to bear children at an early age, thus further burdening the school system.

Junior high school curricula, services and goals have never come to grips with the onset of puberty. Especially critical is the increasing rate of early sexual activity among boys and girls of junior high school and high school age, creating both immediate and long-term social and educational problems and needs associated with adolescent childbearing.

Decline in Enrollment

The national decline in enrollments does not imply universal distress—nor is it a universal phenomenon. A decline is occurring predominantly in the Midwest, Mid-Atlantic, and Pacific states,

Lone student works in an empty classroom. Declining enrollment may make scenes like this more common.

Photo: Joe Di Dio, National Education Association

while the South and Southwest are experiencing a boom. To complicate matters further, both enrollment declines and increases often occur in the same state, with different small districts experiencing both shrinking and growing student populations. Especially hard hit by the general trend will be the big cities, already in great fiscal distress.

Thirty-seven states have experienced enrollment declines since 1970. Sixteen of these states have lost at least 4% of their students. Simultaneous with the declining enrollments has been an increase in minority enrollment in big cities. In the period between 1968 and 1974, the average student minority enrollment was 67.1%. School enrollment in the 27 largest cities peaked in 1970, and is now back at the level it was in 1962. The exodus seems to have occurred primarily among middle-class

Bringing the School to the Worker

Employers around the world are recognizing the need for employees to have more than mere technical training, according to a report by the Organization for Economic Cooperation and Development (OECD).

If an employee is given an opportunity "to develop his whole personality" and engage in "creative self-expression," the report says, he will contribute more to the economy: "Progress towards industrial democracy depends upon the existence of well-informed employees."

Part of the movement to combine education and training is based on the growing belief that changing jobs or social classes is a social right. But the need to absorb greater amounts of information just to keep up with technical matters is barring most employees from taking the time and money initiative to enroll in nontechnical courses. The OECD argues that the employee requires financial support, and the chance to devote some of his working hours—or an extended sabbatical leave—to concentrated study. In the future, the report states, the employer will provide on-the-job study facilities—places where a worker can study during the working day, without loss of income. For those who are unemployed, governments will sponsor training programs that lead directly to available jobs.

A major problem facing most adult education systems is their failure to attract the uneducated. According to the OECD, the majority of adults enrolled in courses have already had more than 16 years of formal education. Present systems often have course prerequisites, or courses that are beyond the capacity of the uneducated. Many courses simply have no practical relevance to workers' careers. The OECD report says that adult education in the future will need to re-design methods of certification and accreditation to meet the needs of those wishing to catch up with the national educational level. Adult school systems will also need to take into account the differences in learning characteristics between adults and children: Too many systems are based on traditional schooling methods that remind former unsuccessful students of their unhappy school careers. Thus many adult dropouts avoid repeating the shame and embarrassment of their youth.

In order to accommodate the undereducated worker, adult schooling will be more accessible and will be complemented with specialized, industry-based, guidance counseling systems. Teachers may be replaced by part-time educators recruited from the ranks of professions and industrial leaders. Courses will be geared toward functional literacy, second-language courses for immigrants, vocational retraining, and civic and cultural literacy. They may be taught in mini-courses conducted at the workplace, with correspondence courses, or through learning machines and texts located in industrial lunch rooms and recreation areas.

Innovative adult education systems, the report claims, may revolutionize world attitudes toward education. Governments and industries may come to see adult education as a means of fostering true democracy by giving all workers the opportunity for personal, career, and cultural advancement.

Regional Incomes

Change in per-capita personal income as a percentage of the U.S. average, 1929-1974. Regional income levels are becoming more equal as the South and Midwest begin to catch up with the traditionally dominant northeastern and far western states. Broader national distribution of income will tend to equalize regional educational differences.

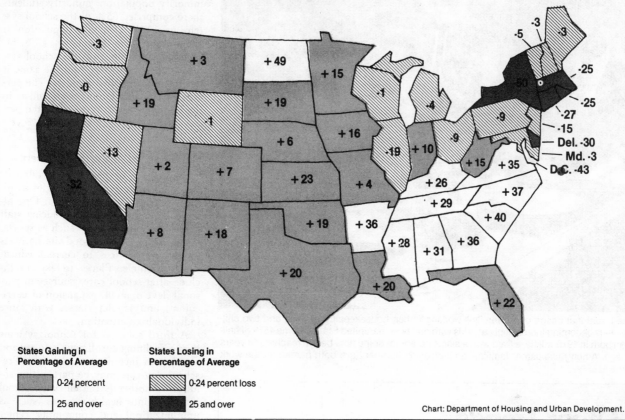

States Gaining in Percentage of Average

| | 0-24 percent |
| | 25 and over |

States Losing in Percentage of Average

| | 0-24 percent loss |
| | 25 and over |

Chart: Department of Housing and Urban Development.

Urban Enrollments

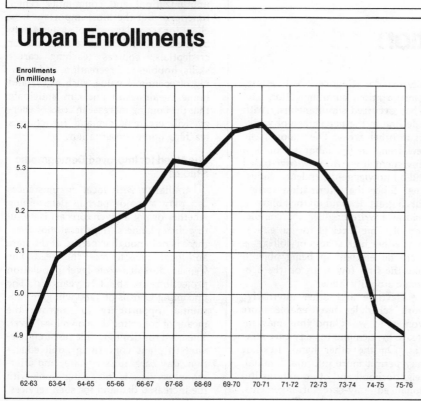

Enrollments (in millions)

School enrollments in the 27 largest American cities have declined to the level they were in 1962, and they may drop even further. This change may transform urban school systems in the future.

Chart: Council of the Great City Schools.

Students leave school building. Declining population in major cities—along with the exodus of the middle class from urban centers—is causing city schools to deteriorate.

Photo: Joe Di Dio, National Education Association

The traditional image of the family—working father, housekeeping mother, and two children—is becoming increasingly at odds with reality in the United States. Some 45% of children born in 1976 will have lived with a single parent for some time before reaching 18 years of age. Among two-parent families, an increasing number have both parents in the work force.

Photo: USDA

and white students. Looking at a sample of those 27 cities, one finds that the percent of minority school enrollment in almost every case is substantially above the percent minority population in the city. For example, Atlanta has a 52% minority population; minority students there comprised 85% of the school system in 1974. Denver's population is 11% minority; in the schools, 47%. St. Louis is 41% minority; the school system is 70% minority. And the same is true of impoverished families. The percent of students from poor families in the big cities is far in excess of the percent of families in poverty: 33.4% versus 11.6%.

Response to Decline in Enrollment

In the face of declining enrollment, there are three general strategies available to school administrators: One alternative is to shrink by reducing staff and the so-called "frills" such as sports, music, and art. The second alternative is to expand services to current educational clientele. Places to expand include after-school care, courses in personal development, expansion of curriculum, and smaller classes with more individualized attention.

A third solution for school systems facing declining enrollment is to expand services to include new clientele. Preschool day-care may be part of this solution. Another is the entry of school functions into health services (such as immunization) and community center functions. But the most important new client for secondary school systems may be the adult. Adults have the need for credentials, courses teaching career skills, hobbies and recreation, and training of economic value, such as car and home repair. And one can anticipate that the coming increase in costs of energy will create a demand for courses teaching home conservation.

The Need for Improved Demographic Studies

Familiarity with local circumstances can play a major part in determining whether or not a given forecast is useful to policy planners. In general, however, there is not enough expertise at the state and local levels to meet this need. The Census Bureau's state-level population projections are about 10 years old. The upcoming Census of 1980 will give substantial opportunity to improve the means of collecting data on a local level. The need for demographic research relevant to plans concerning adult education, day care, nursery care, and after-school services is increasing along with the increased demand for such services. Such demographic data is essential for the wise policy-making needed to build effective educational systems for the future.

Other Trends Affecting Education

A variety of non-demographic factors are likely to interact with demographic trends to change the schools of the future.

• **Energy** will have many impacts on education. Direct effects include fuel costs for heating, transportation and busing; long-term effects on the structure and design of school buildings; and a movement toward larger-size school districts to allow for larger buildings. Indirect effects include a reduction in the discretionary income of families, which may affect the amount of expenditures taxpayers will allow schools. Scarce energy may increasingly encourage people to live closer to the areas where they work—and perhaps bring the middle-class back to the city.

• **Civil rights movements** have increased the percentage of children bused to and from school. Increasing busing costs may cause curtailment of other school costs in a time of shrinking budgets and inflation.

• **The rise of the knowledge indus**tries—trade, finance, real estate, transportation, communication, etc. —has occurred simultaneously with a decline in the percentage of workers in other areas. The major, basic new trend in the labor sector is a movement toward knowledge-based and knowledge-dependent industries. Since the information society puts a great demand on the ability to read and write English, the completion of some level of formal education, either high school or college, is a crucial element in being able to take the first few steps on the economic mobility ladder.

• **Flextime** and other alternative work schedules may enable more women to work and thus may increase the demand for day-care services. On the other hand, flextime may permit more informal familial, neighborhood and other non-institutionalized day-care arrangements, which may *reduce* the demand for childcare services in schools or other formal institutions.

Work in the Year

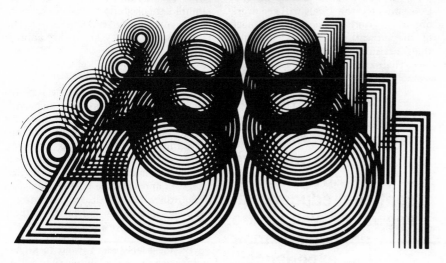

by William Abbott

Technological breakthroughs will continue to change the world of work in the years ahead. But the workplace may be affected even more by the continuing revolutions in values, consciousness, knowledge, and equality. These changes are already transforming labor unions and universities, and have brought about an unusual alliance of Big Business, Big Labor, and Big Government.

Although the work environment will expand in the next few decades to include outer space and the depths of the oceans, the most important changes in the workplace will be considerably more down to earth. Those changes will involve how the worker prepares for his job, how he updates his training, and how he interacts with management as part of the decision-making process.

Skilled workers will have to attend school at least four times in their lives to be *totally retrained*. Frequent retraining is already necessary in a number of trades. For example, members of the Graphic Arts International Union must now be retrained three or four times during their working lives, according to Union President Kenneth Brown. The International Brotherhood of Electrical Workers now has 57

of its members rewriting textbooks because about 10% of the technical knowledge in the industry becomes obsolete each year.

Industrial workers will be employed in autonomous work teams, making their own production decisions. Factory work will be organized horizontally, with employers and employees making joint production decisions. This "unimanagement" is already occurring in a few factories as a result of agreements between the United Auto Workers (UAW) and the Harman, Rockwell, and Dana Corporations. At Harman Industries in Bolivar, Tennessee, worker-supervisor core committees plan production within each department, subject to review by a plantwide union-management work committee. At a Dana Corporation plant at Edgerton, Wisconsin, production committees of workers and foremen elect a union-management screening committee, which sifts the production committee's suggestions as to how best to organize the factory's production. In Europe, co-determination has made rapid strides. A 1973 Swedish law put union representatives on corporate boards. A 1976 West German law gives workers the right to elect half of the directors of firms employing over 2,000 people. Worker participation in management is increasing dramatically in a number of Western and Eastern European countries. The reason behind this movement, according to Andre Thiria, International Secretary of the Swedish Confederation of Trade Unions, is that "demands are being raised for a better work environment and more satisfaction on the job, while at the same time mechanization and streamlining of production makes it more difficult to meet these demands." Joint labor-management decision-making is an attempt to solve this dilemma.

Workers will schedule their own hours under flexitime. Many will work at home. Most workers will probably hold two jobs or go to college on a part-time basis. (The need for lifelong learning will be a generally accepted principle.)

Economist Eli Ginzberg points out that 45% of employed Americans now work less than full-time for the whole year and that 30% of all work is performed by less than full-time workers. This trend is likely to continue.

Collective bargaining will continue, but fist-banging will give way to joint problem-solving task forces and arguments over the interpretation of data in books and budgets that are open to labor as well as management. Labor relations will increasingly become a battle among intellects. Union leaders are going to college, and are beginning to run for office by pointing to community college degrees in labor as a qualification for elected office. Some go on for a four-year education. In at least one instance, company executives and union leaders sit in the same class as they pursue a labor studies two-year degree at Black Hawk College in Moline, Illinois. In 1976, faculty, staff, and administration at Federal City College (now the University of the District of Columbia) ran a joint program where labor played the role of management and vice versa.

In order to keep their identity and the loyalty of the members, unions will become more a way of life than a simple bread-and-butter organization. UAW sends entire families to its extensive Walter and May Reuther Family Education Center at Black Lake, Michigan. Husband, wife, and children are all taught union leadership. Retirees now play an integral role in the union's program. Increasingly, the kind of leadership UAW is talking about is that of meeting the needs of the whole personality. Next in the union's bargaining program, according to President Leonard Woodcock, is a sabbatical leave just like that of university professors.

Multiple Revolutions Transform the Workplace

On top of a continuing technological revolution in the 1970s, the decade has been marked by several concurrent revolutions: the Equality Revolution, the Knowledge Revolution, the Value Revolution, and the Consciousness Revolution.

The Equality Revolution, while far from complete, nevertheless has brought some giant employment strides. Blacks and other ethnic minorities have made gains largely through the impetus of the civil rights struggles of the 1960s, often consummated in affirmative action legislation. In the 1970s, women have also demanded equal treatment. In employment, while the number of employed males has increased 26% since 1950, the number of female workers has soared 93% during the same period.

By the year 2001, there will probably be new battles launched by those struggling against established orthodoxies. Social utopia will remain elusive as solutions to old problems create difficulties anew. People with

an ideological, emotional, or material investment in what is established will be confronted by an imaginative avant-garde pressing for ever greater rapidity of change.

If one accepts Arnold Toynbee's definition of the proletariat as that group which feels itself disinherited, the "lower class" may be that which gets pushed aside in the Knowledge Revolution, which is beginning to mix practical work values and a liberal education together into a new recipe for success, leaving behind those who cannot put the two together inside their personalities. To a greater degree than ever before in history, tomorrow's worker will have to become something of a scholar, and today's scholar will have to learn communication, administration, and other practical skills to stay on top. Consequently, the 1980s will see more organized groups clamoring for a piece of the educational action, insisting that institutions gear themselves to meet their special needs.

> ## "Many of the best ideas for the future may come from senior citizens, who will have the advantage of continual educational renewal as well as the richness of their experience."

In 1976, apprentices in the skilled trades began to ask for two-year college degrees which included English, humanities, and social sciences as part of their training. The Operating Engineers Union responded by initiating a dual enrollment program—a worker could study either for a college degree or for the traditional certificate. Under this program and others, job training has tended to take on the character of a general education.

A related development has been the rapid proliferation of community colleges in recent years. In a period during which many of the more traditional universities have been going through doldrum agonies, the community colleges have been thriving. In 1974, community college enrollment was up 12.1%; in 1975, it increased an additional 15.4%.

The rise of the community colleges has been accompanied by the birth of a new kind of educator who goes into

the neighborhoods, plans courses with adult students, and learns to communicate with them in their language. He or she is part teacher, part recruiter, part administrator, part counselor, part planner, part innovator, and, on the whole, quite successful in these roles. This new educator does his job on campuses, in neighborhood drop-in centers, in churches, union halls, factories, and storefronts, and in homes. In the future, he may reach many people in their homes through various electronic media, as well as through personal visits.

The flaw in the new form of higher education is that research and materials development have not kept up with the innovations. The challenge to universities is to provide scholarship synthesized with non-esoteric communication styles to uphold this redefinition of education. The community colleges need the universities if they are to accomplish their mission.

Workers Demand Education

In the 1970s, the Equality Revolution has taken a social-class turn, with workers beginning to demand the same educational opportunities enjoyed by other classes. They are being attracted by colleges that count their work experience as credit toward degrees and that are best equipped to help them as adults to update or change their skills and broaden their life as well as work options.

Business also has turned to higher education for help. Industry spent at least $10 billion on its own training program in 1975. But even this staggering amount was not enough to do the job. To meet its more pressing training needs, business has looked to the higher education institutions with the most flexibility; more often than not, they have been the community colleges. Earlier this year, for example, the National Automobile Dealers Association announced a unique two-year degree program at community colleges for aspiring auto mechanics. The dealers are convinced that simply learning how to repair a car is no longer enough. An auto mechanic must also have a greater knowledge of society and be able to communicate effectively.

The UAW, in recent years, has negotiated tuition assistance ranging from $450-$700 a year. In 1976, the union bargained an increase to $900 per member per year from the Ford Motor Company. This year, the UAW expects to extend this $900 benefit to over a million workers.

Nationwide, a total of two million members of various unions are covered by such tuition aids; an additional four million unionists benefit from apprenticeship training funds, a substantial amount of which finds its way into community colleges.

In 1976, Bernard DeLury, then U.S. Assistant Secretary for Labor-Management Relations, expressed hope that the number of workers receiving such aid would soon be much higher. DeLury called for "a negotiated careers program" which would use "collective bargaining as a means of opening the door to clerical, technical, professional and management jobs for workers in the bargaining unit." Counselors would be available to advise the worker on "the need for good reading ability and language skills" and to recommend colleges and universities that could best satisfy his needs. The counselor would also "talk with management about providing opportunities to learn about the overall production in the plant and the various departments related to it . . . . The counselor would work with training and higher education institutions to develop a tailor-made, work-integrated program for this worker which leads to a credential, and perhaps even a degree in Business Administration." The International Union of Electrical Workers has already run a successful experiment for its membership in this type of counseling.

The flow of workers into college is taking place in Europe, too. A 1971 French law gives educational leaves to most of the nation's work force. The faculties of France's overcrowded universities have not been wildly enthusiastic about the idea of catering to swarms of workers. The British government has also attempted to open up higher education to the common people, and met similar faculty resistance. As the Organization of Economic Cooperation and Development's Centre for Educational Research and Innovation dourly noted, "There is no evidence that any impetus for educational leaves of absence came from the education sector itself." British historian Harold Perkin observes that while left-wing majorities now dominate many German universities, working class students are discouraged from attending them. "Left-wingers," says Perkin, "are as academically conservative and elitist as the rest."

Thus a new class struggle has shaped up, with government, business, and more pragmatic-minded unions attempting to get the lowly commoner into college, while academic ideologues, both left and right, team up to pour cold water over such a move.

Colleges Begin to Emphasize Community Service

The burgeoning community colleges and the faltering universities in the United States and Canada have engaged in some struggles over turf; however, as early as the late 1960s, survival-minded four-year institutions quietly began a shift in emphasis from the traditional academic pattern to that of community service.

A good method of measuring this change is to compare "faculty" to a new breed of professionals providing services to the academic as well as the larger community. At the University of Hawaii, the regular faculty members are called "nine-month employees," while professionals engaged in year-round service-type duties (which could mean anything from teaching to program planning to administration—or a combination of those skills) have been labeled "11-month employees." In 1973, the 11-month personnel numerically edged out the nine-month faculty as the university sought to provide more services to more people of varying ages and walks of life. This is the mark of a "communiversity," for in 1973 one out of every 16 men, women, and children who lived in Hawaii participated in some program of the University system.

Education has taken a totally new direction. People of all ages and social classes will continually have to seek an updating of their education simply to cope with the fast-paced changes swirling within the world of work. If they are to avoid drowning in the whirlpool of change, they will have to return to school recurrently to update their skills. Many of the best ideas for the future may come from senior citizens, who will have the advantage of continual educational renewal as well as the richness of their experience.

In 1976, the American Board of Family Practice made 1,400 family doctors take tests to see if they had kept abreast of advances in the field. If they failed, the Board would not renew their certification. No line of work is safe now from the demands of lifelong learning.

It should be clear that the separation between work and education is disappearing. By the year 2001, most Americans will not be able to separate one from the other very easily, and perhaps there will also be no clear demarcation between education and ordinary living.

To cope with living in today's society, 17 million people have enrolled in adult education classes. This figure may appear impressive, but it fails to match the need. A University of Texas study concluded that twice that number of people are functionally incompetent to cope with their personal consumer economics. The study warned: "If the requirements change and the individual does not adapt by either acquiring more or different knowledge and skills, then that person becomes less competent."

Simply remaining proficient at living requires lifelong education, according to Edmund J. Gleazer, President of the American Association of Community and Junior Colleges.

The Knowledge Revolution is described best by Robert Hillard, educational broadcasting specialist for the Federal Communications Commission:

"At the rate at which knowledge is growing, by the time the child born today graduates from college, the amount of knowledge in the world will be four times as great. By the time that same child is 50 years old, it will be 32 times as great, and 97% of everything known in the world will have been learned since the time the child was born."

Many jobs will become obsolete so quickly that no one will think in terms of career education but rather of a lifetime of multiple careers.

Knowledge Workers Will Proliferate

One of the largest vocations will be knowledge workers, many of them condensing torrents of new information into frequent newsletters and tapes for all manner of national organizations, local affiliates, and individuals. "Capsi-Knol" (capsuled knowledge) will employ several

"Hierarchy will vanish in offices, to be replaced by autonomous self-directors who will probably waste too much time at meetings coordinating themselves."

Do-Goodism: A Growing "Industry"

"There will be more people making a career out of helping other people in the year 2000 than there will be in any other occupation," predicts William Abbott in a recent article in CAREERS TOMORROW.

U.S. Census Bureau statistics show that the number of volunteers helping other people increased from 24.3 million in 1964 to 36.8 million in 1974. Among these volunteers, reports Abbott, were "church members helping to fix up dilapidated homes in Appalachia, businessmen working out plans for a self-help cooperative with ghetto blacks, union carpenters donating free time to build low-income hous-ing, a biology instructor giving free yoga lessons to young people, a doctor coaching a Little League team, and a welfare recipient organizing an arts and crafts club."

This increasing interest in helping others will also lead to a greater number of paid jobs in altruistic fields, Abbott says. As evidence for this trend, he cites the types of job training now offered by community colleges. "In the paraprofessional field alone, one can get a degree as a social work technician, a legal technician, a planning technician, or a health technician. Most of these new opportunities have cropped up in the last three years and they often involve low-income people who several years ago could only look forward to mopping floors or sweating in small workshops."

"Do-goodism is becoming such a powerful force in our society that it may bring about a fundamental political realignment," concludes Abbott. "Future partisan battles may be fought between 'open-minders' and 'closed-minders': the first group oriented toward unfettered experimentation, the other group more prone to doctrines and authorities." Those battles could determine how large a role altruism will play in government policy-making in the year 2000.

hundred thousand readers, researchers, interpreters, writers and technicians.

Typists and file clerks will dwindle as speakwriters (typewriters that take dictation) and robotized filing machines take over routine office work. Hierarchy will vanish in offices, to be replaced by autonomous self-directors who will probably waste too much time at meetings coordinating themselves. There will be bursts of creativity before the iron law of oligarchy stultifies workers in an organization, at which point Albert Camus's idea of permanent rebellion against what exists will pick up a large following.

The alliance of Big Government, Big Business, and Big Labor in bringing about some of these changes in the workplace has created suspicions among some people who feel that the "little person" is increasingly at the mercy of giant forces. Due to their fears, the resisters have not recognized the need for rapid educational change, and thus have programmed themselves into the vortex.

People who feel powerless will form new organizations and coalitions in the years ahead in order to cope with the tidal wave against tradition and to protect the interests of the average individual in the emerging new society. They will demand decentralized, grass-roots economic and social planning where their voices can be heard and their input counted. Popular Participatory Planning (PPP) for more or-derly social change (Alvin Toffler calls it "anticipatory democracy") may be as universally revered in 2001 as the Fourth of July is today in the United States.

New Values Affect the Marketplace

Concurrently, we are in the midst of a Value Revolution. For many people, the acquisition of material symbols no longer is the primary goal in life. A President of the United States wears blue jeans; the rich move out of the suburbs into the city's inner core; compact cars are favored by those who have long ago arrived and want to go someplace else; Ph.D.'s sneer at advanced degrees.

In gaining the world, many discovered they had misplaced their souls. While much of the population is still laboring mightily for orthodox middle-class goals, the children of the well-to-do stick an irreverent finger into the air at such strivings. This value gap caused much hostility between "hippies" and "the establishment" in the 1960s. But in recent years, in a less ostentatious manner, more people have accepted nonmaterial values, albeit rather clumsily, because of a general uncertainty about what values should replace those being discarded.

In the future, the search for ways to fill one's leisure time with fun will intensify greatly. Alvin Toffler writes of future "experiential industries," including simulated environments that would be enclaves of the past and would allow people to experience the kind of life their ancestors lived. "Thus," Toffler says, "computer experts, roboteers, designers, historians, and museum specialists will join to create experiential enclaves that reproduce, as skillfully as sophisticated technology will permit, the splendor of ancient Rome, the pomp of Queen Elizabeth's court, the 'sexoticism' of an 18th-century Japanese geisha house, and the like."

Tourism, already big, will become bigger in the years ahead. Two decades from now, many tours may begin with an audio-visual panorama that will brief tourists on the sights they will see and get them in the right mood to visit the sites. There will also be "consult-a-historian" services where tourists can enter private counseling rooms for an in-depth talk with an expert. Regional craft people will not just show tourists how they weave rugs or fashion pottery, but will teach tourists the skills. A mark of status in the year 2001 will be to have a home furnished with the objects that you yourself have constructed.

The search for roots in a turbulent world will make history more popular than ever before, and indeed, parallels will be found between the cult of self-improvement of the 1830s and 1840s and that of the 1970s and 1980s. Perhaps history moves in cycles: The new cooperation between labor and management in the latter 1970s, coupled with way-of-life unionism,

Mystic Seaport, Connecticut, recreates 19th-century maritime life. In shops like those on Seaport Street (above), craftsmen still ply their trades in support of the shipbuilding, whaling, fishing, and shipping industries. In the year 2001, craftsmen may be teaching their skills to tourists, not simply demonstrating them.

Photo: Russell A. Fowler, Mystic Seaport, Inc.

Tourists wait their turn for a stagecoach ride in Old Tucson, Arizona. This replica of 1860s Tucson was originally a movie location set, but is now also a major tourist attraction with shops that are permanently in operation. A town like Old Tucson could have important educational applications in the future, with students learning their history lessons by "living in the past" for a few weeks or months.

Photo: Courtesy of Tucson Chamber of Commerce

Visitors ride in a horse-drawn carriage through the streets of Colonial Williamsburg, Virginia, a restored community which includes 88 original 18th- or 19th-century houses, shops, taverns, and public buildings. Such enclaves of the past may be increasingly popular as people search for roots in a turbulent world.

Photo: Colonial Williamsburg

Experiential Communities May Thrive in Future

"Enclaves of the past" may be very much in demand as tourist attractions in the year 2001, says author William Abbott, because "the search for roots in a turbulent world will make history more popular than ever before." People may take great pride in visiting such a community and mastering some of the skills of their ancestors. "Regional craft people will not just show tourists how they weave rugs or fashion pottery, but will teach tourists the skills," says Abbott. "A mark of status in the year 2001 will be to have a home furnished with the objects that you yourself have constructed."

Alvin Toffler, author of the bestseller *Future Shock*, has suggested that people suffering from future shock could retreat to enclaves of the past similar to Colonial Williamsburg, Virginia, Mystic Seaport, Connecticut, and Old Tucson, Arizona, where they could live for periods ranging from a few days to several years. Living and working in one of these enclaves could also be a valuable educational experience for students. "Such living education would give them a historical perspective no book could ever provide," Toffler declares.

Toffler speculates that "computer experts, roboteers, designers, historians, and museum specialists will join to create experiential enclaves that reproduce, as skillfully as sophisticated technology will permit, the splendor of ancient Rome, the pomp of Queen Elizabeth's court, the 'sexoticism' of an 18th-century Japanese geisha house, and the like."

Work Newsletter

For those who wish to keep informed about the latest developments in the area of work and careers, the World Future Society is now publishing a bimonthly newsletter called CAREERS TOMORROW. The eight-page newsletter contains articles on work, labor unions, compensation, job opportunities, industrial relations, and workplaces. CAREERS TOMORROW is available for $6 a year for Society members and $9 for non-members and libraries.

bears some striking resemblances to the old-time guilds.

Consciousness Revolution Will Continue

And the quest for inner peace has led to another revolution—the Consciousness Revolution. "Psychenauts" (a term coined by behavioral scientist Jean Houston) are currently probing inner space to help people find levels of consciousness to better communicate with themselves and with others. Already, there are 8,000 methods advocated as the right road to happiness. Werner Erhard has already sold his "est" to 83,000 individuals at $250 each for a 60-hour "experience" in discovering alternative realms of consciousness within oneself. Awareness, a big business now, will get bigger.

People will invest heavily in psychic process classes, in meditation and other methods of inner development, finding and using senses they may have never been aware of before.

Already the consciousness movement is being co-opted to a significant degree by churches, colleges, and other established institutions who see survival or institutional progress in their ability to keep up with change. The

Author William Abbott, editor of the World Future Society's CAREERS TOMORROW newsletter, reports that unions are beginning to seek increased educational opportunities for their members, so that they can keep up with changes in the workplace and in society.

U.S. military is researching telepathy since the Russians are also doing it.

Spiritual development and organized religion may not be quite the same in the year 2001, but humans are social in nature and they need the reinforcement of others to identify themselves. All social beliefs which attract sizeable followings, including communism, have religious overtones; hence, nothing in the future is likely to wipe human religiosity out.

The prognosis for the future can look bright with one important proviso. If the heavily industrialized nations ignore the multiplying problems of developing regions, a titanic struggle could take place between the haves and have-nots. The powerful countries of the world could make a better future guarantee if they would pool their resources to wage the only war worth fighting—the war on human misery and degradation.

William Abbott, editor of the World Future Society's CAREERS TOMORROW newsletter, is also Director of the Service Center for Community College-Labor Union Cooperation of the American Association of Community and Junior Colleges, 1 Dupont Circle, N.W., Washington, D.C. 20036.

Will Diplomas Need To Be Renewed?

In the future, university degrees may expire automatically unless they are renewed after the degree-holder's abilities are checked.

The rapid increase in new knowledge creates a need for continuous updating of professional skills, according to Leland R. Kaiser, comprehensive health planner with the University of Colorado.

"The credential loses most of its meaning in a period of rapid knowledge obsolescence," Kaiser says in an article in the January-February issue of *Hearing and Speech Action*. "A piece of paper representing an academic or any other formal qualification can only assure competence for a short period of time. The emphasis will be upon demonstrated competence retested at frequent intervals."

People will need to be "life-long learners," Kaiser says, and institutions will need to offer programs of continuing education and self-directed learning "to meet the challenge of rapid educational recycling."

Already in many localities physicians and school teachers, among other professional groups, must show proof of continuing education for periodic recertification.

Kaiser also foresees an increase in education for sensory enrichment.

"New emphasis on quality of life," he says, "is moving us towards a positive definition of health. Positive health means actualization—development of the highest potential. Since the sensory organs connect the human being to the external world, the quality of life depends upon sensory enrichment and awareness training." He expects that this kind of training will be especially beneficial to older people.

The percentage of older people in the population will increase, Kaiser says, as medical services become more advanced and more available, and as the birth rate continues to decrease. The elderly increasingly will become a political force in the United States.

Kaiser expects the United States to adopt some form of national health insurance, in order to solve some of the problems of increasing cost and une-

qual access to health services. He also looks for a continuation of the trend toward transfer economics—that is, federal monies being returned for distribution by the states and counties in the form of revenue sharing and other local distribution plans.

Increasing accountability of human service agencies will result from rising costs and the disappearance of philanthropic funds, plus the existence of a better-educated public. As the health goals of society far outstrip its resources for health care in the years immediately ahead, Kaiser sees much more use of quality standards, agency assessments, cost-benefit analysis, and peer review. Voluntary not-for-profit health organizations may lose their tax-exempt status unless they can show that their services are of real benefit to the community.

A growth of consumer advocacy may lead to public regulation of the health professions and their schools. "The image of the health professional is becoming increasingly tarnished on television and in the newspapers," Kaiser says. □

AMERICA'S EDUCATIONAL FUTURES

1976-2001

The Views of 50 Distinguished World Citizens and Educators

by Harold G. Shane

What will the world be like at the start of the next century and how should educators help people to prepare for it? To answer this question, the National Education Association, which represents about two million U.S. teachers, sought the opinions of a group of carefully selected leaders. In the following article, a futurist-educator summarizes their conclusions.

In 1972 the National Education Association established a Bicentennial Committee to commemorate the principles of the American Revolution, and also to consider the *next* 100 years of U.S. education in an interdependent global community.

As one of its goals, the Bicentennial Committee sought to determine whether the "Seven Cardinal Principles of Education" are valid for the 21st century or how they should be revised.

The Cardinal Principles were a statement of educational goals that were first published in 1918 and became perhaps the most important guidelines ever to appear; their influence on U.S. schooling, at least, has been enormous. The goals of education, according to the 1918 statement, are: (1) development of health, (2) command of fundamental processes, (3) worthy home membership, (4) vocational competence, (5) effective citizenship, (6) worthy use of leisure, and (7) ethical character.

After much careful discussion, a Project Pre-Planning Committee selected a panel of about 50 distinguished persons, both in the U.S. and from overseas, to be interviewed. The participants were asked to respond to three questions:

1. In broad terms, and barring such catastrophes as nuclear war, what are some of the charac-

teristics of the most probable world you foresee by the 21st century?

2. In view of this image of the future, what imperative skills should education seek to develop? Also, in anticipation of the 21st century, what premises should guide educational planning?

3. Have the original (1918) cardinal principles retained their merit? If so, what are the new ways in which they now should be interpreted, amended, or applied in anticipation of changing social, economic, and political conditions in the world community?

While no attempt was made to secure a scientific sample, the Project Pre-Planning Committee endeavored to include panelists whose ideas commanded respect, who represented the views of persons in other countries, who were geographically widespread, who were representative of the polycultural and multiethnic fabric of American society, and who were active in many different fields of human endeavor.

Among the panelists were Roy Amara, President of the Institute for the Future in Menlo Park, California; sociologist Elise Boulding; economist Lester R. Brown; McGeorge Bundy, President of the Ford Foundation; Wilbur J. Cohen, former U.S. Secretary of Health, Education and Welfare; Israeli political scientist Yehezkel Dror; Willis W. Harman, Director of Stanford Research Institute's Social Policy Research Center; Theodore M. Hesburgh, President of the University of Notre Dame; and David Rockefeller, President of the Chase Manhattan Bank.

To provide a "youth view," a panel of 96 high school students were asked what they hoped to be doing in 2001 and how they felt that education could help them attain their future-focused role images.

More than 80 hours of individual panelists' tapes were recorded. An additional 18 hours of dialogue were obtained from youth, who were mainly interviewed in small groups.

The Next 25 Years

What sort of world did the panelists foresee in 1976-2001? While the sophisticated international participants in the NEA inquiry recognized the hazards if not the impossibility of over-precise or extravagant predictions, their speculation proved highly interesting and as plausible as any social prophecies that reflect highly informed opinion.

Without exception, the respondents recognized that not only the U.S. but the world as a whole is passing through the greatest tidal wave of transition in history. Our era is so confusing that we get a severe case of cerebral cramp if we attempt to study the undercurrents of the tidal changes and their implications for life in the next millenium. The panelists clearly recognized that *anyone's* problems *anywhere* had become *everyone's* problems *everywhere*, and generally felt that mutually *planned* interdependence and "dynamic reciprocity" (Barbara Ward's phrase) could do a great deal to improve relationships in the human community.

> ## "We have gone overboard with our monstrous cars, our waste of food, and our consumption of raw materials. Someone has said that the world could not stand two Americas. I am not sure it can stand one."
>
> *Rev. Theodore M. Hesburgh*
> *President of The University of Notre Dame*

Despite the near-chaos of the present discontinuity in the old order of things, the panelists agree on certain points:

• *Accelerating change.* The panelists did not all foresee the same events, and those who did sometimes thought in different time frames. But the panelists concurred that an increasingly rapid rate of change could be anticipated.

• *Increased complexity.* Complexity, an apparently inevitable concomitant of rapid change, promises to be with us for the decades under consideration. Trade, communications, armaments, international relations, the subtleties of pollution problems—all promise to demand of the human community its best coping skills.

• *Twilight of the hydrocarbon era.* From secondary school students to presidents of national gas companies, it was widely recognized that we are running out of such inexpensive and convenient sources of energy as natural gas and oil. Lacking foreign oil imports, the U.S. could exhaust (at current consumption rates) all of its known domestic reserves, including off-shore and Alaskan pools, in approximately 3,500 days. The threat is not only to our transport system—our "wheels"—but to the agricultural productivity which has become a world resource. Besides great quantities of fuel needed for farm machinery, enormous quantities of petroleum and natural gas are needed for some of our widely known types of fertilizer.

• *New concepts of "growth."* In view of resource depletion, and with due allowance for human adaptability and wit, the panel felt that the "growth is good" doctrine would be carefully reviewed—probably before the 1990s. The task, apparently, will be to define "reasonable" or "selective" growth so as to give due recognition to the limits of the earth's bounty and to make trade-offs that will lead eventually to a dynamic equilibrium between humans and their environment as Nobel physicist Dennis Gabor suggested years ago in *The Mature Society.*

• *Continued crowding and hunger.* Project participants were impressed by the problems of hunger and by the stress placed on planetary resources by a population that recently passed the four billion mark. One panel member likened the earth to an old resort hotel of faded grandeur—its carpets frayed, its hangings faded, and its plumbing increasingly unreliable—overbooked by impoverished guests who could not pay the room rates that the hotel would need to charge if it were to restore its former standards of service.

As of the late summer of 1976, world food conditions did not offer much hope in the 1970s for improvement of the conditions. The world's inability to get sufficient food to the right places at the right time, according to Father Hesburgh, led to the death, by starvation, of more than one million humans during 1975. Another ten million, he noted, were physically impaired or brain-damaged due to lack of proper nutrition for expectant mothers and too little food for infants during their early years of life.

• *Third World pressure for equity and for a new economic order.* The NEA tapes stressed that the next two decades will continue to be characterized by growing Third/Fourth World pressures for a greater share in the material goods of which the developed nations—the U.S. in particular—are overwhelming consumers.

These pressures seem to add up to more than a "new deal" in which payment for raw materials and for labor are more fairly rewarded. There are likely to be pressures for an entirely new order in which resource-rich Third World countries seek industrial power so that they can process, produce, and promote finished products. If and as such a new economic order develops, the entire political power structure of the planet could change significantly.

• *Troubled international waters.* Prospects for international tranquility during the period previewed by panelists—1976-2001—seem slim. As Elise Boulding pointed out, the world we will have to put together will be very different from the one we have now if the images of the future of the Celtic League, the Bretons, and the Basque Separatists are considered!

Two decades from now, peacekeeping machinery will probably be improved, regional economic alliances perfected, and such matters as oceanic mining rights arbitrated, but basic problems will remain to test human skill in economic and political innovations and relations as we seek to cope with the "international chemistry" that will seethe at least during the 25-year period ahead.

• *Welfare, debt, and freedom.* At first glance, welfare, debt, and freedom appear to be disparate topics, but certain relationships between them began to surface during the interviews. Let us comment briefly on each, then consider how they are linked together.

The participants felt that the years immediately ahead will bring to America such welfare provisions as a guaranteed annual wage, appreciably improved medical care at least partly at federal expense, and guaranteed employment. The happy promise of improved human welfare was diminished, however, by the potentially fractious problems of increasing debt in the 1980s and 1990s. America's investment in welfare increased by 738% between 1964 and 1974 and, during the fiscal year which ended last July 1, various subsidized programs (medicare, veterans' benefits, and the like) required $116 billion in federal support. Data from the U.S. Office of Education indicate that another $108 billion was invested in public and private education from early childhood through the post-secondary level during the same 12-month interval.

Reduced paychecks due to withholding provide evidence of the increasing cost of Social Security—a program which will need additional, massive infusions of money for an indefinite period. The ratio of workers and Social Security recipients was seven to one in the early 1970s. By 1985 there will be approximately one recipient for every two workers contributing to the program. When the large number of baby boom workers reach retirement some 25 years hence, the strain on our system of Social Security benefits becomes difficult to imagine.

Welfare guarantees also called to many panelists' minds the potential dangers of "regulated freedom." If employment is assured, for instance, presumably some agency will need to *enforce* participation either in a position for which one is qualified, or in job training, perhaps in some environmental cleanup-and-repair activity in the tradition of the Civilian Conservation Corps introduced in the 1930s to aid unemployed youth.

• *A post-extravagant society.* The 40% decline in the dollar in ten years, the prospects for sustained 6% to 8% unemployment, severe international problems, and alarm over resource depletion motivated a number of the panel members to conceive of a post-extravagant society by 2001. While more sanguine than economist Robert Heilbroner, who warned in 1975 that affluent Americans would need to give up a great many of our expensive privileges, panelists saw the need to phase out the "throwaway society" (Toffler's phrase), to incorporate recycling and "voluntary simplicity" in lifestyles, and attain a prudent balance in export-import policies. In short, America may be able to avoid a gray-toned post-*affluent* society by striving *now* to create a post-*extravagant* era not too different from the "wear it out and make it do" lifestyles of our grandparents prior to 1920.

• *Work and leisure.* The survey revealed a distinct split in opinion as to what the future might hold for work and leisure. John Johnson, Editor and Publisher of *Ebony* magazine, simply replied, "Leisure? Most blacks don't have it!"

McGeorge Bundy, President of the Ford Foundation, commented that "As far as the use of leisure is concerned, I think there is going to be a trend toward spending more time making or growing what people used to buy in the marketplace."

Other panelists suggested an era of less leisure because of diminishing energy sources and a consequent return to more labor-intensive production. For the most part, a shortened work-week of perhaps four eight-hour days was foreseen as industry, farming, and services gradually reduce (to perhaps 40%) their need for participation by the work force.

An aging population—up from 22 million in the over-65 group in 1975 to 31 million in 2000—also seems certain to influence both leisure and work (not to mention politics). Other factors likely to be of influence are: (1) increased production or lack of it, (2) more women in the work force, and (3) inflationary pressures which might motivate larger numbers of persons to hold down two or even three jobs.

• *Future-directed planning*. A need for future-oriented planning was expressed repeatedly by virtually all survey participants. They also expressed concern because so little "future-think" is being done. Fred Jarvis, head of Britain's National Union of Teachers, put it this way: "Decisions about the future [in Great Britain] are being made without any attempt to picture society as it's going to be 10-to-30 years hence."

Presumably the study of the future promises to become a more influential part of life in the U.S. if the panelists' views prove to be self-fulfilling prophecies! The trick will be to obtain the benefits of long- and short-range planning while avoiding dangers implicit in the concern expressed by Sterling McMurrin: "The future is going to be marked by automation, mechanization, cybernation, and certainly by an increase in bureaucracy," he noted. "All of this, I am afraid, adds up to a great threat to individuality."

The Viewpoints of Youth

The concepts which high school age youth had of the next 25 years tended to parallel those expressed by adults who participated in the inquiry. Evidently their schools and other media of instruction had provided a substantial amount of input with respect to such endemic problems as pollution, resource depletion, nuclear dangers, and so on.

In the youth dialogues, three points came through repeatedly and clearly:

1. In a frustrating and sometimes frightening world there is a great need for *coping* skills and techniques. Good guidance and better preparation are needed in the skills of human relations, in dealing with uncertainties, and in learning to choose wisely among alternatives.

2. Young people want to attend schools in which people *care* about them, and the "good" teacher is a person who radiates warmth and genuine interest.

3. Help was sought in *communicating*—in finding at least a few people (teachers, peer group members, parents, etc.) with whom to share concerns, hopes, and aspirations.

"Schools have to teach people how to change —give us an open mind so we can cope with change when it comes."

New York senior high school student

When questioned about the work-roles they hoped to fill ten or more years hence, the juniors and seniors showed little interest in managerial, ownership, or executive roles, but frequently expressed an interest in service or professional positions. There was least interest shown in clerical, sales, or factory work—except for short periods of a year or two to finance various types of post-secondary preparation.

Interestingly, while high school youth anticipated huge social, political, economic, and technological changes, the personal lives that they expected to lead often were projections of present lifestyles with some of the imperfections and defects removed. In short, they saw their own futures as being very like the present but better because of improved human relations.

Education for a New Millennium

Space limitations preclude anything like a complete review of the educational premises proposed for a new century in the 80 hours of tapings. High spots can, however, be inventoried.

For one thing, panelists almost universally agreed that *education* was of supreme importance but that it would involve much more than conventional schooling during the 25 years between 1976 and 2001 with which the NEA inquiry concerned itself. Willis Harman, for instance, pointed out that pressing social decisions and reforms must be contemplated in the next two decades and that children and youth, for the most part, would still be too young to participate and to offer leadership during this interval. Other media are needed, Harman argued, to provide continuing adult education in the 70s and 80s for the ill-informed, the biased, the selfish, and the stubborn, and to do so in the shortest possible time.

Lester R. Brown made an analogous comment during lunch with the writer. Referring to the diners in a club frequently patronized by prominent Washingtonians, he commented that most of them could give an hour-long extemporaneous talk on such problems as resource depletion and pollution, topics which were not in the curriculum 20 or 30 years ago. Media other than the schools, he felt, are needed to update continually the backgrounds of learners of all ages with respect to information that is just becoming available.

On the subject of education, most panelists seemed to agree on the following points:

1. The need for educators to develop a spirit of global community—of planned interdependence and dynamic reciprocity—which respects multi-ethnic and poly-cultural differences both in the U.S. and abroad.

2. Recognition of the need to make education a continuing, lifelong process.

3. The need for flexibility in instruction and for the *merit* of learning experiences rather than the *route* followed in attaining them.

4. The importance of recognizing that a wide range of performance is to be expected among learners, both young and old.

5. The importance of understanding that students' aspirations and motivations are best served when learning is at least partly self-selected rather than dictated by teachers.

6. The need for continuing education on a worldwide basis that would serve both mature (past 30) and senior (past 60) learners.

LESSON
14
LANGUAGES

7. Teaching and learning should not occur only in schools.

8. The need to understand that occupational education should transcend vocational training and requires the encouragement of greater versatility among members of the work force through such techniques as better general education.

9. Recognition that traditional patterns of home-school relations need to be modified because of changes in the home.

10. The view that problem-preventing education begun in early childhood is distinctly superior to compensatory education provided at a later time.

11. The point that instruction in subject matter fields should instill an understanding of contemporary threats to the biosphere and emphasize socially useful service—by persons of all ages—in maintaining the biosphere and achieving a balance between humans and their environment.

12. Promotion of "human geography"—a grasp of planetary cultures as they exist today.

In summary, emergent educational development, 1976-2001, presumably would help young learners acquire a knowledge of the *realities* of the present, an awareness of *alternative solutions*, an understanding of *consequences* that might accompany these options, development of insights as to wise *choices*, and help U.S. youth to develop the skills and to acquire the information that are prerequisite to the *implementation* of examined ideas, policies, and programs. In short, five terms to remember in developing new curricula are: realities, alternatives, consequences, choices, and implementation!

The Classic 1918 Goals of Education Reexamined

As indicated earlier, the NEA panelists were asked whether the goals for U.S. education—the "seven cardinal principles of 1918—were valid after 60 years. With no more than two or three minor exceptions, the 50 participants agreed that the *goals* remained suitable, but the *meanings* of the goals needed modernizing.

> **"We must remember that the children of 2050 will be just as valuable as our children are now ... They deserve the best of our time and energy now."**
>
> *Robert J. Havighurst*
> *Professor of Education*
> *University of Chicago*

The development of *health*, for example, was seen as still an appropriate goal, but teachers now should help the young learn how to survive in a carcinogenic society, to understand the causes of cardiac illness, the importance of mental health practices, and to understand that opportunities for healthful living need to be extended to the world's millions who do not see a physician from birth to death.

Command of fundamental processes, largely limited to the 3R's in 1918, was expanded by 1976 to encompass human relations skills, development of cross-cultural insights, developing a knowledge of sources, understanding computer languages, learning to cope with increasing complexity, and developing "anticipatory skills" such as the power to see relationships and to make correlations.

Worthy use of leisure. The line dividing work and leisure is likely to become even more blurred. Complexity—demanding more time for the tasks and routines of daily living—

was singled out as a factor of the future along with the likelihood that more items now bought in the market place (e.g., canned soup) would be made "from the ground up" in the home and that householders would do more of their own repairing and servicing of equipment and appliances.

Worthy home membership, according to survey participants, was related to an understanding of changes occurring in the status of the family; recognition that traditional families consisting of a mother and father and two or more youngsters living in a neat little frame house was the exception rather than the rule in present-day America. While the importance of a family or comparable "affinity group" was emphasized, it also was conceded that the influence of family bonds has decreased appreciably since 1918.

The meaning of *vocational competence* also was deemed to have changed with the passing years. Panelists noted:

- *Specific* vocational skills are difficult to foresee in a changing society.
- A good *general* education is a prerequisite to the vocational skills of operating theater, supermarket, or factory.
- Lifelong learning is a vocational skill.
- There is a need to develop a new breed of workers who see their jobs in an ecological context.
- Occupational education must not lock people into the wrong jobs.

Citizenship skills, many consultants felt, should embody a measure of loyalty to the planet as well as to the nation, and a consciousness of the need to study and to improve the inequities existing between the have and the have-not worlds. Some participants also saw a need to introduce the young to ways of making positive use of power and the need for people to be better informed when they sought to exercise it.

Ethical character. Everyone was in favor of the seventh cardinal principle as a developmental goal. Of particular interest was the emphasis by a large plurality of panelists on (1) the need to recognize again the value of self-discipline in learning, (2) the merit of rules to live by as distinct from unrestricted permissiveness, and (3) the importance of protecting and improving the biosphere. These concerns may serve as sources of secular commandments or guidelines for better lifestyles during the coming decades.

The need for adults to set suitable examples, to serve as mature models for the upcoming generation, also found frequent mention.

Concluding comment. A quality of cautious optimism with respect to the next 25 years tended to pervade the inquiry. The panelists seem to feel that the world's peoples have sufficient time to clean up the "planetary nest" they have befouled and the potential to demonstrate that they are the missing link between animals and civilized man.

It would seem, in Pogo's immortal phrase, that "We have met the enemy and he is us." How we cope with "the enemy" largely will determine whether the children and youth of 2050 live in a better, more humane world or find themselves wallowing in a tragic low-technology re-run of the 10th century!

Harold G. Shane

Harold G. Shane is University Professor of Education, Indiana University, Bloomington, Indiana 47401. For further information, see *Today's Education*, September-October 1976, published by the National Education Association, 1201 Sixteenth Street, N.W., Washington, D.C. 20036, U.S.A.

The Educational Significance of the Future by Harold G. Shane is available from the World Future Society Book Service. Phi Delta Kappa, Inc., Bloomington, Indiana, 1973. 116 pages. Paperback. $4.20.

Prolongevity:
The Extension of the Human Life Span
by Albert Rosenfeld

Scientists are making good progress toward learning the secrets of aging, and may begin to control it within the lifetimes of people living today.

In ancient Greece, the average life expectancy was something like 22 years. Individuals did live to ripe old ages, but their number was small enough to render them an elite group in most ancient societies, where their seasoning was rare and their wisdom prized. A Greek who reached the age of 70 in the fifth century B.C. had just as many years to live—perhaps more, since he had to be tougher to have survived so long under such conditions—as does the 70-year-old of today, who has merely reached his average life expectancy.

Sophocles wrote *Oedipus Rex* when he was 75, and won the last of his many dramatic prizes at 85, still going strong. And he needed no contemporary equivalent of Masters and Johnson to tell him that men of that age were still sexually viable. He not only kept his bed and bones warm with the famous hetaira Theoris (who was succeeded at an even later date by Archippe), but also became a father again. This is not to say that vigorous longevity such as Sophocles' goes unmatched today, but simply that it is still rare. The maximum life span has *not* been extended. And our contemporaries who reach 70, 80, and 90 probably have just as many aches and failings as the ancients did, though there may be a few more medications available to ease their more troublesome pains.

The fact that so many of us do reach 70 and beyond is what makes us more aware than ever how universal are the ravages of the aging process—ravages that made even Sophocles, for all his honors and amours, a thoroughgoing pessimist in his declining years. Observing the inexorable nature of these changes, their variety, their sheer multiplicity, and their interlocking complexity, most traditional gerontologists have maintained an unshakable conservatism despite the boldness of their stated goals. The prevailing view, understandably, has been that, considering the multifaceted nature of the aging process, it would be foolish to count on any significant progress toward final answers until countless further generations of painstaking experimentation shall have passed.

Typical of this cautious outlook, even among scientists not reputed as especially conservative, is the conclusion of a 1962 paper in *Proceedings of the Royal Society*. Its author, anatomist P. L. Krohn of the University of Birmingham, after describing a brilliantly original series of experiments designed to study the effects of transplantation on aging tissue, finally appends this demurrer: "Nothing has been said to imply that problems of old age are likely soon to be solved by this approach .... The solution will probably come as slowly and insidiously as the aging process itself."

Control of Aging May Begin Soon

Gerontologist Bernard Strehler of the University of Southern California represents a spirited avant garde of scientists who vigorously dispute the cautious, pessimistic views of the medical traditionalists. They believe that significant progress can be made toward the control of aging, perhaps in our own lifetimes or within the current century. The more confident gerontologists are hopeful of buying a little extra time for themselves personally while waiting for the larger advances to be accomplished—much as a leukemia victim might hope for the larger breakthroughs to occur while he is in remission.

Scientists who a few years earlier would have deplored such speculations as being in the realm of the quack and the con man are now distressed that the general public just won't give serious credence to the new possibilities. If people begin to believe in them, progress will certainly occur more rapidly. Gerontologist Alex Comfort is convinced not only that a project to slow down aging is feasible but that it could be carried out for relatively modest sums of money.

In any case, because the older explanations of aging leave so much still unexplained, interest in the avant garde view has been growing in research laboratories all over the world. This view is easy to summarize. Though even avant garde gerontologists differ in the details of their schemes and their persuasions, they are clearly coming together in the common convictions:

(1) that there does exist within ourselves an identifiable "clock of aging," a genetically determined program which dictates that we will age and die, and the rate at which this will occur;

(2) that we have an excellent chance of discovering the location (there may be more than one) of the clock of aging, as well as the nature of its operating mechanisms—and how to interfere with them to our own advantage;

> **"I will venture to predict that by the year 2025—if research proceeds at reasonable speed—most of the major mysteries of the aging process will have been solved, and the solutions adopted as part of conventional biomedical knowledge."**

(3) that, moreover, all this can begin to happen, not centuries from now, but *now,* if only the research can be carried out;

(4) that senescence may thus be started on its way to obsolescence.

Research on Aging: Many Promising Approaches

Let us assume that gerontological research does hold out a valid promise of additional good years of life. In that case, each of us is bound to wonder whether the hoped-for advances will occur in time to add good years to our own lives—and to the lives of those we wish to share ours with; and, further, what we might meanwhile do to enhance the probability that we will still be on hand to take advantage of whatever breakthroughs may occur.

It is impossible to set forth a timetable of upcoming gerontological achievements with any assurance that these events will occur on schedule. This is true even for a given theory or a given investigator. Suppose, as one example, that researcher Donner Denckla succeeds in his quest for the thyroid-blocking hormone, and it turns out to be *the* death hormone, as theorized. How long would it take for the results to start doing us any good? Denckla has recently made some careful calculations, considering each painstaking step along the way: isolating and purifying the hormone (if indeed only one hormone is involved), discovering its structure, synthesizing it, devising some molecular means to inhibit its action; perhaps identifying its releasing factor in the hypothalamus—the smaller molecule that induces the pituitary to release the larger one—and going through the same sequence of procedures with it; getting a sufficient supply of the inhibiting agent to test it on animals; carrying out the necessary animal trials; then—with Food and Drug Administration approval and the informed consent of the subjects—conducting some preliminary human experiments, followed by broader and more conclusive human trials; and finally getting the new drug on the market. Denckla figures that, even with good luck, going at his present maximum pace it will take him 40 years to complete the work. With stepped-up funding and expanded facilities, he feels he might do it in 20. Thus it is not preposterous for Denckla, who is now only 40, to maintain a reasonable hope that he could become a direct beneficiary of his own research.

Most gerontologists doubt that substantial advances will be made within their own lifetimes. But many do not share this skepticism, and they encourage a cautious optimism in others. Modest progress—much more modest than that envisioned as the finale of Denckla's overall program—might still offer a slowed-down rate of deterioration, enhanced vigor and enjoyment in the later years, some alleviation or even reversal of overt aging symptoms—in a word, a significant postponement of old age as it is customarily experienced (and feared in advance). Human beings who are very young today may hope that, if they remain in reasonably good health through, say, their middle years, they may become the first people in history to have their life spans extended by artificial means—by how many years, no one can say. Gerontologists such as Comfort and Strehler have held out a long-shot hope that, if you can hang on a little longer, and then a little longer, perhaps helped in each case by some of the smaller breakthrough events, it is just barely possible you could still be here and a candidate for further prolongevity when the larger breakthroughs arrive.

The pace of progress in gerontology should quicken as the National Institute on Aging begins to support programs on a broader scale. Within the next decade or so, I believe we will see the proving out of some of the potential anti-aging substances known at this time as well as others yet to be discovered. At least a few should prove to be effective, with acceptably minimal side effects.

A number of antioxidants are already at hand, and some are safely ingestable—among them Vitamin E. Vitamin C is also an antioxidant, though less so; and it is supposed to amplify the effects of Vitamin E. A much more powerful antioxidant than either is the element selenium. Traces of it are present in many of our foods, and perhaps we already get all of it that we need—or is good for us. More is not necessarily better. But "supernutrition," as Richard Passwater calls it, the administration of unusually large doses of vitamins and minerals, is a popular trend among biological investigators, and some purely dietary aids to age resistance may well be developed. Selenium will undoubtedly be among the substances studied for that purpose.

The usefulness of antioxidants will depend on the validity of the free radical theory of aging. This does not mean free radicals will have to be shown to be *the* cause of aging, only that they represent an important factor in wear-and-tear damage. We have at least indirect proof that this is so. As researcher Richard Hochschild reminds us, "Animal studies show that deficiency of vitamin E in the diet leads to damage of exactly the kind predicted. Age pigments pile up faster. Mitochondria, the power houses of the cell, swell and eventually disintegrate, knocking out the energy generating ability of the cell. And lysosomes break open, releasing their digestive chemicals to digest the entire cell. Thus a small amount of free radical damage is multiplied into a devastating sequence of pathological events."

Much of this damage is prevented or repaired by the body's own self-protective mechanisms as well as by antioxidants naturally present. But, as the studies cited by Hochschild—including those of A. L. Tappel—indicate, an antioxidant deficiency clearly reveals extensive free radical damage. When there is such a clear-cut deficiency, antioxidant therapy can definitely reverse the damaging trend. Moreover, substituting one equally effective antioxidant for another will accomplish the same result, proving that it *is* the antioxidant function at work.

Should you therefore begin taking Vitamin E and other antioxidants? Many people do, including some gerontologists—but the latter have large reservations about taking Vitamin E in the massive doses often recommended. The fact that Vitamin E will counter a specific antioxidant deficiency is not proof—again—that more is necessarily better. Some feel that, with so much still unknown about the precise actions of Vitamin E, there could be some hazard involved. For instance, suppose we were to prevent *too many* of the cell's oxidation reactions; it might impair the cell's functioning in some vital way. So I would recommend caution until such time as more conclusive experiments have been carried out. (I take 100 units of Vitamin E a day myself, on the grounds that, like chicken soup, it isn't likely to do any harm.)

I do feel optimistic, however, about the potential use of antioxidants in aging, and, because investigators like Harman and Comfort believe the definitive research could be carried out in reasonably short order if sufficiently funded, I include antioxidants as being among drugs probably available in the next decade.

Other good bets for such availability are hormone preparations (such as thymosin), lipofuscin inhibitors (such as centrophenoxine), and lysosome membrane stabilizers (such as the DMAE with which Hochschild has been getting such encouraging results). The same is true of cross-link inhibitors. Robert Kohn, for example, has—in collaboration with F. S. LaBella of the University of Manitoba—had some success with a substance called beta-aminoproprionitrile. Kohn has investigated other possibilities, too, as has Johan Bjorksten. Even though the prevention or reversal of cross-linkages may (like antioxidant therapy to combat free radical damage within cells) fail to get at the basic cause of aging, such an outcome could still prolong the good years of life through "symptom relief." If a drug were to appear that could do no more than uncross-link collagen molecules in the connective tissue outside the cells, the benefits could be considerable.

Collagen makes up some 30 to 40% of the body's protein. Its universal presence in the body's framework is what has led scientists of Kohn's stature to suggest that the aging of collagen could be a primary factor in the overall aging of the organism. Nutrients going from the bloodstream to the cells must pass through collagen in order to get there. The same is true of waste materials going in the other direction. If collagen becomes dense and rigid, it also becomes less permeable (perhaps even impassable in some cases); hence the cells have a harder time getting their food and getting rid of their wastes, and heart and lungs probably have to work correspondingly harder. Changed collagen molecules could also invite autoimmune attack.

So it is clear that the loosening up of collagen via uncross-linking (or preventing cross-linkage in the first place) could help keep the body younger longer. This would probably be true of appearance as well, since much of the skin's aging and wrinkling could be due to collagen changes. It is even conceivable, as Hochschild further suggests, that it could slow down the graying and falling out of hair. The next decade could be an exciting one, then, in terms of the first visible steps toward anti-aging medications.

Many substances under investigation, such as the temperature-lowering agents of Rosenberg and Kemeny, will undoubtedly take much longer to test because so much is still unknown about the effects of chronic cooling on living organisms. But it is possible that, within two decades, we would know whether such medications are feasible or not—and, if they are, we should by then also have a good idea when we might expect our physicians to be able to prescribe them for us. During this same 20-year period I think we will also be getting close to arriving at some effective enzyme mixtures and other compounds that would supply substances that were running short and counteract substances that were in damaging oversupply.

During this 20 to 30 years, a multitude of lines of investigation will be followed simultaneously, and surely some of them will bear fruit. Work such as Denckla's is problematical, depending on good luck and adequate funding. But I am more optimistic than most about seeing significant progress in hormonal research, in understanding the hypothalamo-pituitary role in aging, in understanding and controlling the on-off switching of genes, and in the general area of genetic engineering. I will venture to predict that by the year 2025—if research proceeds at reasonable speed—most of the major mysteries of the aging process will have been solved, and the solutions adopted as part of conventional biomedical knowledge; and that some of the solutions will by then already have come into practical use to stave off the ravages of senescence.

What You Can Do Now To Live Longer

So you are ready to do whatever is possible to enhance your chances of being around to enjoy the benefits personally? I'm afraid that the only advice I can offer at this point is the same old-fashioned advice you have always received from your family doctor: Take good care of yourself.

This is always easier to say than to do. Nor is there anything like universal agreement as to what constitutes taking good care of yourself. Even such factors as diet and exercise are controversial—though Alexander Leaf, the investigator who has studied most closely those celebrated pockets of longevity in Ecuador, Hunza, and Soviet Georgia, was able to pin down only two common factors (as reported in his *Youth in Old Age*): all those old folks eat frugally (though nutritiously) and continue to exercise and work hard.

Whole books, indeed whole shelves full of books have been written, on how to take care of yourself. They are not, needless to say, in total agreement. But it is possible to list some general points I have noted in many years of reading, and of talking with members of the various biomedical professions.

In the realm of diet, the best advice is: Eat lightly. Obviously, even very old people still require a well-balanced and nutritious diet, but the quantity does not have to be large. Obesity is a handicap, especially as you grow older. With your strength diminishing, your heart and lung capacity declining, and your blood-vessel spaces narrowing, you don't need to carry around any extra weight to add to the burdens of your cardiovascular and respiratory systems—to say nothing of the extra tissue that also needs oxygen and nourishment and adds an additional burden to the same overworked systems. So go easy on calories.

Go easy on fats, too. We have by now all heard the bad news about cholesterol and its probable role in cardiovascular diseases and heart attacks. Cutting down on foods loaded with saturated fats (eggs, fatty beef, fat-rich dairy products) is undoubtedly a good idea. But, considering what aging research has taught us about polyunsaturated fats and their probable role in the production of excess free radicals, I wouldn't feel safe in eating unlimited quantities of those either. My own stance is to be prudent

"Within the next decade or so, I believe we will see the proving out of some of the potential anti-aging substances known at this time, as well as others yet to be discovered."

about all fats, not be fanatical about avoiding them entirely but simply to eat them sparingly.

The same is true of sugar. Research results are contradictory and inconclusive, but excess sugar intake may have a role in heart troubles and even in the buildup of cholesterol, not to mention lesser adverse effects such as causing tooth decay. We can probably get all the sugar we need by eating fruits, preferably fresh fruits.

In sum, we don't need a *lot* of any kind of food (except in special cases where the doctor advises otherwise for specific conditions). We should eat well-balanced diets, including at least the recommended daily minimum quantities of vitamins. Fish and seafood provide excellent protein, although some seafood, such as shrimp, is high in cholesterol while low in fat. Poultry is another good source, although it's well to avoid the skin of the chicken or turkey, where a lot of the fat lies. When you eat meat, select the leaner cuts wherever possible. As for dairy products, drink skim milk rather than whole, make your cheese cottage or pot or low-fat whenever you can. Cereals (preferably unsugared) are good for both nutrition and roughage. You can eat bread and other carbohydrates—whole wheat or vitamin-enriched—but not in large quantities; practically all the fresh fruits and vegetables you want, within reason. As for rich desserts—pies, cakes, pastries, ice-cream dishes, and the like—you're better off without them. Try to avoid them, except as an occasional treat.

How you prepare foods is of course important too. Boiled, poached, baked, roasted—almost any other means of cooking is preferable to frying. The typical short-order service of cheeseburger with french fries and apple pie with ice cream is one of the dumbest kinds of meals you can eat, especially if you're getting on in years and have either a high-cholesterol or weight problem.

"Human beings who are very young today may hope that, if they remain in reasonably good health . . . they may become the first people in history to have their lives extended by artificial means."

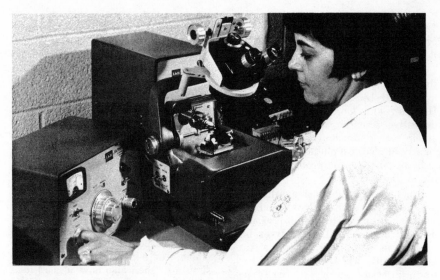

Laboratory technician prepares to slice tissue section with an ultra microtome for viewing under an electron microscope, in research on aging at the U.S. National Institute on Aging's Gerontology Research Center in Baltimore, Maryland.

Photo: NIA Gerontology

What of exercise? For most people who do not participate in regular vigorous athletics, it's best to find some congenial way of getting a moderate amount of exercise *regularly*. An occasional spurt of hard exercise or physical work which may be unavoidable, such as the necessity of shoveling snow, or pushing a stalled car, or running to catch a train with a heavy suitcase, can be very dangerous if you haven't been doing anything else for a while. The weekend athlete is a notorious example of someone courting heart trouble. Exercise, if not every day, should occupy a little of your time at least three or four times a week. It should not be so strenuous as to tax you unduly, but strenuous enough to keep you reasonably fit. Here again, books and exercise systems (from aerobics to yoga) abound; almost any of them is better than nothing. In addition to whatever you do at home, you ought to do something outdoors, something fairly easy and enjoyable but preferably something that exercises your whole body: bicycling, swimming, jogging, skating, dancing (this one is mostly indoors, of course), or even just taking long and not-too-leisurely walks. The main point is to move enough to keep your body from becoming stagnant and lethargic. When you're active, your mind works better too. We have placed great emphasis in our society on labor-saving devices, all the way from pushbutton garage doors to golf carts. Saving labor is fine if you're really overworked or just plain worn out. Otherwise it doesn't save a thing. It costs.

Keep moving. Be sensible and moderate about alcohol. Don't smoke. There simply is not a good thing to be said about smoking. If there is a body system it hasn't yet been shown to be bad for, it's because it hasn't been measured yet.

Life-style is a difficult thing to define. I guess a principal element, in terms of aging, is how well you can organize your life to deal with stress and challenge—enough to keep you interested and on your toes, but not so much that you can't cope with it.

What of environment? There is not much you can do about it personally, except to avoid undue exposure to environmental hazards and pollution when possible. For everyone's good, refrain from doing anything to add to pollution. Otherwise, act wherever you see the opportunity in clean-up or prevention campaigns.

Everybody has always "known"—except for a few cranks and crackpots—that extending the human life span is and always will be a pipedream. That is why I have devoted the major space in this book to spelling out the research and theories that suddenly transform the pipedream into at least a feasible fantasy, and perhaps a reality we can plan for. Unlike Shaw's Barnabas, who was relying on the sheer power of wishful thinking to bring about his extended life span, we will soon have in our hands the biological tools to bring about, in a practical manner, the long-sought elixir of life, in one form or another. Old age will be a disease you can go see your doctor about, if, indeed, prophylactic measures do not virtually eradicate it.

Our species is at a critical transition point in its history on this planet. To fear the consequences of further knowledge—and thus decide to halt further research—would be the surest road to a non-solution of our problems, and thus to disaster. We do not begin to know all that we need to know. So why not take up, with some anticipatory exhilaration, the challenge of pursuing whatever path may bring us to our full humanhood?

The foregoing article was excerpted from *Prolongevity* by Albert Rosenfeld. Copyright 1976 by Albert Rosenfeld. Reprinted by permission of Alfred A. Knopf, Inc.

U.S. Establishes National Institute on Aging

The U.S. Congress focused national attention on the problems of aging by establishing the National Institute on Aging in October 1974, as one of 11 National Institutes of Health administered from Bethesda, Maryland.

The new Institute incorporated the already-existent Gerontology Research Center in Baltimore, Maryland, as its main research facility. A coordinated program is now underway to learn the secrets of aging and minimize its ravages.

Volunteer takes test to measure nerve conduction velocity at Gerontology Research Center. The test can detect nerve dysfunction which may be related to diabetes.
Photo: NIA Gerontology

A complete program of research on aging is planned for the new Institute, including studies on molecular biology, genetics and chromosomal change, cell and tissue aging, and immunologic and endocrine changes as well as social and nutritional variables.

For further information, write: National Institute on Aging, National Institutes of Health, Bethesda, Maryland 20014, U.S.A.

The new Gerontology Research Center in Baltimore, Maryland. This is the main research facility of the National Institute on Aging.
Photo: NIA Gerontology

The Gerontology Research Center brought to the new Institute a longitudinal study on aging, begun in 1959 with 650 male volunteers, aged 20 to 96. Women and minority group members are soon to be added to the study. Participants are given thorough medical and physiological examinations at regular intervals and the information is fed into a data bank on aging. Useful information from the study is expected to increase rapidly as additional data is gathered.

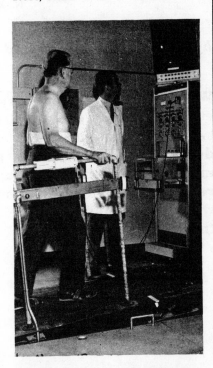

Volunteer walks on treadmill in electrocardiology test at Gerontology Research Center. Test can detect coronary damage in heart.
Photo: NIA Gerontology

The Pleasure Bond: Reversing The Antisex Ethic

by Robert T. Francoeur and Anna K. Francoeur

Western society is on the verge of developing a new sexual ethic based on pleasure, caring, and mutual growth, say two experts on marriage and sex. They predict that, despite antiquated laws and mores which uphold monogamy and fidelity, a "pleasure bond" ethic of non-reproductive sexual relationships outside of marriage will fundamentally alter society, the family, and values in the future.

For 3,000 years, people in western society have been nervous about most things sexual.

In the early Christian era we denied sex in our religious traditions by extolling female virginity and recommending celibacy for all. We have ignored sex by claiming only married people should do it, and then only to conceive children.

We've put down sex by talking about "private" body parts, by our uncomfortableness with nudity, and by our constant attempts to hide sex behind bedroom doors and the dark of night.

Much of this antisex mentality started when the Hebrews were influenced by the Persian cult of Mithra during the Babylonian captivity. That religion, a type of gnostic dualism, said the body was evil, a prison for the divine soul. The world was split into black and white, and sex was definitely black.

In early Christianity, a similar antisex influence came into the new religion from the disciples of the Greek philosopher Plato. Again dualism divided humans into a good soul and a not-so-nice body.

Christians fought this heresy, but like the Hebrews, they were often unconsciously influenced by it. In the third century, Augustine joined a gnostic group, the Manicheans, and kept a mistress. Later he converted, became a bishop and a great Christian saint. When many were denying sex and labeling it evil, Augustine argued that sexual pleasure was permissible if it were used as God intended, as an inducement for a husband and wife to go through the trials and tribulations of parenthood. Progeny redeemed sex.

The Three R's of Sex

Nine hundred years later, as the battle to segregate sex from life continued, medieval theologians finally spelled out our basic sexual ethic, the Three R's of Sex. Sex with the Right person, your spouse; Sex for the Right reason, children; and Sex in the Right position,—male prone—female supine (the "missionary position").

A hundred years ago the medical profession endorsed this commonly held view and introduced physical education programs into our public schools. If we were going to keep our kids in school instead of letting them work in the fields, mines, or factories, we should keep their minds and hands off sex. "Idle minds and hands are the devil's workshop," was a commonly held view. A fatigued boy or girl has little time or energy for playing around.

In America, the western frontier was built on this philosophy. The best remedy for concupiscence and lust is good hard work, and plenty of it. Instead of playing with himself, a young man was urged to chop down an oak. If he masturbated anyway, what better way to work off his guilt and get out of his childish fixation on play and pleasure than to cut down two more oaks?

Cornflakes Reduce Lust

Graham crackers and cornflakes came out of this tradition of denying sex in the same era. Sylvester Graham, an advocate of dietary reform, believed that Americans in 1850 were going the way of Rome— down, and fast. Spicy cooking, too much meat, and hot foods, he said, promoted excessive sexual indulgence. The remedy, besides hard manual labor, was an organic, nutritious and bland diet of Graham bread or crackers three times a day. Stimulants, coffee, tea, alcohol, spices, meats, and all animal products were discouraged. For variety, there was always Dr. Kellogg's cornflakes without benefit of milk or sugar.

This antisex philosophy continued well into this century. Doctors often recommended removal of the clitoris to suppress unwanted sexual drives in women and spiked penile rings to discourage males from masturbating. Marital intercourse was recommended only for males over 30 and then never during pregnancy, nursing, which lasted 18 months, or during the mother's six to eight month recovery period after weaning.

Antisex Ethic Lingers On

In 1976 this history of our sexual values sounds either pathetic or ridiculous, or both. But our parents and grandparents lived like that, and so do we in a less obvious and extreme way. The antisex tradition is still with us.

Our laws still make criminals of millions of Americans who engage in non-marital and non-reproductive sex. Oral sex is punishable by a year in jail or $1,000 fine in New York, in New Jersey by 20 years or $50,000! Same-sex relations are outlawed because homosexuality is unnatural, meaning non-reproductive. Heterosexual relations before or outside marriage are unnatural because they are non-marital and should be non-reproduc-

tive. But if no contraceptive is used, they are immoral because of the risk of illegitimacy.

So do we really have a sexual revolution?

The real meaning of the sexual revolution, we believe, is the fact that despite our antiquated laws and changing mores, we are really tossing overboard the marital-reproductive-female property ethic. In its place we are beginning to develop a new ethic, or new aesthetic, based on communication, pleasure, relationship, and recreation.

The revolution began when Freud challenged the Victorian belief that women and children were somehow entirely innocent of any sexual desire or enjoyment. And it really caught hold in the 1960s when the birth control pill and the socioeconomic liberation of women became a part of our lives.

We can't turn back without reversing all our technological, social, and economic advances. But going ahead is not easy either. A lot of us get nervous, even frightened, just thinking about what life would be like if we honestly decided to stop trying to segregate sex from everyday life. We get uncomfortable thinking about what life and society might be like if we become truly comfortable with our sexuality. What would life in South Dakota be like if we eroticized our businesses and politics?

Lack of Rules Marks New Sex Ethic

The old life-styles and antisex mentality had a nice, neat compartment for sex, with very clear licenses, precise rules, and definite penalities for infractions. The new world is not so well defined. In fact, a lack of rules and guidelines seems to be the only rule in a society that is comfortable with sex. Durkheim, the sociologist, called this condition *anomie*, "normlessness."

The new values we are finding in sexual relations and behavior are varied. Sex alone or with others is for self-knowledge, for pleasure, for friendship, for enjoyment, for variety, for learning, and for mutual growth and support.

There are several specific areas in which this shift in values has concrete meaning for us as individuals and for our society.

Sexual Experience Among Youth

The most obvious form of non-reproductive and non-marital sex today is found among youth. College

cohabitation and its off-campus parallel are common and becoming more so. On many campuses one-quarter or one-third of the students are living with an opposite sex partner at any one time.

A White House survey taken in 1973 revealed that over 50% of America's 19-year-old single women were sexually experienced. In 1969, 66% of Americans polled said premarital sex was wrong; by 1973 disapproval was down to a minority of 48%. Among those under 30, disapproval was only 29%. Eight percent more Catholics approved of premarital sex than Protestants. Other surveys indicate that single women are much more sexually active than the same-aged single male, an interesting inversion of the old "double standard."

For many adults, especially parents, this is an uncomfortable reality. The young are marrying later and later in life and reaching sexual maturity earlier and earlier—four months earlier for girls with each passing decade. We recognize this, often reluctantly, but we continually try to ignore it. Instead of creating relaxed, positive settings for our youngsters' first sexual experiences, we shove them back-handed into a cheap motel, the back seat of a car, the hypocrisy of a college dorm, or the anxiety of home before a parent returns.

Middle-aged Singles Sexually Active

Non-marital cohabitation is also common among middle-aged Americans. Over half of Americans between ages 18 and 39 are single, divorced, separated, or widowed. How many of these are sexually active? A good number, no doubt.

For Americans over 50 or 60, non-marital cohabitation is encouraged by social security and pension laws. Many retirees on fixed income know that marriage will cut their income in half. So Grandma lives with her boyfriend, and their kids blush.

In the year 2000, just 25 years from now, the first of the post-war "baby boom" generation will be retiring. Our birth rate has dropped like lead from 2.7 children per fertile woman 10 years ago to under 1.7 today. If this continues to drop, or even stays constant, we will soon reach the time when the average American is over 50. Unless our pension laws and social security change, non-marital living together may become more common than marriage!

Sex and the Mentally Retarded

Several million Americans live in institutions—the mentally and physically handicapped, the aged, the law-breaker. What kind of sex does our society allow these persons?

The mentally retarded of all ages are commonly segregated according to sex. Until recently very little was done to deal with their sexual needs and rights. They can, are, and perhaps should be, protected from the responsibilities of parenthood they cannot handle. But we can protect them from unwanted pregnancies without denying them the psychological and emotional support normal non-reproductive sexual relationships could give them. Why do we limit them to secretive masturbation or a closet homosexual experience? Allowing these persons free expression in loving sexual relationships that are non-reproductive could make their lives much richer, more fulfilling, and probably better adjusted.

Aged and Handicapped Have Sexual Needs

The same can be said about the sexual needs and rights of the physically handicapped and aged—the stroke victim, the paralyzed victim of automobile and other accidents, the 120,000 quadriplegics and paraplegics, those suffering from neurological and muscular disorders like muscular dystrophy and multiple sclerosis, and the aged. In one home for the aged, inmates lose their privileges for five days if they are caught in the room of another inmate of the same sex. The penalty is 10 days if the person is of the other sex!

Criminals Denied Normal Sexual Outlets

We claim to rehabilitate the criminal, but in this rehabilitation we deny them the emotional and psychological support of sexual relations with their spouses. We even expect the mate to be there waiting patiently and faithfully to resume normal marital life five, 10, or more years later. Our penal system is carefully designed to cut the criminal off from all sexual relations and expression, save masturbation and homosexuality.

Masturbation Shapes Sexual Self-image

Masturbation is the most common and least acknowledged form of sexual expression. It can and does occur within hours of birth. It is common in early childhood, preadolescence, adolescence, young adulthood, mid-dle, and old age. Kinsey reported that 98% of husbands do it, at least occasionally, and many married couples do it together. Engaged or dating couples who want to "save themselves for marriage" do it. Still we deny its existence and practice, especially for women.

"Know thyself," Socrates urged us. Masturbation—self-exploration, self-learning, self-pleasure, self-knowing—can play an important role in the image we develop of ourselves as sexual persons. How can you tell another person what to do to turn you on unless you have gained some knowledge of yourself? Many women's consciousness-raising groups highly recommend self-examination and self-pleasuring for women. Sometimes this is a negative expression towards men, but more often it is a healthy development designed to put the woman in touch with herself and help her communicate better with her man. Masturbation, both alone and with a partner, is an important exercise in many sexual therapies.

Homosexuality Slowly Gains Acceptance

Between five and 10% of the U.S. population is exclusively homosexual in orientation, most studies indicate. And many researchers believe that a much larger percentage, 70 or 80%, is potentially, if not actually, bisexual or ambisexual in their enjoyment of sex. If this is true and we are indeed shifting from a marital-reproductive-property ethic to an aesthetics based on communication, pleasure, friendship, enjoyment, variety, and mutual growth, then why are we still so uptight about the logical application of these values to sexual relations between two or more males, two or more females, or any combination thereof?

Ten states are in varying stages of adopting "consenting adult laws" which hold that any sexual activity between two or more consenting adults is legal, provided it is not a public nuisance or disturbance. Even the Vatican recently authorized publication of a book by a noted Jesuit theologian which reinterprets the morality of homosexual relations in terms of "loving concern" or its lack in the relationship, rather than on the basis of unnatural acts of sodomy, anal or oral sex, or any other form of non-reproductive behavior.

Americans Teach Young Guilt About Sex

For well over 100 years, Americans have tried to protect their children from the primal scene of mating. The result has been generations of youngsters totally puzzled by a basic aspect of life. Sex becomes a mystery and a problem, instead of a joyful, wonderful part of their lives.

In most cultures today, sex is not a great taboo secret. Children are raised with a natural comfortableness with nudity and sexual behavior of all kinds. In many cultures, children are encouraged and even taught to explore their bodies. When they discover what turns them on, their elders rejoice. Children are often allowed, even encouraged in playful explorations of love-making and intercourse. Playfully they prepare for their adult life.

In America we show our children every form of violent behavior on television. But God help the kid who accidentally walks in on his parents making love. We drive our children's natural curiosity underground. We load their natural explorations with taboos and our own guilt and shame. We do everything we can to create a negative, "forbidden-fruit" image of sex. Many children never overcome this negative learning. They end up gutted adults, incapable of appreciating one of the richest sources of pleasure and communication we have.

Removing Taboos from Sex

Why can't we have a ritual to celebrate a girl's first menstrual flow, or a boy's first wet dream? Why can't we parents share with our children the anxieties, insecurities, and joys we find in sex? Why shouldn't a son or daughter feel free to discuss his or her hesitant explorations of sexuality with a parent?

Western society needs to be more open and accepting of the human body and its ability to experience sensual pleasure, according to Robert and Anna Francoeur. They recommend open discussion of sex among parents and children and feel that parents should encourage the natural expressions of their youngsters' sexuality.

Photo: George A. Francoeur

We toss our children into one of the most important areas of human communications with a few words about sexual plumbing and a few abstract instructions about good and bad. We refuse to admit sexuality to our children until they marry and can have kids, instead of seeing their natural sexuality as a process which may or may not lead to marriage and/or parenthood.

Monogamy vs. Sexually Open Marriage

A final issue is raised by the value shift to sex for communication, pleasure, friendship, enjoyment, variety, learning, and mutual growth: the question of monogamy.

Several noted theologians and a fair number of marriage counselors, sociologists, and psychologists are suggesting today that we have gone far enough down the devastating path of trying to save monogamy with no-fault divorces.

Divorce today is far more socially and religiously acceptable as a modification of the "until death do us part" vow than is a sexually non-exclusive marriage which maintains the commitment of a lifelong bond but modifies the "forsaking all others" to include others. It is about time we ask ourselves which of the two values is more important in a good marriage, and whether modifying one or both will lead to a fuller, more human life.

In this perspective some theologians are suggesting that maintaining the long-term commitment while expanding the circle of love to include others may be a viable Christian option.

Can a man and woman have a lifelong, healthy, growth-oriented, open and trusting marriage that allows each to have supporting friendships, even when these are sexually and genitally involved? Can a good marriage be enriched and strengthened by satellite or comarital relations? Does all extramarital sex have to be destructive forbidden fruit?

Alternatives to Monogamy

There are many ways a couple can modify traditional sexual monogamy. These include couple-front swinging, group marriages, and intimate networks based on the acceptance of the possibility of any friendship involving the sexual and erotic. Another alternative is a sexually open marriage, where the amount of information about the satellite or comarital relationship that comes back to the other spouse can vary from simple knowledge it will happen sometime, to

the name of the person and some brief details about him or her, to mutual friendships developing between the satellite and the other spouse. This variety has been carefully documented in several recent books: Francoeur's *Eve's New Rib*; the Francoeurs' *Hot and Cool Sex*; Rogers' *Becoming Partners*; Bartell's *Group Marriage*; Myers' *Adultery and Other Private Matters*; Clanton and Downing's *Face to Face to Face*; the Lobells' *John and Mimi*; and Ramey's *Intimate Friendships*.

James Ramey's research is perhaps the most interesting in our context here. Director of the Center for the Study of Innovative Life Styles, Ramey has examined the "intimate networks" that develop when happily married couples and contented singles accept the legitimacy of sexual expression as part of traditional friendship. Some of these networks have been in existence for 30 or 40 years. The existence of such intimate networks and their durability suggest that this form of marriage may prove a good alternative for some to the serial polygamy, divorce, and remarriage that is now our most common pattern. (See Ramey's articles, "Intimate Networks," THE FUTURIST, August 1975, and "The Multi-Adult Household: Living Group of the Future?," THE FUTURIST, April 1976.)

The environmental situation we face today in America is quite different from what existed 100 years ago. What worked then in terms of marriage patterns, sex roles, and sexual values is obviously no longer working today. Yet we still have some basic human needs: for intimacy, support, growth, communication, and pleasure.

The old pattern of the extended multi-generation family still survives in some rural areas. But in our vast urban-suburban regions we have millions of isolated, fragmented nuclear families, often single-parent families. The psychological, emotional and economic support we once drew from our aunts, uncles, cousins, grandparents who lived nearby or next door no longer exists. What, if anything, can replace this support?

Opening Up the Pleasure Bond

Sex researchers Masters and Johnson in their latest best seller, *The Pleasure Bond*, say that there is no need to replace this support network. They argue that if only a husband and wife work at their mutual commitment and recognize the growing erotic

pleasure bond between them, they will not need outside support or enrichment. In their Victorian, reactionary conservativism, they argue that a healthy, committed marriage cannot exist without sexual exclusivity. For them, the suggestion that we might develop a new definition for fidelity and commitment in marriage not based on sexual exclusivity is, in their words, "to encourage the dangerous and self-serving malady of megalomania" and "the most seductive of rationalizations."

Actually, our sexual ethics have been constantly evolving over the centuries. Our marriage patterns have also evolved, because behavior patterns and values that worked well in one era may not work at all when the environment changes. Of 185 cultures in today's world studied by Beach and Ford, America from 1930 to 1960 had one of the most restrictive and anti-sexual.

Given the overall pattern of marriage in western civilization and our current trends in both behavior and values, it may be wise to allow more freedom of expression to what William Masters and Virginia Johnson call the pleasure bond.

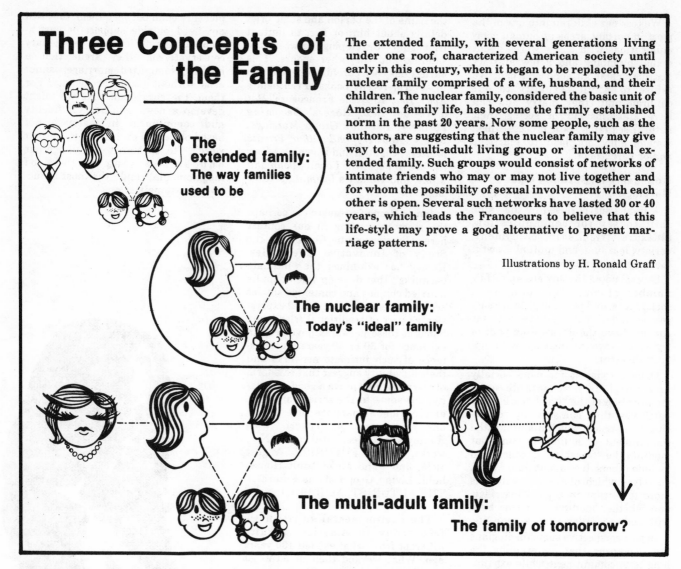

Three Concepts of the Family

The extended family:
The way families used to be

The nuclear family:
Today's "ideal" family

The multi-adult family:
The family of tomorrow?

The extended family, with several generations living under one roof, characterized American society until early in this century, when it began to be replaced by the nuclear family comprised of a wife, husband, and their children. The nuclear family, considered the basic unit of American family life, has become the firmly established norm in the past 20 years. Now some people, such as the authors, are suggesting that the nuclear family may give way to the multi-adult living group or intentional extended family. Such groups would consist of networks of intimate friends who may or may not live together and for whom the possibility of sexual involvement with each other is open. Several such networks have lasted 30 or 40 years, which leads the Francoeurs to believe that this life-style may prove a good alternative to present marriage patterns.

Illustrations by H. Ronald Graff

New Sexual Values to Shape Future Society

It seems likely in the future that American society will be more concerned with parenting. The laws have always tried to protect children and assure their proper upbringing. Maybe in the future, the laws will focus on this aspect and leave the non-reproductive sexual relations of consenting adults alone, in the private sphere. In this event, our laws will ignore the whole realm of premarital, comarital, postmarital, nonmarital, homosexual, bisexual, adolescent, and infantile sexual behavior, provided the behavior is non-reproductive.

In a zero-growth society where children are rare, where blood relatives are few and scattered, where mobility, contraceptives, and the economic liberation of women are accepted realities, our needs for intellectual, emotional, psychological, and sexual support may no longer have to be met exclusively by one person, our spouse. We may find that the old intimate network of blood kinships with its incest and adultery taboos is already being replaced by the pleasure bond of non- or comarital, non-reproductive relationships. This new intimate network, a kind of intentional family without incest and adultery taboos, may be even more supportive and creative than blood kinship because it is not determined by birth, but rather is open to creative spontaneity and new additions as we encounter new persons and new needs.

The pleasure bond will very likely be the foundation of our future society, marriage and family, but it will be with a whole new set of values and life-styles which we are still struggling to develop and articulate. The central issue we will have to face in developing these new values and life-styles is two-fold. On the philosophical and religious plane, there is our need for a whole new philosophy and theology of play, pleasure and non-goal-oriented human activity including non-reproductive and non-marital sexual behavior of all types. On the social and economic plane, we will have to deal with the impact of this new aesthetic on our American capitalistic (property-oriented), consumerist (competitive) Puritan work ethic. In simple words, can our present society survive the shift to a person-oriented, non-competitive value system that accepts play and pleasure as prominent realities in life, equal to—or superior to—work?

Robert T. Francoeur, a professor of human sexuality and embryology at Fairleigh Dickinson University, has authored and edited eight books and over 140 articles on marriage, alternative life-styles, theology, and evolution. His most recent books are *Hot and Cool Sex* and *The Future of Sexual Relations*, which he co-authored with his wife, Anna K. Francoeur.

Anna Francoeur, a member of the Groves Conference on Marriage and the Family, is researching the history of sexual customs in America. The Francoeurs live at 2 Circle Drive, Rockaway, New Jersey 07866. □

Part 4
THE FUTURE AS INVENTION

"Inventing the future" has become a popular phrase among futurists. They do not see the future as something that just happens to people; instead, people create the future by deciding what they want and then working to achieve it.

Recycling People:
Work-Sharing Through Flexible Life Scheduling

by Fred Best

The world of the future will likely require more flexibility in the way we schedule education, work, and leisure over a person's lifetime. If this can be done successfully, the way will be open for each individual to realize many personal dreams.

For most persons in our society, the activities of education, work and leisure are arranged in what might be called a "linear life plan." We march through school in youth, work or child-rearing in mid-life, and retirement in old age. This pattern of life may have worked fairly well in the past, but there are signs that it now is stifling the vibrance and productivity of our lives and perhaps even draining away the productive potential and financial solvency of our society.

For most of the 1970s, over 7% of the United States labor force has been unemployed. The cost of this unemployment in human misery, lost productivity, and inflationary tax-raising income maintenance programs is horrendous. If we cannot create enough jobs for those who wish to work, might it not be better to find ways to allow persons in mid-life to reduce or temporarily leave their jobs and thus share their work with others? Furthermore, the competition for work has pushed young persons into ever longer years of schooling and older persons into increasingly earlier retirement.

Beyond the psychological problems resulting from this pattern, the compression of work into ever fewer years of mid-life has created years of non-income earning time at the extremes of life which are leading to poverty, ever higher welfare and student support costs, and the possible bankruptcy of Social Security. Might it not be better to distribute income earning work time more evenly over the total life cycle? Besides unemployment, we must now contend with *under*employment. Between 1960 and 1975, the portion of persons 25 years and older who had graduated from a four-year college increased from 7.7 to 13.9%. But today we are finding that our society, as presently organized, has little need for the vast numbers of better trained and educated workers now available. As a result, there is an awesome waste of productive human potential, growing discontent due to the failure to provide equal opportunity through education, and the possibility of widespread institutional stagnation due to the lack of individual opportunity. If we cannot create enough quality jobs to match the skills and aspirations of our population, might it not be better to rotate the more attractive positions among qualified persons?

Lifetime Scheduling Trends

The current predominance of the "linear life plan" can be attributed to three major causes: First, the natural dynamics of the human life cycle are such that a person gains physical maturity and learns basic skills in youth, works in mid-life when abilities and responsibilities are at their peak, and retires from work as abilities and responsibilities decline in old age. Second, the consistent shortage of jobs in the United States over the last several decades has fostered fierce competition for work between age groups which has pushed young people into increasingly extended school and older persons into even earlier retirement. Third, the tremendous growth of economic productivity brought about by industrialization has allowed tremendous growth in the average person's time away from work.

Some elaboration of the extent to which non-work time has increased within industrial societies may be helpful at this point. Rough estimates computed by the Metropolitan Life Insurance Company of the years of total lifetimes spent on major activities during different stages of societal development serve to dramatize this growth of non-work time. Work absorbed about 33% of the average person's lifespan in primitive times (before 4000 B.C.), 29% during the agricultural era (4000 B.C. to 1900 A.D.), and about 14% during the industrial era (past-1900 A.D.). In the 20th century, worktime for American males, as a proportion of their overall waking and sleeping lifetimes, was cut almost in half between 1900 and 1970 from 23.7 to 13.4%, according to esti-

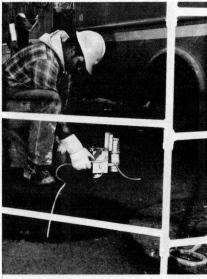
Utility worker checks level of gas in manhole in New York City.
Photo: Consolidated Edison, New York

Village barber in Bangladesh trims the hair of a young customer.
Photo: Agency for International Development

American office worker enters punched card into business machine.
Photo: U.S. Department of Labor

mates computed from U.S. Bureau of Labor Statistics data.

A large measure of the increase in non-work time during the 20th century has come in the form of a reduced workweek. Specifically, the average U.S. workweek has declined from approximately 60 to 39 hours over the last century. However, during the last three decades the workweek has remained remarkably stable with significant increases in non-work time taking the form of longer vacations and more holidays, more years for education during youth, and earlier retirement in old age. Chronologically, the growth of non-work time over the last century first took the form of reduced workweeks and increased vacations for those in the mid-years of life and then began to expand in the form of schooling and retirement for persons in the early and later years of life. In this way, both the options and constraints of advanced industrialization have led to the compression of work into the middle of life.

Between 1900 and 1970, the percentage of the average U.S. male's "lifetime" spent primarily on work or looking for work decreased from 66.6% to 59.7%. Computations based on average life longevity, years of school and average age of retirement indicate that the time spent primarily in work has been increasingly compressed into mid-life, and non-work time has increased substantially in the earlier and later years of life. This trend was caused partly by a dramatic increase in longevity before 1940. Since 1940, life expectancy has remained relatively constant, but the compression of work into an ever smaller proportion of mid-life has continued. If current trends continue unabated, the average U.S. male will, by the year 1990, be spending 44.2% of his lifetime in non-work activities during youth and old age.

The trends of lifetime distribution of education, work and leisure raise two important questions: (1) Are we approaching or perhaps beyond the point of "diminishing returns" for the "linear life plan"? (2) What alternative ways of scheduling education, work, and leisure over total lifetimes might be pursued?

Alternative Lifetime Patterns

There are a number of alternative ways to distribute education, work and leisure over a total lifespan. Three major alternatives are:

• **Continued expansion of the linear life plan.** The forces which have determined life patterns in the past may continue and work years may be increasingly compressed into mid-life.

• **Reduction of the workweek and part-time work.** The average workweek might be reduced and the average worklife might be spread over a larger portion of the life span. This would reduce non-work time in youth and old age, and presumably allow time for part-time education in mid-life.

• **Cyclic life plans.** Current time spent on education in youth and retirement in old age as well as any further gains in non-work time could be redistributed to mid-life for extended periods away from work for education or leisure.

None of these alternatives would meet everyone's needs, and there are numerous reasons why the United States may move toward generally increased flexibility in scheduling working lives which may include the above and other life scheduling formats.

Assuming a moderately slow but constant economic growth rate of around 3% and a general willingness of the average worker to exchange about 25% of future economic growth for more free time, the scheduling of work for the average person might resemble the following by the year 2000:

Single and Non-Offspring Years:
Longer workweeks of 45 to 50 hours with annual vacations ranging from eight to 14 weeks and some sabbaticals.

Early Child-Rearing Years:
Shorter Workweeks of 25 to 40 hours with moderate vacations of two to four weeks.

Late and Post Child-Rearing Years:
Moderate to long workweeks of 40 to 45 hours with long annual vacations of five to eight weeks and extended sabbatical leaves.

Old Age:
Short to moderate workweeks of 25 to 40 hours and long vacations and sabbatical leaves.

Life Schedules in the Future

Such scheduling of work and non-work time over the human lifespan would require major shifts in the fabric of American society. Indeed, we may well ask whether the problems and

Women Pour Into Labor Force

The rapid entry of women into the labor force in recent years has been one of the major factors spurring more flexible work schedules.

As recently as 1960, women comprised only 33% of the U.S. labor force. In 1970, the number had climbed to 38%, and by 1976 the figure had reached nearly 41%.

Economist Eli Ginzburg, chairman of the National Commission for Manpower Policy, has called the flood of women into the work force the single most outstanding phenomenon of our century."

"The long-term implications are absolutely unchartable in my opinion," Ginzburg says. "It will affect women, men, and children, and the cumulative consequences of that will only be revealed in the 21st and 22nd centuries."

Many reasons can be given for the relatively sudden surge of women into the labor force. Among them:

• Television and other mass media have created such high standards of material well-being that a husband's salary no longer suffices to meet a family's perceived needs.

• Religion has declined as an outlet for women's energies and aspirations, and careers are sought as a substitute.

• Divorce rates have risen sharply. The U.S. now has a million divorces a year. The instability of marriage has made women realize that they cannot be certain of having a husband to support them.

• Effective contraceptive methods, together with legalized abortion as a "failsafe" measure, are now far more easily available in a variety of forms. In addition, there is a widespread attitude that having children is not necessarily good for society.

• Marriages are occurring later in life. Even after marriage occurs, childbearing is often postponed—sometimes permanently.

• Widespread higher education has increased women's awareness of and qualifications for various occupations.

About the Author

Fred Best, a specialist on work scheduling, is currently a Research Associate at the National Commission for Manpower Policy in Washington, D.C. He holds an M.B.A. and will complete work on a Ph.D. in sociology this year. He has held a number of research and administrative positions, and is now completing a book titled *Recycling People*, which will be published in 1978. He has also edited *The Future of Work* (Prentice-Hall, Englewood Cliffs, New Jersey, 1972. Paperback. 179 pages. $2.95. Available from the World Future Society book service.).

shortcomings of current lifetime patterns are really great enough to move us toward alternative patterns. Powerful forces—natural life cycle dynamics, competition for work, etc.—have fostered the development of institutions and life patterns that support the linear life plan, and many of these forces continue to exist. We must therefore ask whether the problems and shortcomings of current lifetime patterns are great enough to offset those forces and to combine with emerging new forces to move U.S. society toward more flexible and cyclic patterns of life.

Let us now assess some of the major social forces for their likely impact on future lifetime patterns. These social forces include unemployment, attitudes toward income and free time, methods and scheduling of education, education and the desire for social opportunity, social change and life junctures, sex roles and family structure, developmental stages of adulthood, and problems of old age and retirement.

Unemployment and Work Sharing

Of the social forces which may foster more flexible life scheduling, none is more pressing than unemployment. Recent unemployment rates have been excessively high, and the prospect for improvement over the next few decades is dim. Technological advances continue to foster increased productivity in many sectors of the economy, and thus create situations in which economic growth may fail to generate as many jobs as in the past. At the same time, prospects for economic growth itself are dampened by international competition, depletion of key raw materials, and the indirect costs of technological "diseconomies" such as pollution. Furthermore, the proportion of the U.S. population which is working or seeking work is growing faster than the most rapid rates of job creation in our history.

The rapid rise in the working population can be attributed to several causes: The labor force participation rate of women has been increasing at a rate of

Years Spent on Life Activities

These charts show how human life span has lengthened (most rapidly during the early 20th century) and how the amount of time each person spends on different activities has changed. Perhaps the most important change is the sharp decline in relative amount of time devoted to work.

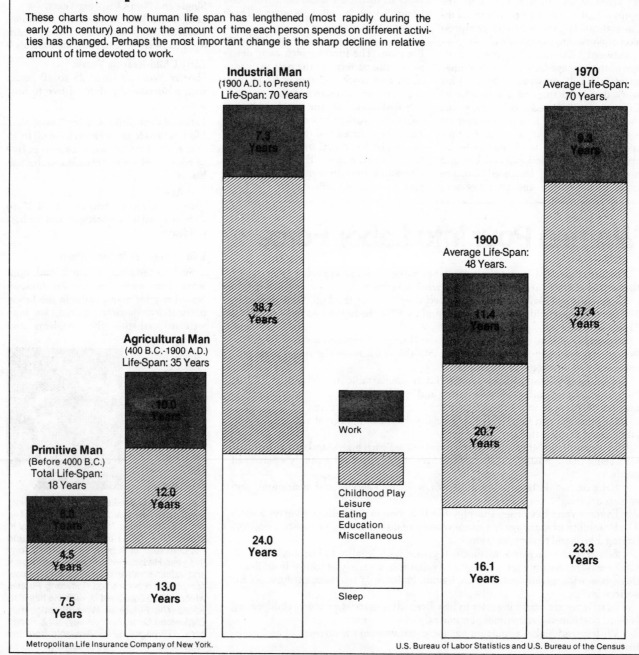

Metropolitan Life Insurance Company of New York.

U.S. Bureau of Labor Statistics and U.S. Bureau of the Census

about 1% per year. The influx of the unusually large post-World War II "baby boom" generation into the labor force has swelled the ranks of the working population still further. Adding to the "over supply" of workers are the older workers, who are resisting retirement, and an estimated six million illegal aliens now working within U.S. boundaries. In terms of hard statistics, the overall labor force participation rate rose from 59.2 to 61.2% between 1960 and 1970, and is projected to rise to 63.2% by 1985. While views vary in degree, there is a growing consensus that the U.S. economy will not be able to create enough jobs for all those willing and able to work during the next few decades.

The burden of unemployment is shared unevenly among age groups. For example, the 1975 unemployment rate for persons aged 16 to 19 was 20.1% as compared to a rate of 6.7% for those over 20 years old. People aged 20 to 24 also had a high unemployment rate—14.3%. Furthermore, the number of young persons who have ceased looking for work due to a sense of futility or who have returned to school for a lack of alternatives adds further "hidden unemployment" to the already high rate of this group. At the other end of the life cycle, older persons without work commonly enter early-retirement rather than linger in a state of unemployment.

High rates of unemployment also result in declining promotion opportunities for workers in mid-life, and when the career progression of mid-aged workers becomes blocked, younger workers will find it difficult to obtain entry-level positions with advancement potentials and older workers will be pushed into ever earlier retirements.

What can be done to reduce unemployment and to achieve a more equitable distribution of work among various groups, particularly among age groups? Three somewhat traditional solutions come to mind: (1) economic growth, (2) public jobs and job training programs, and (3) work-sharing, which reduces work time for those with jobs and redistributes work opportunities to persons at the fringes of the labor market. As already noted, the traditional job-creating strategies of economic expansion and public job programs might not be enough. Although these approaches will undoubtedly remain the principal ones, their limitations are likely to create a demand for other solutions, such as work-sharing.

The idea of work-sharing is not new. Consciously and unconsciously, the U.S. has pursued work-sharing in a number of ways. The common approach has been to limit or reduce the workweek. Since the 1930s, the length of workweeks has been limited by the Fair Labor Standards Act, partly to

spread available work more evenly among the labor force. In addition, public and private policies have encouraged young and old persons to stay out of the labor force, thus increasing job opportunities for those in mid-life. Clearly, over the last half century the U.S. has pursued de facto work-sharing policies.

Today, there are indications that past work-sharing approaches may be inadequate. We have reached or passed the point where more non-work time at the extremes of the life cycle would be desirable, and there are signs that most workers have little interest in exchanging income-earning work time for a universal shorter workweek. There is, however, evidence that many workers in mid-life would welcome opportunities for free time scheduled to meet their individual needs.

If ways could be found to allow workers to choose among various forms of free time, enough work might be foregone to reduce unemployment significantly. Hypothetically, a decision on the part of 50% of the labor force to forfeit 2% of their annual income for an additional week of paid vacation could open up enough jobs to reduce unemployment by 1%, as could a decision by 7% of the labor force to exchange 14% of their earnings for one paid year off every seven years. Of course, many workers would not choose to give up

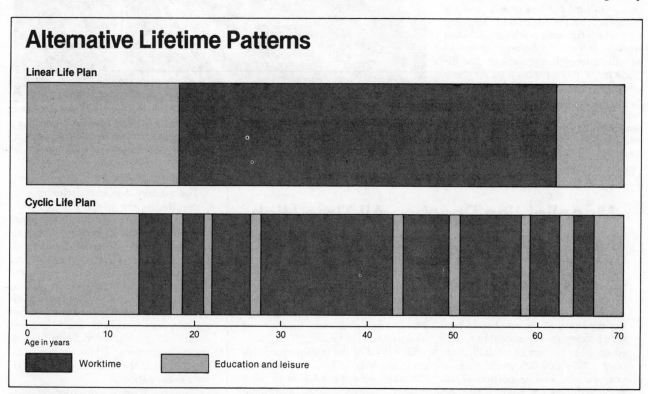

Linear Life Plan (the way life is now organized): An extended period of non-work at the beginning of life is followed by a solid period of work years and then another period of non-work. Under this plan, most increases in non-work are taken in the form of reduced workweeks and expansion of the time for education during youth and leisure during old age. Such expansion reduces the compressions of work into the mid-years of life but maintains the linear progression from school to work to retirement.

Cyclic Life Plan (the way life may be organized in the future): Non-work time is redistributed through the middle years of life to allow extended periods of leisure or education in mid-life.

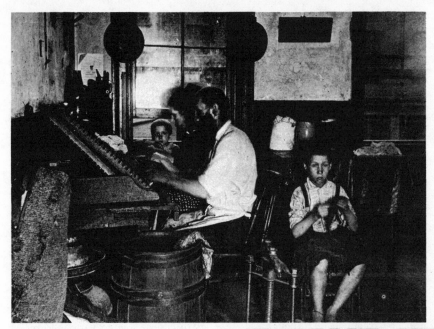

Changing Patterns of Work

Left: Much manufacturing once occurred in the home, with all family members participating, except for the very youngest. This Bohemian family is making cigars in their New York City tenement about 1880. Shoes, clothing, foodstuffs, and many other articles were commonly prepared in such cottage industries for sale on the market.
Photo: Jacob Riis. Courtesy: Library of Congress

Below: When work moved out of the home to the factory, women and children often joined men in tending the machines. This is a cotton mill in Lancaster, South Carolina, about 1908. The young girl in the foreground is described as "Sadie Pfeiffer, 48 inches high. Has worked half a year. One of the many small children at work in Lancaster Cotton Mills." During the early 20th century, laws were passed to prevent the hiring of young children as workers.

any earnings, but others might give up substantial amounts.

Changing Attitudes Toward Time and Income

For many decades, scholars of industrial society have rather adamantly proclaimed that the average American worker is not willing to give up income-earning work time for more free time. However, some recent evidence suggests that the willingness of workers to exchange income for free time is strongly influenced by the forms and flexibility with which free time is scheduled. When workers are asked whether they would be willing to exchange some of their income for a shorter workweek or some undefined form of free time, the vast majority express a preference for income. However, when workers are presented with a choice between income and a number of equally costly forms of free time, only a small portion prefer income as opposed to free time. More

Photo: U.S. Department of Labor

notably, the largest portion prefer extended time away from work in the form of longer vacations. One survey of 2,000 workers found that extended

vacations and work sabbaticals were the most preferred of 15 fringe benefit options.

Changes in Education

The massive democratization of education during the 1960s, fostered by a larger and more diverse educational constituency, forced a widespread recognition that different individuals learn best with different methods and time frames. The result has been a wave of educational innovations such as student-initiated courses, non-graded studies, academic credit for work and other experiences, vouchers and "learning contracts," residential colleges, decentralized campuses, ethnic curriculums, programs for the elderly, and equivalency examinations.

"Non-traditional" education is generally conducive to more flexible life patterns, and its likely growth will tend to increase the scheduling flexibility of schooling, thereby facilitating departures from the linear life patterns.

Moonlighting Reaches All-Time High

While many workers are seeking to work less, others are trying to work more—as evidenced by the recent increase in the number of moonlighters.

The U.S. Bureau of Labor Statistics reports that the number of persons holding two or more jobs reached an all-time high of 4.6 million in May 1977—600,000 more than a year earlier. The proportion of all employed persons holding two or more jobs rose to 5%, about the rate that prevailed in the late 1960s and early 1960s.

"While the multiple jobholding

rate of men continued much higher than that of women, the increase in the moonlighting rate from May 1976 to May 1977 was much sharper for women," the Bureau said. "For the first time, their rate exceeded 3%. Women now make up over one quarter of all the moonlighters."

One third of the multiple jobholders in the May 1977 survey reported that they held second jobs to meet regular expenses. An additional 5.3% cited a need to pay off debts. One fifth said that they moonlighted because they enjoyed the work on their second jobs.

Mechanization: Friend or Foe? Workers have long had mixed feelings about machinery: On the one hand, they recognized that the machines spared them much back-breaking labor; on the other, the machines were seen as taking away the workers' jobs. This 1882 cartoon portrays mechanization as a monster, spelling doom for the workers.

Who Will Do the Dirty Work?

Labor experts have noted a rapid increase in recent years in the feeling of workers that they are entitled not just to a job, but to a *good* job—one that is financially and psychologically rewarding.

And the image of a good job rises constantly: A woman who once felt proud of earning money independently as a typist has, in recent years, sometimes been made to feel like a victim of oppression—or guilty of "failing to live up to her potential."

Newly minted law school graduates demand fantastic jobs, says University of Denver Law School Dean Robert Yegge. "There's a perception that lawyering is working for a larger firm, making $100,000 per year, and there is nothing else for a lawyer to do," Yegge says. When they cannot get a dream job, Yegge says, some law school graduates wind up tending bar.

Though society may now have a larger number of interesting jobs than in times past, the fact is that most jobs are still rather uninspiring. As a result, society faces a "dirty work" problem: Who will do the humdrum tasks that society requires for its everyday functioning?

One proposal was offered in the 19th century by Edward Bellamy in his utopian novel *Looking Backward: 2000-1887*. Bellamy proposed a two-year compulsory national service in which young people would wait on tables and take out the garbage.

Education and Social Opportunity: The Problem of "Overeducation"

The failing link between educational attainment and occupational advancement is fostering social tensions which may lead to more flexible life patterns. In previous decades, the rising need for a highly skilled and educated labor force made extended years of schooling the central avenue for social mobility. For many years, schooling represented the "meritocratic" ideal: The rewards and valued positions in society would be distributed on the basis of proven effort and skill as evidenced primarily by educational certification. Today we are beginning to realize that the developed skills, not to mention the undeveloped potentials, within our population are considerably greater than the demands of the labor market. Nonetheless, young people are continuing to stay in school longer in order to first avoid and then overcome competition with older workers and each other.

The increasing problem of "overeducation" may be seen by comparing the growth in the proportion of college graduates in the labor force with the growth in the number of professional and technical jobs (the kind which most college graduates get) as a percentage of total civilian employment. This comparison shows that while the proportion of workers who are college graduates will continue to grow during the 1975-85 decade, the percentage of professional-technical jobs will remain approximately constant (about 15%). This translates into a labor market surplus of millions of college graduates. The rather conservative estimates of the U.S. Bureau of Labor Statistics project a surplus of 1.6 million college graduates in 1985. Other analysts project an even greater oversupply. Joseph Froomkin, for example, assumes a lesser demand for professional-technical and managerial jobs than BLS because of technological advances and automation and a greater supply of college graduates due to the increased labor force participation and educational attainment of women. His figures project an oversupply of from six to eight million college graduates. The growing magnitude of the imbalance may have serious consequences.

Projected levels of "overeducation" will not only result in widespread suboptimization of human resources, but political discontent, job dissatisfaction and the counterproductive effects of dampened occupational aspirations. The signs of this crisis are rapidly becoming apparent. According to two recent surveys by the U.S. Department of Labor, one-fourth to one-third of American workers feel overqualified for their jobs. Since feelings of overqualification are one of the strongest correlates of overall job dissatisfaction, an increase of such feelings could well result in poorer worker morale and decreased productivity. It was argued in the 1960s by Theodore Schultz and other "human capitalists" that investments in education were investments in the gross national product. These economists felt that upgrading the workforce educationally would lead to high productivity as underqualified workers were replaced by those with greater skills.

But Ivar Berg in his book *Education and Jobs: The Great Training Robbery* (Praeger, New York, 1970) has argued that the reality is quite different from the economists' model. What actually happens is that more highly qualified workers may be forced to stay in or accept jobs not utilizing their education and bump slightly less qualified workers from their jobs. No increase in productivity occurs because the nature of the jobs is usually such that they do not require higher skills. Productivity may actually drop because the more highly qualified worker is likely to be dissatisfied with the job. In sum, increasing the educational level of the workforce above a certain level, without concomitant changes in the structure of work to capitalize on the increased capabilities of workers, will probably exert a slightly negative impact on productivity.

On the positive side, the increasing overqualification of workers, who,

ironically, have the educational backgrounds to articulate their dissatisfactions, could result in an overall improvement of working conditions, the creation of more interesting jobs (as employers consider how to adjust the demand to fit the supply), and greater amounts of industrial democracy with more workers sharing in corporate decision-making. Though the increasing educational attainment of the labor force has not had such an impact thus far, we must remember that the oversupply problem is still somewhat new, having begun only in the past five years.

In the future, it may be necessary to develop new channels, and perhaps new definitions, for social opportunity and personal achievement. The problem and the solution will lie primarily with the world of work rather than education. In a society in which human capacities surpass the opportunities for achievement, it becomes necessary to either expand or redistribute opportunities or confront stagnation. Since the structural realities of the U.S. labor force are not likely to allow a significant expansion of opportunities, it may be necessary to redistribute opportunities by moving toward some type of rotational system for sharing not only the number of jobs, but the quality of work. In this sense, a flexible life pattern, in which most persons open work and ad-

vancement opportunities to others by periodically leaving their jobs for extended periods, may well become the next step in America's traditional pursuit of achievement and equal opportunity.

Sex Roles and Family Structure

Today there is cause to believe that changes in sex roles and family structure will be critical forces in fostering more flexible life patterns.

The increase in women workers, particularly working wives, will enable more male "breadwinners" to decline income-earning work time in favor of more free time. Correspondingly, the decline of family size and dependents will likely decrease parental chores, thus freeing more time and income for non-work activities.

While women today are working more during and shortly after pregnancy, the physiological necessities and preferences of women workers to take at least some time away from their work activities for both pregnancy and child-rearing will likely have the effect of increasing the flexibility of work hours and work years for both men and women as the proportion of women in the labor force rises.

Husbands and wives are becoming increasingly flexible in exchanging work, household and child-rearing responsi-

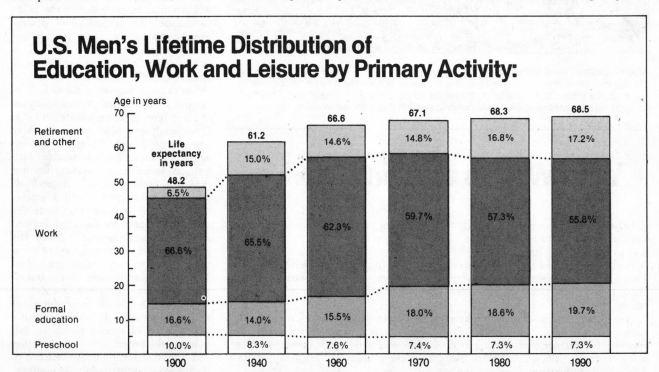

U.S. Men's Lifetime Distribution of Education, Work and Leisure by Primary Activity:

Primary Activity	1900	1940	1960	1970	1980	1990
Life expectancy in years	48.2	61.2	66.6	67.1	68.3	68.5
Retirement and other	6.5%	15.0%	14.6%	14.8%	16.8%	17.2%
Work	66.6%	65.5%	62.3%	59.7%	57.3%	55.8%
Formal education	16.6%	14.0%	15.5%	18.0%	18.6%	19.7%
Preschool	10.0%	8.3%	7.6%	7.4%	7.3%	7.3%

This chart, based on data from such government agencies as the Bureau of the Census and the Office of Education, includes projections of worklife and life expectancy from unpublished computations provided by Howard N. Fullerton, Bureau of Labor Statistics.

Figures were computed for U.S. males only because of fundamental differences in current lifetime patterns between men and women which made consolidation of figures for both men and women inadvisable. Parenthetically, when "homekeeping" and "child rearing" are considered as "work," the life pattern differences between men and women become more similar. Additionally, while women appear to be pursuing longer and more continuous "worklives," it is unlikely that the average woman will develop a worklife which consumes a longer portion of total lifetime than the average man. In this sense, male lifetime activity estimates present a conservative indication of the "linear life plan."

Based on a chart that originally appeared in "Education, Work and Leisure: Must They Come in That Order?" by Fred Best and Barry Stern, *Monthly Labor Review*, July 1977.

The Disappearance of Work

The substitution of animal—and later mechanical—power for human labor made it possible to accomplish more with a smaller expenditure of human labor.

In recent years, instruments and control devices have increasingly taken the place of human perceptual and intellectual abilities, making it possible to have highly productive factories that require only a small number of workers.

Above: Nepalese family farms together; he tills and she sows.

Photo: Agency for International Development.

Left: Tractor cultivates cotton in the United States. A field like this once required scores of slaves to do the job that one man and a tractor can do today. Mechanization of the cotton fields of the U.S. South deprived millions of blacks of their jobs and sent many of them into the ghettoes of the North.

Photo: U.S. Department of Agriculture

Below: Control room of a modern food factory. This is the nerve center of the Gaines Pet Food plant in Topeka, Kansas. Checks are made of the readings of monitoring equipment which keeps watch over the entire processing and packaging operation of the plant.

Photo: General Foods Corporation, White Plains, New York

bilities. While past sex roles required men to be "breadwinners" and women to be "housewives," increasing sex role flexibility is likely to expand the opportunity for spouses to rotate roles and thus free each other from the linear life patterns of the past.

Developmental Stages of Adulthood

Over the last few years several scholars have proposed that adults experience developmental stages, as do children and adolescents.

There appears to be some consensus that most adults progress through successive phases of stabilization and consolidation followed by change and growth as they pursue new goals and confront the changing crises of different stages. If so, cyclic life patterns might correspond more to the needs and rhythms of adulthood than linear patterns. In fact, the prevailing linear life plan may be robbing society of much of the creativity and productivity which occurs among adults during mid-life junctures.

Social Change and Life Junctures

There is evidence that considerable change is occurring in American society, and that it will likely continue if not increase. In societies where there is a rapid rate of social change, individuals constantly confront new opportunities and new problems which require significant changes in their life-styles. In the future we can expect that social change and its attendant changes in individual life-styles will be an ongoing force moving U.S. society toward more flexible life patterns.

Old Age and Retirement

The conditions confronting persons in the later stages of life will likely create powerful forces for the development of more flexible life scheduling. Older persons today are living longer and there are increasingly more of them. The life expectancy of a person aged 65 increased from 12.8 years in 1940 to 15.3 years in 1970. The percentage of persons aged 65 and over in the U.S. will increase from 9.7% in 1970 to some 14.6% in 2020, and 17.3% in 2030. We can expect a major social realignment when the post-World War II "baby boom" generation begins to withdraw from the labor force in the year 2000. Since the younger generation behind them will be significantly smaller, there may be an inadequate number of persons to fill the jobs developed by their predecessors. As a result, younger persons are likely to be drawn out of schooling and older persons detained from retirement to fill the demand for labor. These forces will be highly disruptive and possibly destructive to the continuation of the "linear life plan."

The Social Security System, which has allowed most elderly persons to retire with a basic income and more recently fostered early retirement at age 62, may face continuing financial trouble. The tax-paying population is declining relative to the retired population and inflationary pressures are at once reducing the financial base of Social Security while the demand for large expenditures is rising. Proposals for later and flexible retirement are already being made and it is highly possible that the emerging financial limitations of the Social Security System will not only halt the trend toward earlier retirement but foster continuous or intermittent work activity further into the stage of life now called "old age."

In addition to the demographic and financial forces that are limiting the length of retirement, there are complementary signs that many elderly persons are resisting withdrawal from work activities. A combination of longer life expectancy for older persons, better health, declining physical demands of most work, and financial considerations appears to be fostering a desire on the part of many persons for gradual or in-

termittent rather than mandatory and earlier retirement. As one indication of changing preferences toward retirement, a 1970 Social Security Administration survey found that one half of the men who were subject to compulsory retirement wanted to return to work one year after withdrawal from the labor force. Changing preferences and emerging trends are likely to foster both flexible retirement and work patterns during the later stages of life.

Institutional Constraints and Options

While there are a number of social forces afoot which may foster or allow movement toward more flexible lifetime patterns, there are also strong forces of institutional inertia that may make the emergence of more flexible life scheduling more fantasy than reality. Ultimately, we must confront the critical question of whether or not the constraints and options of most work organizations and other influential institutions can be adjusted to new patterns of life.

Among the obstacles to more flexible patterns which might be expected from work organizations and the persons

The Four-Day Week

The workweek, long standardized at five days, has shown signs in recent years of shrinking to four.

Between 1973 and 1977, the number of U.S. workers on a four-day workweek increased by more than 50%, the Bureau of Labor Statistics reports. However, they still represent only a tiny percentage (1.4%) of the U.S. labor force.

During the same period, workers having workweeks greater than 5½ days declined from 17.3% of the labor force to 15%. Occupational groups that stand out as working long weeks include managers, sales workers, and transport equipment operators. Local government workers constituted the group most likely to be on a four-day workweek.

Increase in Part-Time Workers

The category of "permanent part-time workers" is one of the fastest growing segments of the U.S. work force. Almost nonexistent in 1900, it now includes close to 17 million people, mainly women.

The rise of the "permanent part-time" workers has facilitated the growth of the temporary help industry, which provides typists, secretaries, clerks, and a wide variety of other workers to fill temporary vacancies.

Union leaders generally oppose attempts to substitute part-time workers for full-time workers, on the grounds that more workers may be lured into the job marketplace at a time when jobs are scarce and the wages of full-time workers will be depressed.

New Terms for New Work-Styles

Job Sharing: The sharing of a single job by two or three persons who cooperate in carrying out the responsibilities of the job.

Work Sharing: Reduction of worktime so that more employees can have some employment. Instead of laying off 10% of its employees, a factory could reduce the hours—and wages—of all employees by 10%.

Flexitime(or flextime): Flexible work scheduling which allows employees to start and quit work at times that best meet their personal schedules. In general, flexitime maintains a certain "core" period when all or most employees are expected to be present—typically in the late morning and early afternoon. Flexitime normally does not imply any reduction in the total amount of time worked each week, but only a flexibility in the period of time during which the work takes place.

who manage them are problems of organizational discontinuity, threats of losing trained personnel and possible business secrets to competitors, administrative costs of coordinating non-continuous employees, and fears by employees of all levels that they may lose both their jobs and organizational influence.

Of course, more flexible life patterns may also have positive impacts. For example, extended non-work time may allow both self-renewal and retraining of employees, worker morale and productivity may improve, non-productive and "dead-ended" workers may find new and more suitable jobs to the benefit of themselves and their old organization, and tax burdens for unemployment and welfare services may be lowered. Whether these problems and benefits can realistically be managed or actualized, and whether the net effect would be positive or negative upon organization, is perhaps the most critical question to be answered by those concerned with the future distribution of education, work and leisure over the human lifespan.

In evaluating the adaptability of work organizations to cyclic life patterns, it is important to recognize that their constraints and options vary tremendously. The product type, size, structure, and

stability of organizations are important considerations. For example, the work scheduling flexibility of organizations concerned with continuous, year-round mass production is different from those concerned with seasonal or batch production. Similarly, a small firm will face different constraints and options than a large corporation. Likewise, the level of capital investment and nature of technologies will influence organizational flexibility. The ways in which employees are organized is particularly important, as is the overall stability and rate of organizational change.

While there is, at this time, no systematic overview of the adaptability of work organizations to cyclic patterns of life, there are a number of indications that suggest widespread adaptations may be possible. The growth of progressively longer vacations is an important case in point, suggesting that large numbers of organizations are finding it possible to adapt to extended absences by their employees. Other more limited and specific examples suggest that organizations have been adaptable to a wide variety of work scheduling innovations such as "flexitime," 4-day, 40-hour workweeks, leaves of absence without pay, extended vacations sometimes approaching 3 months, "cafeteria" time-income tradeoff options, and a

Unpaid Time Off— a New Employee Benefit

Workers are coming to view unpaid time off as a valuable fringe benefit, employment experts report. Since many workers would rather have time off than extra money, workers are generally ready to accept shorter hours during a period of low economic activity rather than see some of their fellow workers completely deprived of work while the rest go on working the same hours as before.

"Work-sharing" thus becomes "unemployment sharing."

variety of work sabbatical programs. On another dimension, a number of organizations experimenting with "job rotation" have reported positive results. While further investigation and experimentation in this area is necessary, these trends and innovations suggest that the institutions of work can be adapted to more flexibility in the short- and long-run scheduling of individual worktime.

Beyond the problems which must be overcome by management are those of organized labor, whose reservations about increasing worklife flexibility may be well-founded in some instances. Over a period of more than 100 years, organized labor has struggled to build a legal and political system which supports the institution of collective bargaining and the rights of individual workers. Widespread flexible worklives might undermine standardized worker rights like overtime pay and job security provisions, and possibly complicate and fragment the worker solidarity needed for effective collective bargaining. Additionally, many union leaders believe that gains in free time should not come at the expense of reductions in worker income, particularly if gains in free time are fostered as work sharing. Any major movement toward flexible worklives is likely to be gained only after thorough assessment of the desires of rank-and-file union members and a careful adjustment of public statutes and collective bargaining agreements so that options for worklife flexibility can be developed without undermining basic union concerns.

Flexible Worklife Policy Options

While the prospect of worklife flexibility has wide appeal, there are many often conflicting ideas on how the general concept might be applied. The notion has value to many groups, almost to the point of offering something for

Age Groups as Percentage of Total Labor Force 1960-1990

Changes in the age mix of the U.S. work force may have widespread impacts. Note the rise in the percentage of workers aged 35-44 as the "baby boom" generation moves into middle age.

Source: *Manpower Report of the President*, 1975

everyone at only moderate costs. Yet the idea does have some costs and possibly dangers, and its benefits could be shared unequally. While there may seem to be compelling reasons for movement toward life scheduling flexibility, there are also a great many unanswered questions. At this stage in the development of the flexible worklife idea, it is important to isolate as many policy options as possible, and stimulate broadly-based dialogue about them. Five general policy options will be surveyed: reduced workweeks, time-income tradeoff options, accumulated leaves of absence, work sabbaticals with pay, and income maintenance payments.

• **Reduced Workweek and Part-Time Work Opportunities.** While a universal reduction of the workweek would present many complications, there is a growing interest in shorter workweeks and part-time work among many groups—particularly working mothers, student youth, and elderly persons. Programs and policies to create a given quota of jobs with reduced workweek hours at all levels of the occupational stratum would be well received by persons at different stages of the life cycle.

Over the last few years, a growing number of efforts have been undertaken to legitimize and increase the role of part-time work. In the U.S. Congress, Representative Pat Schroeder and Senator Gaylord Nelson have introduced joint legislation to creat a fixed proportion of part-time jobs within the federal government. Similar efforts have been undertaken within many state governments, and in California an organization called New Ways to Work is spreading the notion of "job sharing" in which two persons share one full-time position.

• **Time-Income Tradeoff Options.** Private and public sector initiatives to allow workers to exchange income-earning work time for a number of types of free time would increase worklife flexibility. Two examples may illustrate this approach.

A "Time-Income Tradeoff Option Agreement" was developed for employees of Santa Clara County in California by union-management negotiation. Employees could either keep their existing hours and pay or make one of three exchanges: 5% pay cut for 10½ days added vacation, 10% pay cut for 21 days of added vacation, or 20% pay cut for two 21-day vacations per year. One year after implementation, some 18% of the county employees had voluntarily requested one of the tradeoff options, mostly the 5% and 10% choices.

A second similar example is the "Flexiyear Contract" which is gaining popularity in Germany. The basic idea

Photo: U.S. Dept. of Labor

Photo: General Foods Corporation, White Plains, New York

Working conditions: Then and Now. A Pennsylvania coal mine in 1911 employed horses—and young boys. The lad holding the gate had "a chronic cough," the photographer reported. By contrast, a modern factory—the Gaines Pet Food plant in Topeka, Kansas—offers a clean, healthy environment for the employees.

is that employer and employee negotiate individualized agreements annually concerning how much time each employee will work each year and how the work time will be scheduled. Presumably, a worker could negotiate for the right to work full time only six months a year, three-fourths time all year round, or any of a number of other workyear variations. While organizational constraints do not allow unlimited options, numerous German firms are finding that the "Flexiyear Contract" allows for more scheduling options for both employee and employer than would otherwise be possible.

• **Accumulated Leaves of Absence.** Public and private policies could encourage employers to allow their employees the right to accumulate rights to leave from work. As commonly advocated, this proposal would allow progressively longer leaves of absences without pay as an employee's length of service increases. As an illustration, an employee might accumulate the right to take a one-month leave without pay for every year of continuous employment. In this way it would be possible to leave work for a half year after six years service, and still return to one's job.

• **Work Sabbaticals with Pay.** The sabbatical concept entails an extended leave from the job, frequently for a full year, taken after several years of consecutive service. Sabbatical leaves commonly entail continuation of income, though possibly at a reduced rate.

There are many existing examples of applied sabbaticals. The most common examples are academic sabbaticals for college faculty, which are generally taken for one year every seven years and are commonly intended for some academically related activity. Another variation is the "Continuous Service Leave" policy initiated by the Rolm Corporation in California. An employee who has worked six consecutive years can leave work for as much as 12 calendar weeks with pay. Finally, a collective bargaining agreement negotiated by the U.S. Steel Workers in the mid-1960s has provided 13-week "sabbatical leaves" every seven years.

There are a number of proposals for national sabbatical programs. U.S. Civil Service Commissioner Jule Sugarman has advocated consideration of a mandatory "Decennial-Sabbatical Plan"

which would use accumulated personal tax withholdings to provide full pay during a one-year leave every ten years. Workers would lose all or part of their personal tax contributions if they did not take their sabbatical within a prescribed period. The plan was advocated by Sugarman to reduce unemployment. Barry Stern, a policy analyst for the Department of Health, Education, and Welfare, has proposed a less mandatory national sabbatical program which would provide partial income support and be financed totally or in part by general tax revenues.

• **Income Maintenance Payments.** Income maintenance and other transfer payment programs could be integrated to provide some income support for non-working persons at all stages of life on the basis of an employment or income level test. In this proposal, workers might use funds now categorically reserved for unemployment insurance, educational loans, welfare or social security to support or partially support non-work periods during mid-life. The best known proposal of this sort is the "lifelong drawing fund" concept advocated by French consultant Gosta Rehn. This plan would entitle workers to use individually accumulated public retirement funds for mid-life leaves as long as they did not deplete their retirement accounts below a given level. Some advocates of advanced "guaranteed income" schemes have also suggested a similar use of income maintenance programs.

Clearly there are many approaches to more flexible worklife scheduling, each with its unique problems and advantages. Further, there are many variations of the few ideas surveyed, and doubtless whole new ideas yet to be proposed. Some of these approaches will evolve naturally within some portions of the private sector. Others will need government support in the form of information dissemination, technical assistance, tax incentives, regulatory legislation, and possibly income subsidies.

Besides helping to solve many of today's pressing social problems, more flexible life patterns promise new opportunities for human growth and enrichment. Every individual has some desire to explore and possibly change to a fundamentally different way of life. We all have a yearning for what we might have been and may yet become—a yearning to explore things like the art of the classical guitar, the writing of books, the building of houses, or the setting up of a business. Such dreams take time to realize, and one of the promises of more flexible life patterns is that each individual will have a greater choice to explore the countless possibilities of human existence. ☯

College Graduates: Supply Overtakes Demand

	College graduates as a percent of total civilian labor force	Professional-technical workers as percent of total civilian employment
1960	10.0%	11.0%
1965	11.7%	13.0%
1970	13.2%	14.2%
1975	16.9%	15.0%
1985 (projection)	20-21%	14.9-15.4%

This table compares the percentage of college graduates in the U.S. workforce with the percentage of professional-technical jobs, the positions which college graduates have generally filled in the past. The comparison suggests that increasing numbers of workers will be "overeducated" for the jobs they will fill. Compounding the problem is a shrinkage in the percentage of managers—expected to decline 1% to 2% between 1975 and 1985.

Source: 1985 projections by the U.S. Bureau of Labor Statistics and by Joseph Froomkin in *Supply and Demand for Persons with Postsecondary Education*, Policy Research Center paper prepared for the Assistant Secretary for Education, U.S. Department of Health, Education, and Welfare, Washington, D.C., 1976.

The Shrinking Workweek

In the 18th century, when most workers were engaged in agriculture and crafts, the normal workweek was approximately 72 hours long—from sunrise to sunset, six days a week. Even today many farmers still follow that schedule.

After the Industrial Revolution began in England about 1750, workers started traveling to jobs in factories, and the workweek dropped slightly. But in 1860, Americans were still working an average of about 68 hours a week and even by 1900 the workweek had declined only to 65 hours a week.

During the first half of the 20th century, however, a dramatic drop occurred in the length of the workweek. Between 1900 and 1930, the workweek declined from 65 to 50 hours, and during the Great Depression the workweek declined still further, to 40 hours (partly as a means of work-sharing during a time when jobs were scarce).

Since the Depression, the 40-hour workweek has remained the generally accepted standard, though some organizations have adopted a workweek as short as 35 hours. Further shrinkage of the workweek has generally been opposed by workers, who prefer to earn more money rather than have additional time off from work. Recently, however, there have been signs that many workers would rather have time-off than money.

APPROPRIATE TECHNOLOGY

What It Is and Where It Is Going

by Rowan A. Wakefield and Patricia Stafford

A new "appropriate technology" movement is vigorously challenging conventional technology and economics. Proponents argue that the human situation now is quite different from what it was in the recent past, and that is why "the old rules are not working any more." What is now needed is a drastic revision of man's technological and economic systems to make them fit the new realities.

Modern technology developed when natural resources were abundant and human labor was relatively scarce. Since natural resources now are shrinking and worldwide unemployment is growing, society is seeking ways to adapt its technology to the new conditions. That is a major underlying reason for the appropriate technology movement which is now growing rapidly across the world. The movement may be expected to lead eventually to a new technological order, and, hopefully, an easing of the many problems that mankind now confronts.

The specifications for tomorrow's technology are still emerging, but its philosophical outlines already are clear. An intellectual catalyst for many people has been *Small Is Beautiful,* a book by British economist E. F. Schumacher. *Small Is Beautiful*

argues that high technology is thus inappropriate in many situations, and "low" or "intermediate" technology should be used. What is often needed, Schumacher says, is technology that will employ lots of people, be gentle in its use of scarce resources, and serve the human person instead of making him the servant of machines. An "intermediate technology," Schumacher explains, is one that is "vastly superior to the primitive technology of bygone ages but at the same time much simpler, cheaper, and freer than the super-technology of the rich. One can also call it self-help technology or democratic or people's technology—a technology to which everyone can gain admittance and which is not reserved to those rich and powerful."

The term "appropriate technology" is generally used to describe Schumacher's ideal, but there is considerable ambiguity in the phrase. To some people, appropriate technologies include large-scale or high technologies, such as electronic telecommunications or freeze-dried blood plasma if "appropriate" to a given situation.

However, the phrase generally implies the use of indigenous materials and minimal use of non-renewable resources such as fossil fuels. The U.S. Agency for International Development's summary definition states, "In terms of available resources, appropriate technologies are intensive in the use of the abundant factor, labor; economical in the use of scarce factors, capital and highly trained personnel; and intensive in the use of domestically-produced inputs."

The concept of appropriate technology implies a redefinition of economic efficiency. Traditionally, economic efficiency has been viewed as producing maximum output with minimum input or cost. Evaluating the appropriateness of technology emphasizes how production occurs and the consequent implications for the quality of the physical environment and the life of the individual. This new perspective represents a fundamental change in the way people evaluate economic relationships.

Appropriate technology is becoming increasingly popular as a component of development strategy. Both the World Bank and the Inter-American Development Bank have established special procedures to insure appropriate uses of technologies in their programs. The International Labor Organization is showing a keen interest in appropriate technology as a possible approach toward increasing employment opportunities in developing countries. The World Health Organization and the Pan American Health Organization have begun looking for ways that appropriate technology can be related to health delivery systems in places where modern hospitals and ambulances cannot be maintained.

Workshops on appropriate technology at Habitat: the United Nations Conference on Human Settlements last June have led to the establishment of an informal network of organizations interested in common actions and strategies in the international arena. This network, known as TRANET, is one of the organizations seeking to insure that appropriate technology will receive major attention at the 1979 U.N. Conference on Science and Technology. The Conference may well become a bat-

tleground between the friends and foes of appropriate technology.

An International Network for Appropriate Technology was established in Paris last fall to increase communication and coordination among organizations in the field. The core of the Network consists of the "big five" of the major private voluntary

organizations involved in appropriate technology, namely, Volunteers in Technical Assistance (VITA), a U.S. group; the International Technology Development Group, Schumacher's organization in London; Brace Research Institute, located in Canada; a Dutch group using the acronym TOOL, and a French

The 40 Women and the Washing Machines

When the Agency for International Development sent two $32,000 washing machines to the Barranquilla Hospital in Colombia, the hospital administration had the good sense not to hook them up, reports James C. McCullagh. The machines would have displaced the 40 women who did the laundry by hand, thus threatening the life-support not only of their families but of store clerks, bus drivers, and others whose goods and services they bought with their wages.

McCullagh currently is editing an American edition of *Socially Appropriate Technology,* a book originally published in the Netherlands. The book will be issued this summer by the Rodale Press. The laundry incident is typical of many reported in the book. Over and over, technology is misapplied, causing enormous problems.

"Experience gained in some developing countries shows that the application of modern or advanced technology in many cases actually creates more unemployment even when production is increased," says Charles R. Tett, author of one of the papers in *Socially Appropriate Technology.* "In Kenya between 1954 and 1965 manufacturing output rose by 7.6% while employment increased by only 1.1%. This is typical of many other countries which have fallen for the same sales talk."

High technology, McCullagh comments, "often encourages a questionable economic order which prevents much of the world from utilizing its own creative resources." He cites the Case of the Jam Jar, described by P. R. Lofthouse:

"I was horrified," Lofthouse reports, "to get a letter from Chile, saying: 'Please can you find us a

supplier of glass jam jars. For years we have been importing jam jars from the United Kingdom to put our jam in.' The mind boggles at the thought of a boatload of empty jam jars being transported there to be filled with jam and then exported back to the western world. I thought this was absolutely crazy. So I started looking into this.

"I talked to various people, all of them highly technical and very knowledgeable about glass, and amongst them was the Chairman of the Glass Research Association. I said, 'I have done a little bit of homework and as far as I know glass is basically silica, sand, limestone, and soda ash with a few traces of elements like arsenic to clear it. So what is the problem in making glass?'

"He said that the problem is soda ash, which is only produced by I.C.I. (Imperial Chemical Industries), and without soda ash you cannot make good glass. I was feeling just a bit naughty that day, so I said, 'How long has I.C.I. been running—50 years? Could you then tell me how the Egyptians and the Chinese made glass before I.C.I. was ever heard of?'"

The jam jar tale ended happily with the Chileans able to make their own glass. The only difference between high-technology glass and intermediate-technology glass is that the latter will be slightly green and have tiny bubbles in it. It will be the kind that curiosity shops sell for $4 or $5 apiece.

McCullagh currently is Executive Editor of Rodale Press's Intermediate Book Series. "I am interested in receiving manuscripts in the general area of appropriate technology," he told THE FUTURIST. McCullagh's address is Rodale Press, Organic Park, Emmaus, Pennsylvania 18049.

Solar heater, built from salvaged materials, can heat a room. This device consists of a wooden frame holding a plate of glass and a piece of black roofing metal. Sunlight passes through the glass and strikes the black metal, which changes the light energy into heat energy. The air between the metal plate and the window is heated and rises into the room; at the same time, cooler air from the room is drawn through a vent just above the window sill. This device was developed by Chris Ahrens and his colleagues at Friends World College, Huntington, Long Island, New York, under a grant from the Community Services Administration.
Photograph: Sam Love

organization known as the *Groupe de Recherche sur les Techniques rurales* (GRET).

Interest in appropriate technology is greatest in the developing countries themselves. Five African nations—Nigeria, Tanzania, Ethiopia, Ghana and Kenya—have appropriate technology organizations intended to become nationwide focal points, according to a survey by the U.S. Agency for International Development. In addition, more than 100 community development groups, university engineering and agricultural facilities, research institutions, and small industry extension units are active in appropriate technology in 32 African nations. In the 10 East and South Asian nations surveyed, 25 public agencies and universities were identified as being actively involved in appropriate technology. Pakistan, India, and Bangladesh each have appropriate

technology units in one of their central ministries. According to the AID survey, government support of appropriate technology is just beginning in Latin America, but more than 300 organizations, nearly all private, are concerned with appropriate technology in the Latin countries.

One example of an appropriate technology project is the World Bank's effort to develop a manually-operated hand-pump for lifting irrigation water. The diesel pumps now available cost about $1,300 apiece and create maintenance problems due to the difficulty of procuring spare parts. The new irrigation pump, now in the prototype stages, is made of cheap, corrosion-resistant plastic (instead of cast iron), and will cost only about $100. It will operate with human labor rather than diesel power. The use of human labor reduces the need for fossil fuel, thus easing the farmer's capital outlays, his country's need for foreign exchange, and the world's energy problems.

U.S. interest in appropriate technology is increasing, as shown by the recent establishment of AT International, a non-profit corporation created by the U.S. Agency for International Development. AT International draws its support from funds appropriated by the U.S. Congress, under the Foreign Assistance Act, "to expand and coordinate private effort to stimulate the development and dissemination of appropriate technologies in developing countries." AID has also established an internal unit within the Agency's Technical Assistance Bureau to see that appropriate technology is emphasized in AID's own programs.

Congress has mandated the National Science Foundation to establish a program in appropriate technology, and intended to do the same for the Energy Research and Development Administration (ERDA). The ERDA authorization bill, which was approved by the joint House and Senate Conference Committee but failed to be enacted in the closing hours of the 94th Congress, contained a $10 million authorization for ERDA to establish a small grants program in appropriate technology.

Congress has also authorized the creation of a National Center for Appropriate Technology to explore the utilization of appropriate technology in low-income communities. Located in Butte, Montana, and responsible to the Community Services Administration (CSA), an independent federal agency, the Center provides technical assistance and seed grants to local

Community Action Agencies and other community-based organizations working in impoverished neighborhoods. The Center plans to offer technical expertise on such things as wood stoves, greenhouses, and low-cost solar collectors that can be produced locally.

Prior to the establishment of the Center, CSA funded some successful demonstration projects, which—appropriately enough—cost the Government very little. For example, a solar heater which can be utilized by low-income people was built under a $1,000 grant to Friends World College on Long Island, New York. The heater, constructed by Chris Ahrens from recycled materials for less than $50, can be mounted in any south-facing window, and provides most of the heat required to keep a room warm during sunny and partly sunny days. Devices like this window heater can have an immediate impact on the lives of many low-income people, unlike the sophisticated (and generally expensive) solar experiments that are the focus of most government research. In another project, low-income people constructed a solar-powered hot water

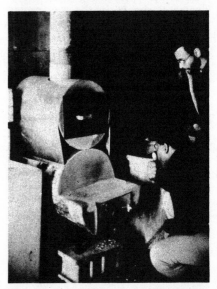

Wood stove has two combustion chambers for greater efficiency. Gases from wood burning in the lower chamber are vented through the upper chamber so that more complete combustion occurs, thus providing more heat. This apparatus was built at Friends World College, Long Island, New York, under a grant from the Community Services Administration. The device was made in a very small shop as a prototype of the sort of stove that a small community group could produce.
Photograph: Sam Love

Substituting Labor for Capital: Laborers in Kenya show how they can do same job as grader. Use of labor-intensive rather than capital-intensive methods makes sense in countries with large numbers of unemployed people—and little foreign exchange.

Photographs: World Bank

heater and a wind-driven electric generator on the roof of a renovated tenement on East 11th Street in New York City. Beyond the energy contribution of the technology, the project is infusing an infectious spirit of hope into the surrounding neighborhood.

At the state level, California has taken the lead by establishing an Office of Appropriate Technology, which reports directly to the Governor. The Office assists Californians in developing cost-saving alternatives to present practices, and plans to help California to develop and use renewable resources rather than non-renewable resources which may not be available in the future. The Office has proposed the installation of solar energy systems on state highway stations, establishment of an appropriate technology skills center, and development of methane-generating plants for urban wastes.

Despite widespread enthusiasm for appropriate technology, there is also criticism. One objection is that the primary goal of technology should be to maximize output—that is, to produce the most with the least—so as to meet urgent human needs as fast as possible. Proponents of appropriate technology reply by pointing out that the introduction of complex mass-production technology, generally in urban areas, has not reduced unemployment and has resulted in goods and services that are too expensive for most people to buy. Another charge is that appropriate technology is "technological imperialism." In the view of these critics, appropriate technology means second-rate technology, and stems from

the desire of developed nations to hoard their most advanced technical devices in order to discourage competitive technological development elsewhere. The advocates of appropriate technology respond by saying that they are not opposed to high technology *per se* but only to its use in situations where people would be better served by a low or intermediate technology. "In some circumstances," notes the AID proposal for AT International, "efficient, labor-intensive technologies may not exist (e.g., petrochemical industries), or competitiveness in export markets may require precision machine-made products." AID concludes that developing countries require a mix of technologies.

Besides the theoretical criticisms of appropriate technology, there are practical objections that may be even more important motives for resistance to the concept. Low or intermediate technologies appear unpromising to many large corporations which must sell their products at a high enough price to cover a large capital investment. For example, the John Deere Corporation found that it could not profitably produce small tractors that would sell in developing countries at prices that farmers could afford. Many small manufacturers, though less influential in government decision-making, may find it easier to produce lower-priced items for the developing countries. Large corporations are showing a growing willingness to sell or license to smaller companies appropriate technologies that the large companies often discover as by-products of their main research and

development work, but decide not to produce, for economic or other reasons.

One approach to improving the dissemination of appropriate technologies is for the local and national governments, assisted by national and international organizations, to take the leadership in helping local people get information they can use in deciding which technologies are the most appropriate to their own situations and how to adapt them. Local people often are more competent than anyone else to choose the technologies appropriate to their own situation. A development specialist in Costa Rica reported that when peasants are queried about the technologies they want to improve their communities, they ask for simple things like better dirt roads, whereas government planners in the capital, San Jose, spoke of airports.

Useful in Rich Areas, Too?

What does the future hold for the appropriate technology movement? For one thing, it is likely to have considerable influence on highly developed societies such as the U.S. During most of U.S. history, land, water, natural resources, and energy were abundant and cheap. The work force was relatively small, even with slavery and mass immigration. By comparison, land, water, raw materials, and energy today are scarce and expensive. Capital is also harder to come by, especially for investment in traditional technologies. But labor is abundant and educated, with the result that the U.S. now experiences chronic unemployment and under-employment. Furthermore, belief in the desirability of high economic growth is widely challenged, and the sheer numbers of people everywhere has led to increased concern about the quality of life and the environment. More and more people feel the need to preserve their individuality in what they perceive to be a sea of people and machines, both controlled by ever bigger and increasingly insensitive institutions. Thus we now seem to have a search for technologies that would not only conserve energy and resources, but also enhance the quality of life and offer satisfying work opportunities in which the individual counts for something.

The appropriate technology movement suggests that some of the technology developed to meet yesterday's needs is no longer appropriate for the U.S. today, and may never have been appropriate for third world countries. The current struggle in today's society is a painful process of changing and adapting technology to meet these new conditions. This process of change will be with us for some time to come.

Appropriate technology will likely continue to grow as a force in society for several decades until the proper mix of high, intermediate and low technologies comes into a new equilibrium with social forces, the marketplace, and the physical limits of the environment. The rapid growth

Can appropriate technology save the cities? Like the underdeveloped countries, Newark, New Jersey, suffers from high unemployment in a population lacking technical expertise.

of the appropriate technology movement, with the establishment of centers and programs throughout the world and the growth of organizations promoting and subsidizing appropriate technology, will increase both the supply of appropriate technology and pressures to market it. Initially, the market may be supplied mainly by Japan, some Western European countries, and by the third world countries themselves which will seek to sell

Simple wool-spinning machine in operation in Peshawar, Pakistan. The device was developed in the laboratories of the Pakistan Council of Scientific and Industrial Research under supervision of Pakistan's Appropriate Technology Development Organisation.
Photograph: PCSIR Labs, Peshawar

abroad the appropriate technologies that they have developed to meet their own needs. China may be the first Communist country to see an export market for innovative low and intermediate technologies. The role of the Soviet Union and Eastern European Community countries is unclear, but a Soviet paper circulated at the international appropriate technology meeting in Vienna last September warned the Third World countries that the appropriate technology movement is a trick by the western countries to keep them underdeveloped, and urged the developing countries to stick to the tried-and-true route of industrial development.

Another reason for believing that appropriate technology will grow as a social force is that it offers a middle ground between accelerated economic growth and no-growth strategies. Poverty-stricken localities in the rich nations may also benefit from appropriate technology strategies. Newark, New Jersey, for example, lacks the resources to purchase expensive energy and high technology, and suffers from high unemployment in a population lacking technical expertise. Furthermore, the people of Newark, like those in an underdeveloped country, have urgent needs that are going unmet. The Office of Minority Business Enterprises of the U.S. Department of Commerce now

recognizes appropriate technology as a promising new growth area for minority-owned and operated businesses, which face heavier competition in most other fields.

The development, growth, and utilization of appropriate technology can go a long way toward satisfying mankind's search for satisfying work as one of the most important elements of a fulfilling life. Moreover, low and intermediate technology offers a partial solution to rising worldwide unemployment and underemployment among the educated as well as the uneducated. This accounts for the strong endorsement of the movement by the International Labor Organization.

Overall, appropriate technology should be seen as part of a larger movement that seeks to improve the quality of life in ways that harmonize with the natural environment and our longings for satisfying and creative work.

The senior author, Rowan A. Wakefield, is President of Wakefield Washington Associates, Inc. The co-author, Patricia Stafford, is a research assistant in the firm.

Wakefield Washington Associates, Inc., is a management consulting firm which provides representation, trend analysis, and forecasting services. The firm's address is Suite 511, 1129 20th Street, N.W., Washington, D.C. 20036.

Social Inventions

The importance of mechanical inventions is generally recognized, and thousands of workshops are devoted to achieving them. By contrast, social inventions receive little recognition or support. In the following article, a Canadian social scientist discusses the importance of social inventions in solving social problems, and explains why special centers are needed to develop these innovations.

by D. Stuart Conger

It has been said that the way people lived in 1900 was more similar to the style of life in Biblical times than to life in the present day. To substantiate this assertion, several examples have been offered: the fact that the common conveyance was the donkey in Christ's time and the horse in 1900, as compared with the automobile today. Again, most major advances in medicine have been made since 1900: the Salk vaccine, insulin, tranquilizers, antibiotics, chemical contraception, to name only a few.

Our technological progress in the 20th century has indeed been astounding, but we have failed to achieve a similar degree of social progress. When we compare the social problems of today with those in Biblical times, we find that they still are much the same and we still are trying to cope with them in the same basic ways. Some of our solutions are more systematic and perhaps more humanitarian, but otherwise not very different, certainly not very different in comparison to the great leaps in scientific technology in the same time.

The Canadian Special Senate Committee on Poverty recognized the need for new approaches to social problems when it wrote recently that "the social welfare structure, so laboriously and painstakingly erected in Canada, has outlived its usefulness."

The whole welfare system, at all levels, costs Canadians more than six billion dollars a year, yet it has not significantly alleviated poverty, let alone eliminated it. Welfare rolls have not diminished. The problems grow, costs go up, and up, and up, and will, in time, suffocate the taxpayer.

Other social problems today testify to the need for new social inventions. Our approach to unemployment still is largely to blame the unemployed for being without jobs: The fact that we train and re-train some 300,000 adults each year is mute evidence that we consider their unemployment to be their lack of skill. We know that our correctional institutions do not reform, but we do not know what to do about them. We have no answer to marriage breakdown, except separation and divorce.

The first strike took place in Rome in 490 B.C. when the Plebs, or common people, struck for certain rights. Today we still have not invented a better method of resolving labor disputes. Striking Canadian workers usually lose 5,442,000 working days each year in about 535 strikes. We are not even experimenting with new methods of resolving strikes.

There is at present a serious gap between the national desire to produce social change on a massive scale and the necessary educational, welfare, technological and manpower resources to meet this objective. More than money is needed; more than reallocation of resources is needed; a change in approaches, methods and institutions is required.

Canada (like the rest of the world) needs better methods of human and social development to achieve a just and equitable society; neither surveys nor armchair techniques can create them. They can be developed only by means of action-research, which conceives, develops, tests and evaluates various methods in real life situations among the people. Experience with manpower re-training programs has proved that training, while necessary, is frequently not enough to enable the poor person to extricate himself from poverty. The multi-faceted problem of poverty must be attacked by an integrated and comprehensive program of services. This requires a marked change on the part of many social institutions currently providing single solutions based upon the methods of a single profession; there is a need to develop multi-disciplinary integrated programs to deal effectively with poverty.

Our social problems are going to be with us until we invent better solutions, but we are not even trying.

We know that we need research centers to find cures for medical ailments; experimental farms to develop cures for infestations and diseases of plants and animals; oceanographic research stations to study aquatic conditions, but we don't see that we need experimental stations to invent new ways of dealing with our social ailments.

We need research stations to create new ways of:
1. Alleviating poverty
2. Creating jobs
3. Teaching languages
4. Achieving interracial accord
5. Reducing crime
6. Increasing family harmony
7. Overcoming addiction
8. Curing mental illness
9. Providing adequate housing
10. Settling labor disputes

This is not to say that we have made no progress in these areas in the past 2000 or 2,000,000 years. We have made some progress, thanks to the limited number of social inventions that have been made over the years, with little or no official support for the research activity.

Why Social Invention Centers Are Not Supported

We have not supported social invention centers to the same extent that we have funded scientific research for five reasons:

1. We tend to see social problems like poverty, unemployment, crime, and poor housing as resulting from failings in human nature that should be addressed educationally, moralistically, punitively or tolerantly, rather than as ailments in need of more effective techniques of treatment.

2. We have not acknowledged the importance of social technology in developing our society over the years and therefore do not see the potential that social inventions have for the further improvement of society. For instance, we do not realize that schools, courts, legislatures and other institutions were social inventions that resulted in great social progress, and that it is possible to invent new institutions of similar value to overcome present ailments and achieve social progress.

The author, D. Stuart Conger, is director of Saskatchewan NewStart, a social invention that got him interested in social inventions. (See box on NewStart.)

3. We have vested interests in the way things are done now, and are apprehensive about the implications of any tampering with society. The disturbances in the courts and in the streets confirm in our minds that the people demanding changes in our social institutions are more intent on destroying our way of life than on constructively developing it. We do not see these disturbances as signs of the need to invent improvements for society.

4. Social scientists are wary of attempting to create social inventions and generally prefer to analyze change rather than invent ways to bring it about. Consequently, social science has contributed relatively few social institutions to the community. Over the past 70 years new social institutions have come from a wide variety of sources: the Boy Scouts were invented by a soldier; Alcoholics Anonymous, by an alcoholic, and service clubs, by a businessman.

5. We do not understand the experimental process, and are horrified at the idea of experimenting with people—even though people actually like to be experimented with, because they get more attention from the researchers than they usually receive from their ordinary associates.

What Is a Social Invention?

A social invention is a new law, organization or procedure that changes the ways in which people relate to themselves or to each other, either individually or collectively. Examples of laws that are social inventions include:

1. The Poor Law of 1388, which first gave the poor the right to relief.

2. The Indenture of Children Act of 1601, which spelled out the terms under which children were bound to another person or family.

3. The English Bill of Rights (1689).

4. The Compulsory School Attendance Act in Prussia in 1717.

5. The Swiss Unemployment Insurance Act of 1789.

6. The laws against cruelty to children that were enacted in the United States after 1875, at which time the New York Society for the Prevention of Cruelty to Animals demonstrated that it was possible to prosecute parents for the abuse of children under laws against cruelty to animals. (We had laws to protect animals before we had them to protect children!)

Social Procedures vs. Social Organizations

Social inventions include both organizations and procedures.

A procedure is a method that might be used by many organizations in many contexts. For example: examinations, instructional methods, curriculum design, mental tests, guidance, probation, instructional T.V., programmed instruction, and behavior modification.

Organizational social inventions are typified by schools, service clubs, Boy Scouts, mental health associations, women's institutes, child guidance clinics, jails, community colleges, Y.M.C.A., and churches.

Once an organization is invented it seldom concerns itself with inventing new procedural methods for the delivering of its service or objectives. Instead, it becomes consumed with developing methods of self maintenance and extension. The restriction of employment to teachers in educational institutions, to social workers in welfare agencies, etc., is intended to preserve territorial imperatives and prevent cross breeding of ideas or methods. Thus, the

The hospital was a social invention that took place in Epidaurus, Greece, in 600 B.C. The temple of Epidaurus was one of the first to be dedicated to the Greek god of healing Asclepius (Aesculapius). Attached to the temple was a hostel where the priests would treat sick people. The god Aesculapius was represented artistically by a serpent twined around a staff. That symbol—the so-called Staff of Aesculapius—became a symbol of the medical profession and may still be seen in modern hospitals.

invention of teachers' contracts, teacher training institutions, jurisdictions, etc., become the focus for social inventions in organizations. Therefore, most instrumental social inventions will expectably be made outside the institutions in which they should be utilized. This is why we need social invention centers that are separate from service delivery institutions. It is because of the inherent threat to the latter of a new procedure, however, that they do not advocate such research centers. A very interesting example is the College of Education that conducts research on teaching—even on new methods—but does not implement the new methods in its own institutions! The difficulty of a social institution in adopting new ways does suggest the value of establishing alternative social institutions and removing the monopoly given to most existing social institutions.

The use of audio-visual methods of instruction is a very interesting example. The advantages of visual methods are legendary—"A picture is worth a thousand words"—and in recent decades a number of overhead projectuals, films, etc., have been prepared as instructional aids to the teacher. Unfortunately, however, while almost every single school has at least one movie projector and an overhead projector, some are literally never used, while most are used only very occasionally. Those who have watched programs such as University of the Air, only to discover that the television camera takes you to the professor in front of the chalkboard and leaves you there without any of the instructional methods that can be used on television, know the minimal acceptance that teachers have made of audio-visual methods. Documentary television programs review-

ing the history of nations provide a far superior method of teaching social studies than the common practice of memorizing dates of kings and queens. Yet the old practice continues.

Recently, *Sesame Street* has demonstrated the value of audiovisual-directed learning in contrast to audiovisual-*assisted* learning. The invention of audiovisual means of instruction required its own institution (television) to be properly used in fulfilling its purpose. Many other instrumental social inventions are under-used or misused because they are prisoners of old social institutions. Examples of such procedural inventions are:

1. Programmed instruction which is capable of teaching virtually all knowledge without the aid of teachers, classrooms or schools.

2. Achievement tests which are capable of certifying a person's knowledge regardless of whether he got it in school or elsewhere.

3. Human relations training, affective education, or Life Skills training that is offered only in adult remedial programs when it should be a part of primary education.

4. Psychological tests that should be used in schools, welfare agencies, etc., to help understand the clients better.

5. Vocational aptitude, ability and interest tests that should be used universally to help students make career decisions.

6. Audiovisual-directed educational programs which could greatly increase the comprehension of subjects by students.

7. Computer-assisted instruction that provides interactive relationship between the student and knowledge.

Each of these instrumental inventions has been only partially implemented in only a few institutions and demonstrates the difficulty of putting new wine in old bottles. The bottles don't get damaged, they just sour the new contents.

Examples of *organizations* that were important social inventions would include the following:

- Schools in Sumer in 2500 B.C.
- Law courts in the same country in 2400 B.C.
- House of Commons in 1300 A.D.
- Labor union in England in 1696
- Penitentiaries in Rome in 1700
- Adult schools in Wales in 1754
- Y.M.C.A. in England in 1844
- Children's Aid Society in New York in 1853
- Red Cross in Geneva in 1864
- Teachers Colleges in New York in 1894
- United Appeal in Cleveland in 1913

Procedures that represent social inventions would include:
- Charity, 2100 B.C.
- Democracy, 510 B.C. in Athens
- Municipal system, 100 B.C. in Rome
- Licensing of teachers, 362 A.D.
- Training of lawyers, 1292
- Oath to tell truth to courts, 1327
- Hansard (the written record of debates in the House of Commons) in 1608
- Formal steps in teaching, 1838
- Probation in Boston, 1841
- I.Q. tests in Paris, 1905
- Programmed instruction in U.S., 1957
- Computer assisted instruction in U.S., in 1960

A social invention such as the law court, school, municipal government, or prison, spawns many ancillary inventions that ultimately create a social system. For instance, the social system developed around the civil law court includes the judge, jury, lawyer, plea, coroner, justice of the peace, code of law, law schools, etc. Each component of the system was itself an invention, but adapted to fit the system.

Each social system comprises a series of social inventions. Some systems, such as education, are relatively well developed, while other systems, such as intergroup relations, have so few methods to rely on that the system is more a constellation of problems than a cluster of solutions.

Medicine has developed a system for inventing better methods of curing and preventing disease, and people recognize this when they support medical research. By contrast, education does not have a well-developed system for the invention of new methods of education, although there is some investment in educational research, and there are in Canada at least a few centers doing important education experimentation. Other social systems such as welfare and corrections are very stable as far as their technology is concerned because they have not established research laboratories at all, and hence, improvements in these areas can hardly be expected except at a very slow rate.

Some of our social problems in Canada do not even have a system of social technologies to provide relief and hence we can anticipate continued frustration with little hope of improvement. A critical example is the burgeoning problem of racial/linguistic discord in Canada. The social technology for dealing with this problem does not exist and no real efforts are being made to develop it. Among the needed methods are vastly improved methods of (1) teaching languages, (2) overcoming prejudice, (3) creating and sustaining dialogue, and (4) fostering equality between groups. The present methods that are available are so crude that while they may be used to force progress in one area they create a backlash in another. For instance, efforts to make more people bilingual apparently increase prejudice, and, therefore, our programs in the entire area of racial/linguistic reconciliation amount to a zero sum game. The elements or components of the system act to maintain the set status quo rather than encourage progress.

Our present systems of law, education, welfare and municipal government can be directly traced back two, three, four or five thousand years, and changes over the years have modified the system, but not created entirely new systems. Furthermore, social systems, as a rule, operate as monopolies which, of course, tend to be less susceptible to change or replacement. The citizen cannot choose whether to attend a school, jail, court, or welfare agency!

Inventions Fail to Change Schools' Basic Character

Schools were invented in Sumer in 2500 B.C., teachers contracts in 445 B.C, State support for schools in 75 A.D., licensed teachers in 362, schedule of teachers' salaries in 376, teacher training in 1672, classroom instruction in 1684, vocational education in 1695, compulsory attendance in 1717, adult schools in 1754, public schools in 1763, kindergartens in 1837, formal steps in teaching in 1838, educational tests in 1845, guidance counselors in 1909, teacher aides in 1953, educational television in 1956, programmed instruction in 1957, and computer assisted instruction in 1960. All of the inventions, after the invention of schools and universities, made education more efficient, but did not change the essential nature of the institution.

If you consider transportation, you find the citizen has several separate choices of systems that he can select, e.g., bus, train, car, snowmobile, and motorcycle. Each is separately owned and operated, or manufactured and sold, thus giving the citizen real choice. A prime invention spawned each system: the car, for instance, prompted the invention of motels, credit cards, paved highways, service stations, drive-ins, driver training schools, traffic police, parking meters, shopping centers, and automobile associations.

When we look at education today we see signs of people chafing at the monopolistic education system which includes schools, universities, colleges of education, departments of education, and teachers' unions. These act as a constellation interacting in mutual maintenance and stability. It has been said that it is easier to move a graveyard than to change a curriculum, and this describes well the slowness to adopt a new invention, even if it is compatible with the system: There are too many vested interests to contend with.

The invention of programmed instruction might lead to the recognition that education can take place outside formal institutional structures. This could lead to an acceptance of alternative sources of learning and then to the separation of the certification of knowledge from the institutions that teach. Programmed instruction is essentially a self teaching method and does not require a stand-up teacher, but solely a person who can occasionally answer a question or explain a point at the request of the student. Furthermore, programmed instruction does not require a class of students at all and permits students to learn simultaneously even though each student may be at a different point in his studies. All of these conditions are completely foreign to our present educational system, which dictates what material will be covered on what dates, how many will be in the class, etc.

On the other hand, we do have another learning institution that allows people to study at their own pace, and to be left alone unless they want help. This institution places no limits on the number studying and is the ideal institution to use programmed instruction. It could be the alternative school for the student who can learn better by himself

D. Stuart Conger and Saskatchewan NewStart

Author Conger became interested in social inventions while directing a Canadian social invention called Saskatchewan NewStart. He describes it as "a quasi nongovernmental organization established jointly by the federal Department of Manpower and Immigration and the Saskatchewan provincial Department of Education."

Saskatchewan NewStart was created to develop new methods of counseling and training adults. It was established as a society under the provincial Societies Act so that it would be free of administrative and professional constraints imposed on traditionally-organized governmental and educational institutions. The idea, says Conger, was to "provide it with the freedom to experiment and make mistakes in the field of human development."

Set up in 1967, NewStart was given a five-year lifetime, during which it developed materials, techniques, and programs for upgrading human skills. When its five-year lifetime expired in August 1972, the Department of Manpower and Immigration created the Training Research and Development Station to continue, on a permanent basis, the work that NewStart had initiated experimentally. Saskatchewan NewStart continues for the time being as the publishing house for the dissemination of methods created during the past five years.

While serving as Executive Director of NewStart, Conger prepared a booklet entitled *Social Inventions,* which he published as part of a campaign to see experimental centers such as NewStart established on a permanent basis in Canada. Besides *Social Inventions* ($2), other publications currently available from NewStart include *Dynamics of Life Skills Coaching* by Paul R. Curtiss and Philip W. Warren (234 pages, $4.95) and *Life Skills: A Course in Applied Problem Solving* (181 pages, $3.95). (Send orders or inquiries to Saskatchewan NewStart, 101 River Street East, Prince Albert, Saskatchewan S6V 5T2, Canada.)

Before his association with NewStart, Conger served as Chairman of the National Committee on Counseling and Guidance. From 1962 to 1965, he was with the federal Department of Trade and Commerce where he developed and organized the national Small Business Management Training Program.

From 1957 to 1962, Conger was Director of Training for R. L. Craine Ltd. in Ottawa. His community activities during this time included the designing and conducting of a course in association management for members of the boards of directors of welfare agencies.

through programmed materials, books and other self teaching devices than he can in the traditional classroom. The institution I am talking about is the library.

We could switch much of our educational program to the libraries except for the fact that the schools have a monopoly on education. We could make great gains in educational progress and economy if we gave the libraries the same right to issue certificates of knowledge as the schools now have. Students could be given the option of attending either a school or a library. Providing this alternative to the students and this competition to the schools could benefit society.

Studies have shown that it takes about 50 years for a new educational invention to come into use in half the schools. Other social institutions take just as long to adopt new improved methods.

Because of the monopolistic nature of our social institutions and systems, and their difficulty in adapting to new circumstances or achieving a significant measure of self renewal, it may be as necessary to invent new social institutions as to invent new laws or procedures.

At the same time, however, our social problems are growing in severity and people are no longer docile about being in jail, unemployed, poor and discriminated against, and they are using television, strikes, boycotts, demonstrations and even violence to draw attention to their problems.

Agencies Cannot Adapt

Present organizations that are almost overwhelmed by the sheer demand to provide services on a minimum budget cannot be expected to invent new methods. Sometimes such agencies are not able to adapt sufficiently to accept new social inventions. A similar situation would have been to expect the railways to invent a better alternative means of transportation. They were not even prepared to adopt the car when it was invented. We would still be in the railway age, and the car would still be an awkward means of transportation, if the automobile had been given to the railways to develop.

Yet, this is precisely what is done with our social problems and innovations. If a new educational method, such as programmed-learning, is invented, which does not require a stand-up teacher, it is assigned to stand-up teachers to try it out, and naturally, they find it isn't very good.

For the same reasons, there has been little progress in the reformation of criminals since Pope Clement invented penitentiaries in 1700. Research and innovation in prisons has been assigned to prison officials, and they are no more likely to come up with a new method than the railway might have invented the car. Better methods of penal reform will be devised only by people who have no direct or indirect interest in maintaining the present system.

Need "New Improved" Product

It is a fact of commercial life that it is necessary to come up with a "new improved" product each year. Sometimes an innovation is an improvement of substance, sometimes of style. Sometimes the improvement represents a new generation of the product, and sometimes it fails abysmally. The Ford Motor Company devoted huge amounts of technical and consumer research to designing the Edsel, but the car was not popular with the public. As a company, Ford was able to discontinue the Edsel, but if the Edsel had been developed by a governmental agency, it would still be in

Government is a social invention that was old in Roman times. Government evolved out of the necessity to have an authority to mediate disputes, and first appeared in history in Sumer, a region of Babylonia, 5,500 years ago. A modern parliament may use such technological innovations as the microphone, but the social aspects of the legislative process—tax policy, speeches, military problems, political factions, etc.—strongly resemble those of ancient Rome.

production and would be given to under-developed countries as foreign aid or as a bonus for buying our wheat.

When the Edsel failed, Ford did not give up its consumer and technical research, but used them to develop other cars such as the Thunderbird and Mustang, which proved successful.

We must do the same with out social programs. We must see them as stages in the evolution of truly valuable and important social technologies.

One of the problems that we face in stimulating social inventions is the general lack of a recognition that they are necessary. People recognize that cancer can be cured only by medical research, but they do not yet realize that intergroup relations can be resolved through inventing better social methods, and the thing that really is needed is a number of social invention centers to invent these better methods on a continuous basis.

Saskatchewan NewStart's Methods of Invention

One of the pressing needs for a new social invention today is a method of achieving equality between various segments of society. It is a reflection of the way in which organizations bind up jurisdictions that we should assign the major responsibility for equalizing to education and give the schools the job of undertaking a massive re-education program, when in fact the schools had already demonstrated their inability to educate the disadvantaged segment of the population.

Only after several years of adult retraining which was ineffective on many counts, not the least being a drop-out rate of over 65%, was there an acknowledgement that some new methods of training adults needed to be created. This gave rise to the Canada NewStart Program in 1967. The first invention of this program was an organizational innovation that involved both federal and provincial departments entering into equal partnership by means of joint ownership and control of an incorporated society. In this way they were able to overcome the constraints of their own jurisdictions to experiment in comprehensive human resource development methods. The decision to do this was eloquent acknowledgement of the crippling constraints placed by dividing work rigidly into jurisdictions and assigning it to monopolistic institutions. Not surprisingly, however, the NewStart corporations worked only at devising new methods and not at inventing new organizations that could achieve human resource development objectives more effectively than present institutions. Saskatchewan NewStart, for instance, invented methods of individualized instruction and life skills training.

At Saskatchewan NewStart Corporations, we have identified the following stages in the development of social invention:

Stages of Development

1. Concept Study: This initial stage comprises a review of the problem area and the attempted solutions to date. The review includes a study of the theoretical and research literature, a study of the requirements of the situation, and assessment of various theories and methods of intervention. The concept study results in preliminary specifications for the desired outcomes, identifying the skills or other factors required to achieve the outcomes, and designing the broad strategies to achieve these goals.

2. Exploratory Development: This is the preparation of initial program strategies, methods and materials, and an examination of them to evaluate the feasibility of the proposed solutions. This stage may involve a reformulation of the concept study, but in any case, will result in more detailed specifications and cost figures.

3. Prototype Development: This stage comprises the preparation of detailed program strategies, methods, and materials, and an evaluation system, and the training of staff to conduct them. Cost, time and resource estimates are made.

4. Pilot Study: In this stage, the new prototype is tested. Allowance is made for sufficient acquaintance with the problem and the prototype to permit necessary reformulations, including the specification of logical alternatives.

5. Advanced Development: This stage is the redevelopment or further development of the entire program including the strategies, methods, materials, staff training program and evaluation system.

6. Program Experimentation: This stage involves a formally structured, systematic, experimental effort to test alternative program elements, or the value of the program with different groups or under different circumstances. This stage may involve repeated testing of all or selected components of the program.

7. Program Formalization: The program development process is essentially a sequence of trial-revision interactions with modifications after each test to approximate the consequences being sought. The cyclical nature of the process means that each stage to this point may have been repeated several times. The preparation of the program into a formal model which can be used elsewhere with predictable results must take place at the optimum time considering results of evaluation and urgency of need for the program.

8. Field Test: Once a satisfactory program model has been prepared, it is then tested under ordinary operating conditions.

9. Operational Systems Development: The systems are prepared for those who will implement the program, as well as for the administrative support personnel and the monitoring agency.

10. Demonstration Project: This is the first major attempt to foster adoption of the new program.

11. Dissemination: Publicity, seminars, conference presentations, publication of books and other documents are necessary to get academic, professional and administrative groups to support widespread adoption of the product.

12. Installation: The consulting services and staff training are provided so that the program will be satisfactorily adopted.

People Enjoy Being "Guinea Pigs"

Some people believe that it is wrong to experiment with human beings. They argue that a researcher who uses people for his own purposes denies them freedom, dignity, and self-direction and is probably tricking them into believing or doing certain things that are contrary to their nature or integrity.

There is a popular notion that people don't want to be treated as "guinea pigs," but the notion is wrong. People enjoy the special attention that they get when they are the subjects in an experiment. People want to be treated as individual human beings. Workers on the assembly line don't receive this treatment. Typists in a clerical pool seldom get it. A child in a class of 40 students doesn't get it. But subjects in social experiments do get the special attention of someone (the researcher), who pays special attention to them and is genuinely interested in their reactions. Indeed, the good feeling that the experimenter creates in his human guinea pigs, because he is really interested in them, has been known to ruin some experiments!

Experimenting with people means that you assess them at some point in time, try a new program with some, and an old program with others, then you assess the subjects again to see if those who followed the new program are any better off than those who took part in the old. Technically, you are not experimenting with people but with programs, because if you find that the people are no better off for participating in the new program, you fault the program and say we have to develop a better program.

We can be assured that people do not mind being subjects in human experiments. They will give their cooperation in the project for the privilege of being treated as human beings!

Saskatchewan NewStart has experimented with up to 110 people in its laboratory at one time. Our program has traded two things for the cooperation of these adults: (1) a commitment to help them meet their objectives in further education and (2) some greater attention to them as people.

At the present time we in Canada are doing little to invent better methods of reducing poverty and other social ills. These age-old problems are getting more serious and there is an immediate need for new methods of resolving our present social problems. The methods can only be invented by a process of action-research which conceives, conducts and evaluates new approaches in real life situations— in other words, social invention centers.

The methods that are used today to solve social problems are about 4000 years old, whereas the methods used to solve medical, agricultural, transportation and industrial problems are about 25 years old. If we can establish social invention centers, we can create solutions to our age-old social problems, and can rid society of racial strife, mental illness, crime and poverty. This is a goal worth working for.

(D. Stuart Conger is Director, Training Research and Development Station, Manpower and Immigration, 154 8th Street, East, P.O. Box 1565, Prince Albert, Saskatchewan, Canada. For a copy of his 107-page booklet, *Social Inventions,* send $2 to Saskatchewan NewStart Inc., Box 1565, Prince Albert, Saskatchewan, Canada.)

Social Inventions Through History

The social inventions listed here are selected from a much larger compilation prepared by author B. Stuart Conger to suggest the importance of these innovations in the course of civilization. The data are drawn from generally reliable historical reference works; however, one must bear in mind that authorities may differ on exactly when and where a given social invention occurred.

Social Invention	When	Where	Who	Why
Marriage	Prehistory (Hundreds of thousands of years ago)	Wherever *Homo sapiens* lived	*Homo sapiens*	Against the exacting climatic background of late Pliocene and Pleistocene times, we can picture animal behavior evolving into social conduct; kindred groups become the exogamous clan within the tribe; instincts and habits of sexual intercourse and mating are more and more artificially directed and circumscribed until any infringement of the code gave rise to a social interplay of condemnation and guilt.
Religion	Pre-history (e.g., 50,000 B.C.)	Wherever Paleolithic man lived	*Homo sapiens*	As man's consciousness drew him apart from nature, he was bound to look at nature and having contemplated it, seek to explain what he saw, to affect it for his own ends, and finally to regard it with awe and reverence and a desire for reunion.
Life after death (soul)	50,000 B.C.	La Chapelle aux Saints, France	Mousterians (Neanderthal man)	Mousterians put their dead in graves normally dug in the cave where the group lived. General attempts were made to protect the body. Graves were placed near the hearths as if to warm occupants. Departed provided with tools and meat.
Agriculture, farming	6000 B.C.	Jericho (Jordan Valley)	Neolithic man	The earliest inhabitants supported themselves by hunting and collecting, but also growing crops, watered by a perennial spring, and grazing sheep and goats.
Churches (organized sects and priesthood)	4000 B.C.	Sumer	Priests	The priesthood developed from "secret societies" who monopolized fertility and other rituals. Once recognized as a professional, a priest could do much to give concrete form to imaginary beings.
City	3500 B.C.	Sumer	Sumerians	The Sumerian was compelled by flooding of the Euphrates and the need for perennial irrigation to cooperate in an elaborate organization. Thus the Euphrates delta was from the outset parcelled out into a number of agricultural-irrigation units each having its own center of administration. These centers grew into cities.
Factories	3000 B.C.	City-States of Sumer (Ur, Sippar)	Sumerians	There were private, royal and temple factories set up to produce goods for local consumption and for export.

Social Invention	When	Where	Who	Why
Books	2800 B.C.	Egypt	Egyptians	Since papyrus was easier to work with, the "book" must have been invented in Egypt soon after writing was introduced. (Sumerian "books" date to 2500 B.C. and consisted of a series of tablets; Egyptian books were papyrus rolls.)
Libraries	2500 B.C.	Sumer	Priests	Developed for schools of higher education, usually attached to temples. Collected books on various subjects.
Schools	2500 B.C.	Sumer	Priests	First established for purposes of training the scribes required to satisfy the economic and administrative demands of the land, primarily those of the temple and palace. Often attached to temple.
24-hour day	2000 B.C.	Sumer	Sumerians	The organized cooperation of an urban population requires more accurate divisions of time than are needed in a rural village.
Hell	2000 B.C.	Egypt	Upper class	Immortality was open to everyone. Osiris became the judge who determined whether or not an individual might proceed to the celestial regions. Those whom he refused to pass apparently stayed in the old world, in a place full of serpents and fire.
Divorce	1800 B.C.	Babylon	Hammurabi	Laws for divorce first appeared in Hammurabi's code although divorce might have been in existence longer.
Hospital	600 B.C.	Epidaurus, Greece	Priests	The temple at Epidaurus was one of the first to be dedicated to the Greek health god Asclepius. A hostel was attached to this temple where sick people could come and be treated by the priests.
Republic	600 B.C.	Greece	Aristocrats	The king was forced to reply to a council of elders made up of prominent members of the most powerful clans. They gradually forced the king out.
Democracy	510 B.C.	Athens	Cleisthenes	After gaining back control of Athens, Cleisthenes instituted sweeping constitutional changes.
Strike	490 B.C.	Rome	Plebs (common people)	For safeguards for debtors, right to intermarry with patricians, right to vote.
State Supported Schools	75 A.D.	Rome	Vespasian	The first endowment on the part of the state was due to Vespasian, who was the first to give Latin and Greek rhetoricians a stipend of 100,000 sesterces, to be paid from the Imperial Treasury.
University (Modern)	1000 A.D.	Paris	Abelard	It is generally agreed that the work of Abelard contributed substantially to the formation in Paris of a general body of students who had completed the studies provided at the lesser collegiate and cathedral centers. It was out of this body of advanced students that the institution which became the University of Paris was formed.
Circuit Judge: Origin of True Criminal Law	1176	England	Henry II	Henry II reorganized the system and divided England into circuits, which were regularly ridden for this purpose; and taken in conjunction with the Assizes of Clarendon and Northampton their administration of justice may be said to be the origin of true criminal law.

Social Invention	When	Where	Who	Why
Trade union	1699	Newcastle, England	Keelmen: Lighter men in coal industry	Workmen began to combine for purpose of mutual insurance against sickness, old age or death.
Cabinet with Prime Minister	1714	England	Committee of Parliament	King George I was unable to speak English, and soon stopped attending Cabinet meetings. In the absence of the King, a minister took over, who became the Prime Minister.
Compulsory school attendance	1717	Prussia	Frederick William I	The work of France in the preceding century and the rapid development of the Pietistic schools led to the decrees of 1717 in which Frederick William I made attendance in the elementary schools of Prussia compulsory.
Unemployment insurance plan	1789	Switzerland	Town of Basel	Group action to protect workers against the hazards of industrial life began as early as 1789 when Basel Town in Switzerland established an unemployment plan.
Kindergarten	1837	Blankenburg, Germany	Froebel	This was a school which did not have preparation for later schooling as its chief purpose. The kindergarten was a place in which children could grow, develop, and learn in an entirely natural way.
Old age pensions	1908	Great Britain	Parliament	Now for the first time payments were to be made as of right, from national funds to a section of the needy, the elderly, within strict limitations of age and means, but with no test of actual destitution.
Family allowance	1918	France	Certain firms	In France the modern movement began in 1918 with an industrial scheme under which certain firms paid a small proportion of their wages bill into an 'equalization fund' from which payments were made on the insurance principle to the men who had children.
Social Security Act	1935	U.S.	Franklin D. Roosevelt	It provided for unemployment insurance and for retirement and death benefits (extended in 1959 to provide income for dependents of deceased or retired workers). It provided a nationwide framework of incentives, support and standards for financial assistance to persons in three groups—the aged, the blind, and dependent children.
National Health Service	1946	England	Labour Government	A comprehensive service, available to all who wished to make use of it and covering all forms of medical care.
Programmed instruction (teaching machines)	1957	Harvard University	B. F. Skinner	Programming was first employed on a regular basis in 1957 at Harvard University as a part of B. F. Skinner's 'The Analysis of Behavior,' a course designed to teach many of the behavioral principles on which programmed instruction is founded.
"Sit-ins"	1960	Greensboro, North Carolina	Negro college students	In February 1960, Negro college students in Greensboro, N.C., began to 'sit-in' at white lunch counters that refused to serve them. Soon the technique spread throughout the South.

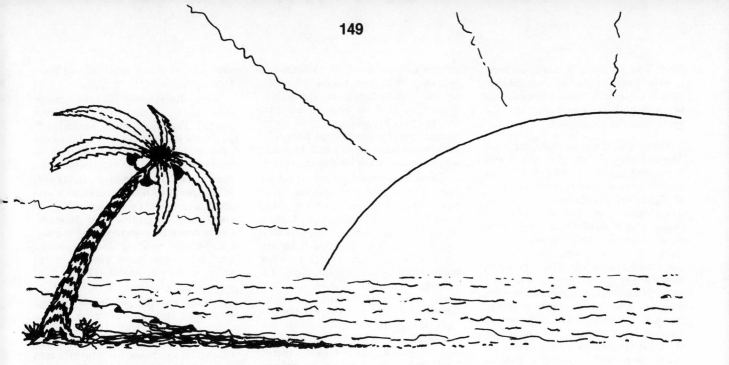

Hawaii's Lessons for the Future

by Bob Krauss

Global village? Limits to growth? Future shock? The people of Hawaii experienced these problems centuries ago and worked out ways to deal with them. The Hawaiian solutions may be worth studying today.

One reason we are frequently surprised, confused, and frustrated by events which affect our lives is an assumption that they are unique. We tend to take for granted that our generation is the first to live under conditions imposed by a global village, spaceship earth, future shock, and limits to growth. The fact is, many humans have lived and prospered under similar conditions. Their experience offers a valuable fund of practical information about the kind of world we are coming into and how to cope with it.

Consider some of the events which led to our assumption of uniqueness. One of these events was the development of nuclear weapons. This intensified a growing condition of global interdependence by making us all more vulnerable to one another. World trade continues to strengthen this web of interdependence. The U.S. is dependent on Arabian oil. Russia is dependent upon U.S. wheat. Developed nations are dependent upon undeveloped raw materials. Developing nations are dependent upon manufactured imports. The only unique aspect

of this condition is its global dimension. Tighter interdependence has been a fact of life for many humans in the past.

Another event was the first space flight around the earth. It took an hour and 48 minutes. Driving around Tahiti takes longer. So our planet has shrunk in concept from an inconceivable enormity to the size of a small Pacific island. Spin-offs from space flight have shrunk our world in other ways. Computers speed up the flow of world credit and provide instantaneous hotel bookings halfway around the globe. Boxing fans can sit in Manila and have ringside seats for a bout in Africa. Such a small-scale world is unique for many of us. Other humans have known no other kind of world.

A third event was exploration in space. So far, nobody else is out there. Nothing illustrates this better than a photo of earth taken from beyond the atmosphere where we live. There we are, all alone together. The enemy is no longer the tribe over the next hill. The enemy is ourselves. Such a sense of group isolation is unique to people

used to escaping over the horizon. For many humans, there was no escape for thousands of years.

A fourth event was the gas shortage. Suddenly we discovered there might be a limit to oil and metals and land and water and every other basic resource necessary to our survival. Such limits are unique to the growth of the West. Similar limits are old hat for other civilizations.

As we each plan for our own tomorrow, it would seem logical to seek advice from ancestors who survived conditions we must face. Every society in the world has such an ancestral resource. All *homo sapiens* once existed in small groups in their own isolated worlds. Each world was highly interdependent, small in size and limited in resources. Practical living experience under these conditions is available in the literature of all sorts of diverse people: Eskimos, jungle tribes, plains Indians, river and desert dwellers.

Pacific Islands Offer Parallels

Probably the closest parallels to our computerized, technological, space age world are Pacific islands scattered like a galaxy of inhabited planets over a universe of empty blue water. The parallels are less exact today than they once were because the isolation of the islands has been compromised by modern transportation and communications. The limitation of island resources has been lifted by contact with the outside. As a result, the islands have become in many respects exotic extensions of continents. Parallels to the space age become much closer when we go back, say, 300 years into Pacific history.

There are many reasons for this. The Polynesians who discovered and populated the most isolated of these worlds were a relatively modern people. They provide the most thoroughly documented recent example of sophisticated civilizations existing in deep isolation under conditions of tight interdependence, small space, and limited resources. The population densities of these peoples and their impacts on their island environments compare to world population densities today and the impact of 20th century humans upon our globe. In addition, the mild climate on many of these islands permitted a lifestyle free of hardships which technology has been able to overcome only in recent decades in highly industrialized states.

One word of caution: There are obvious differences, as well as similarities, between the space age and the ancient Pacific. Our tools are different. The ecology of size, both in population and distance, must be considered. Another complication is the fact that different Pacific islanders used different solutions for similar problems. Not all islanders were Polynesian. Japanese solutions for coping with interdependence described by Ruth Benedict in *The Chrysanthemum and the Sword* are considerably different than the solutions described by Margaret Mead in *Coming of Age in Samoa*. The Tikopian solutions for coping with limited resources described by Raymond Firth in *Primitive Polynesian Economy* are somewhat different than those described by Bronislaw Malinowski in his classic work on the kula system in New Guinea.

However, this variety of adaptations to conditions we must cope with is all to our advantage. It gives us a wide choice of models. If we must not copy, we can creatively adapt. Our method is to approach modern world problems as a Pacific islander would approach them based on his experience with similar problems. This is a fascinating exercise that offers rich rewards in practical instruction.

Islands Had "Limits to Growth"

For example, we must conclude at once that The Club of Rome is very properly concerned with limits to growth. Island experience offers abundant cause for concern as well as ex-

amples of how economic systems can operate within these limits. Island experience offers practical, day-by-day lessons in how to deal with future shock. These lessons amount to an integrated, multidimensional picture of what's happening to us and why, and what we can do personally to survive.

Island experience indicates that we can expect a complex combination of power concentration at the top and more freedom of action at the bottom of our societies. While it appears that technology is homogenizing the globe as tradition and religion once homogenized smaller areas, island experience indicates that people will cling fiercely to regional, ethnic, family, and other identities. Islanders have things to teach us about the future of our religions, sex, our concept of privacy, population control, land use, warfare, and a wide range of other human concerns. The value of such instruction lies not only in past successes but in past failures as well.

Let us now see how an island people, the Hawaiians, handled one of the conditions modern humans are facing—a highly interdependent world. It may be comforting, as we lament our lack of control over the future, to realize that the old-time Hawaiian must have felt the same way. He could lose his life at the whim of a chief. The vagaries of weather, a shift in the coastal current, affected his diet. He was always at the mercy of his neighbors. If he had a fight with his wife at breakfast, it was village gossip at noon. This interdependence extended over the entire Hawaiian chain. When Captain James Cook stopped overnight at the westernmost island of Niihau in 1778, his sailors celebrated the discovery of Hawaii by giving native women venereal disease. A year later, when Cook stopped off the island of Maui, he recognized the symptoms of venereal disease among Hawaiians in the canoes that came out to greet him.

Think what this meant. What had happened on Niihau one night a year before between half a dozen people had already affected citizens on another island far away. These people, isolated in their tiny world, were at the mercy of one another. This is the problem of interdependence. It is obvious from the number of techniques evolved by the Hawaiians to cope with the problem that this was a major source of aggravation. So the first lesson we can learn from the Hawaiian experience is that our new condition of global interdependence will be a major cause of future concern that will occupy a great deal of our

time and consume much of our creative energy.

What did the old Hawaiian do to cope in his tightly interdependent world? The basic thing he did was structure his lifestyle to avoid the kind of confrontations that created friction. What has come to be called the Hawaiian Aloha Spirit in travel brochures must have evolved as a survival technique. People learned to be courteous, hospitable and tolerant, not because they were noble or good, but because courtesy and hospitality and tolerance have high survival value when you are at the mercy of your neighbors.

In such a world, people who are too ambitious or competitive or greedy threaten the survival of everyone. So another lesson the old Hawaiian teaches, if we choose his adaptation to survival in a highly interdependent world, is that we must learn to be less ambitious, less competitive, less greedy. We will do this not because we are noble or good but because we will find it dangerous to be too competitive, ambitious, or greedy.

"There was a feast to celebrate every suitable occasion: the birth of a baby, the building of a new house, the construction of a canoe, the completion of an irrigation system, the arrival of a favorite guest, the harvest of a taro crop."

Hooponopono—"Making Things Right"

The disease of interdependence is alienation. Samoans call it "musu." The Hawaiian term is "huhu." It is expressed then as now in resentment, stubbornness, outbursts of pique. If allowed to fester, it can result in serious antisocial behavior that threatens the public health and safety. We can assume that this disease was common in old Hawaii because the Hawaiians evolved sophisticated techniques to combat it. One technique was called *hooponopono* or "making things right."

Hawaiians evolved many techniques for expressing hospitality, tolerance, and courtesy—virtues that are needed in an increasingly interdependent world. These women perform for visitors in 1816. The artist is Louis Choris, who sailed with Lt. Otto von Kotzebue.

Hawaiian war canoe with masked paddlers. Invasions of neighbor island were forbidden during the Makahiki season. Date is 1778-1779. The artist is John Webber, who sailed with Captain James Cook.

The armor of today's invasion forces is more substantial. However, modern nations have not yet become as sophisticated as the old Hawaiians in establishing rules for limited warfare. Here U.S. Marines move ashore in amphibian tanks.
Photo: *Honolulu Advertiser*

When the behavior of someone in the community became intolerable, the aggrieved person asked the *kahuna* (wise man or priest) for hooponopono. Upon this request, the kahuna called together everyone affected by the problem. He said a prayer to get the meeting off to a positive start, then asked for discussion. This was a signal to stop being polite and to vent one's feelings. Everyone from toddlers to grandparents could speak. When this was done, the kahuna steered the discussion toward a solution of the problem. He did not dictate this but tried to develop a consensus. If the aggrieved finally forgave the offender, the session was considered a success. If there was no forgiveness, the problem remained unsolved.

There are similarities between hooponopono and modern sensitivity sessions. But one element is different. The kahuna was not attempting to help individuals find their own identities. His concern was the survival of the group. Here, then, is another Hawaiian approach to the problem of interdependence. It is a value judgment that, in this situation, the individual is less important than the group. This does not mean that individuals in old Hawaii were unimportant. From all accounts, Hawaiians were spontaneous by nature and not reluctant to disagree. However, the old Hawaiian tended much more than the European to find his identity as a member of a group, not as an individual. The reason must have been that group membership in his interdependent world had higher survival value than individual independence. This is another lesson we might profit from. Our chances of survival will be greater in our interdependent world if we remember that individual rights are not as important as the good of the community.

We must credit the Hawaiian for being very creative about exploring the benefits of group membership instead of merely inventing solutions for the problems that resulted. He apparently decided that, so long as he was stuck with other people in an interdependent world, he might as well enjoy them. His attitude toward privacy reflects this.

It is an attitude common on all Pacific islands. This attitude created real hardship for Peace Corpsmen in Micronesia. The volunteers from U.S. suburbs could get used to the food and they could learn the language. But the lack of privacy drove them up the wall. In desperation one fellow walked off into the jungle during a party just to get away from everybody for a few minutes. His Micronesian host immediately went out to sit with him so the guest would not be lonely.

Like the Micronesian, the old Hawaiian valued privacy less than the opportunity to be with people. The 19th century English missionary William Ellis reported that the chiefs with whom he ate breakfast became quite congenial and talkative over the meal although they had been silent before. This was normal behavior. The old Hawaiian used mealtime as a period for establishing pleasant relations. Disagreements were forgotten over the poi bowl. It was a time to laugh and enjoy.

A Feast for Almost Everything

The special skills which the old Hawaiian developed in the art of human relations are beautifully expressed in "the feast." There was a feast to celebrate every suitable occasion: the birth of a baby, the building of a new house, the construction of a canoe, the completion of an irrigation system, the arrival of a favorite guest, the harvest of a taro crop. In modern economic terms, the feast represented the restaurant industry, the entertainment industry, the travel industry, and the leisure industry all rolled into one. But it was even more to the old Hawaiian. The feast could serve as a substitute for war in conferring status on the guest of honor. The feast was used to re-establish the bonds of the group from the family to the nation, as at a baby *luau* or on national holidays. In addition to all this, the feast was fun.

The widespread, grassroots attempt by many Americans to celebrate their bicentennial on July 4, 1976, provided an example of how the feast can be translated into modern terms. What became clear on July 4, after months of growing cynicism about commercialization of the bicentennial, was that the success of the celebration could not be measured by its professionalism. What really mattered was the amount of cooperative community effort expended and the enthusiasm displayed. The shared experience made us all feel a bit better about ourselves and each other, and soothed the wounds of factionalism.

The same shared experience of effort and fun made the feast a survival technique in old Hawaii. The lesson seems to be that we must learn all over again how to throw a party. Having it catered doesn't help. The success of a party as a technique of

Sharing the fun of a festival can still provide an escape from the pressure of enforced togetherness. This photograph was taken during Aloha Week in 1975.
Photo: Roy Ito, *Honolulu Advertiser*

survival in an interdependent world is measured by the intensity of our enthusiasm over the event, the cooperative effort we expend on the arrangements, and how completely we put aside selfish interests in order to have fun together.

On the international level, it would appear that the problem of interdependence was not so great for the old Hawaiian as it is for us. After all, he did not have the bomb, but only spears, clubs, and sling stones with which to wage war. Still, he had his own ultimate weapon: starvation. If a

chief did not give his people nor his enemies time to plant and to harvest, everybody would starve. So the Hawaiians had to cope with a very modern dilemma. Warfare was an accepted method for settling disputes, and the way for ambitious chiefs to acquire power and territory. Commoners could win fame and position in battle. It is obvious from legends and recorded history that Hawaiians fought frequent wars. How did they avoid the ultimate disaster that could have been caused at any time by an overly aggressive chief in a small, tightly interdependent world?

Festivals and holidays, which provided feasting and dancing, helped ease the burden of interdependence in old Hawaii. This scene is dated 1836. It was painted by an artist who sailed with Captain Auguste N. Vaillant.

Limited Warfare Was Waged

The answer is that they waged limited warfare. Before the fighting began, there was always a great deal of diplomatic maneuvering. The *kahuna* of the war god had to consult the clouds or the entrails of chickens. Ellis reported that battle sites were often chosen beforehand and that the date of a battle might be fixed in advance. The fighting seldom lasted more than a day or two. Armies usually disengaged at sundown and resumed the battle next morning. Casualties were numbered in the tens, not in the thousands. All of this is more like a dangerous sport than the deadly, gray efficiency of modern warfare. Hawaiian-style warfare permitted the islanders to enjoy the danger of war and yet to survive. The lesson seems to be that war can be limited, and probably must be limited in the years ahead.

So a more practical lesson for our future may be an understanding of the nature of limited wars and how to win one's share of them. Since it was impossible for the Hawaiians to wage total war, their wars had to be waged for limited objectives. Each side had to make up its mind before going into battle whether the objective was worth the war. That's why it took so long. The kahuna needed time to judge the strength of the enemy and to test the mettle of his own people. Allies had to be consulted. Meanwhile, both sides engaged in psychological warfare. The easiest way to win was to convince the enemy that he couldn't. The approved method was to boast that your war god was more powerful than his war god. This explains why Kamehameha, the last great Hawaiian war chief, spent so much time and energy dedicating temples to his war god. Finally, the Hawaiians were diligent in honing their skills in the art of conventional warfare. Spear throwing and parrying were included in the education of every chief. The fact that the Hawaiians entertained Captain George Vancouver with a sham battle as well as with hulas clearly demonstrates that they honored the warrior as well as the artist.

It is reassuring to discover that, since the advent of nuclear weapons, humans have been waging war much like the old Hawaiians did. The first example was the Korean war when total war advocate General Douglas MacArthur was relieved of his command by President Harry Truman, who understood the rules of the game. A second example came in Vietnam.

U.S. troops never crossed the line into North Vietnam. They never dropped the bomb. This was not because of inherent good manners but because winning the war in this fashion could have been a greater disaster than losing in conventional fashion. Both China and Russia acted with similar restraint.

In Angola the U.S. faced another Hawaiian-style dilemma. Was intervention worth the consequences? Could the U.S. win or had it been outmaneuvered diplomatically? The Hawaiian experience indicates that this decision will be faced over and over again by all nations in a tightly interdependent world. Each decision will be as difficult as it was for the old kahuna. Each decision will have to be made with consideration of the strength of war gods, which today are nuclear weapons. Are U.S. nuclear weapons more powerful than Russia's nuclear weapons? The history of both detente and deterrent is a modern expression of the delicate, uneasy relationship that existed between rival chiefs in Hawaii 300 years ago.

In this dangerous and potentially terminal war of nerves, the Hawaiians not only established traditional ground rules for battle. They apparently felt it was also necessary to provide an annual cooling-off period. This period was the *Makahiki* which fell sometime between November and March when rough seas made invasions of neighboring islands particularly hazardous. During this time the worship of Ku, god of war, ceased. Lono, god of peace and agriculture, reigned. His stick symbol was carried on a long, slow journey around each island. At each land division, Lono's representatives collected taxes from the people for the local chief. Later there was feasting and dancing and athletic competition. Everybody took a long holiday.

Here is another example of the Hawaiian genius in human relations. The Makahiki not only placed a *kapu* (taboo) on war but it also provided attractive alternatives. Until he received his taxes, a chief could not very well finance a respectable war. The Makahiki also served as an annual reaffirmation by the gods and the people of the chiefly system. These were excellent reasons why a chief should observe the peace. For the people, feasting and fun and games served as a reward for the payment of taxes and as a relief from the heavy burden of interdependence. In addition, the celebration provided an outlet for talent in the arts as well as for competitive energy in sports.

This Hawaiian warrior and officer of the high chief is wearing the battle dress and carrying the principle weapon used by Hawaiians to wage their limited brand of warfare. The artist is Jacques Arago, who sailed with Captain Louis de Freycinet.

Modern warriors carry rifles—weapons they use to wage limited warfare on our island earth.

Mealtime is still used as a time for enjoyment as well as sustenance at camp-outs as well as around the banquet table.

Photo: Roy Ito, *Honolulu Advertiser*

In view of his 1,000 years experience in a small, highly interdependent world, what advice might the old Hawaiian give us if we asked how to survive in our own interdependent world? His advice might go like this:

1. Put less emphasis on competition and more emphasis on the positive aspects of cooperation. It is often more important in an interdependent world to get along with people than to win. It is often more important to be courteous than to be right.

2. Put less value on privacy and more value on being with people. Be less concerned with individual rights and more concerned with the good of the community.

3. Work toward developing techniques for preventing alienation in the family, on the campus, across the nation and around the world. One technique is a lifestyle of nonconfrontation. Other techniques involve the creative use of communication.

4. Provide opportunities for enjoying other people. The more parties, feasts, parades, celebrations, anniversaries, holidays, and festivals the better. Such occasions ease the burden of interdependence and also stimulate the distribution of wealth in a world of limited resources. Christmas provides an example of how such an economy can operate.

5. Recognize the need for placing limits on warfare. At the same time, become proficient in the skills of limited war: psychology, diplomacy, deterrent, the use of conventional weapons. Understand that allies are more important than weapons of any kind.

6. Expand the Olympics and all other forms of peaceful international contact. Don't underestimate ping pong diplomacy and cultural exchange. Instead, increase their scope to that of global war. Set aside one month of the year for a vast exchange of musicians, dancers, athletic teams and artists. If this seem visionary, remember the alternatives. For the old Hawaiian, a real alternative to the Makahiki was protracted, wholesale starvation. In our own interdependent world, a real alternative to a creative program for peace is the decimation of humanity. Which alternative is more desirable?

Mealtime in ancient Hawaii was a period for socializing, to forget animosities. This survival technique evolved into "the feast." The Hawaiian mealtime frolic pictured here was drawn in 1837 by J. Masselot, who sailed with Captain Abel DuPetit-Thouars.

Author Bob Krauss, a columnist for *The Honolulu Advertiser*, got the idea for examining Hawaiian history for models for future behavior when he participated in the 1970 Hawaii Conference on the Year 2000.

Bob Krauss is Columnist, *The Honolulu Advertiser*, P.O. Box 3110, Honolulu, Hawaii 96802. He contributed a paper to *Hawaii 2000*, edited by George Chaplin and Glenn Paige. University of Hawaii Press, Honolulu, 1973. $9.95. Available from the World Future Society's Book Service.

CONCLUSION

Towards A Philosophy of Futurism

by Edward Cornish

Do futurists have a unique perspective on the world? If so, what are its underlying assumptions? The editor of THE FUTURIST describes some of the beliefs that he feels are generally found among people who have a serious interest in the future.

The modern futurist movement, which began developing rapidly during the 1960s, appears to be gradually forming a coherent philosophy or world view. The crystallization of this philosophy is far from complete but it is now possible to speak—very tentatively—of certain basic principles that typify the thinking of today's futurists.

Among the emerging futurist principles are: (1) the unity or interconnectedness of reality, (2) the crucial importance of time, and (3) the importance of ideas, especially ideas about the future. Let us take a brief look at each of these principles:

The Unity of the Universe

Fundamental to almost all futurist thinking is the perception that the universe is all one piece, rather than an aggregation of independent, unconnected units. An insistence on the interconnectedness of everything in the world, including the human race in all its manifestations, and on the impossibility of fully comprehending any single entity without considering its place within the whole, are fundamental precepts of today's futurism. This holistic thinking contrasts with the traditional view that man exists in the universe but is not really a part of it. In the holistic perspective of the futurist, man is as much a part of nature as anything else in the universe: individual human beings owe their existence to the operations of the universe and cannot possibly be separated from it.

The unity of the universe is a unity of time as well as space, that is, the world of the future is being created out of the world of the present, and for this reason we can know much about the future world by looking carefully at what has been happening during the recent past. The future is built largely with the materials of the present.

The Crucial Importance of Time

Most people are almost totally preoccupied with their immediate concerns. Thinking about what might happen five or 10 years from now seems to them merely idle

This article is an excerpt from the World Future Society's new book *The Study of the Future: An Introduction to the Art and Science of Understanding and Shaping Tomorrow's World.* The article is followed by a general description of the book.

speculation. But futurists recognize clearly that the problems of today did not appear suddenly out of thin air; they have been building up, often for many years, and might have been dealt with fairly easily if they had been tackled earlier. The crisis that we face today is generally the minor problem that we neglected yesterday.

In addition to discounting the future, most people tend not to recognize *gradual* change. For example, a 2% increase per year in air pollution might attract little notice, yet it means that air pollution will double in 34 years! The doubling of the population of a city over the course of a generation means a drastic transformation of the life of that city for better or worse. Futurists generally want to identify such gradual changes, so that they can be monitored and timely action taken to avoid painful crises.

When a problem reaches the crisis stage—that is, when the pain of the situation has become unbearable—it generally gets attention. But at that point it can be solved only with fantastic expenditures of time and money, and in many cases it simply cannot be solved at all. The damage has been done, and people just have to live with it. On the other hand, a small change that is wisely introduced today can result in major improvements in the years ahead. Such a change may be likened to a seed that is planted in good soil and grows, almost by itself, into a great tree. Thus, time is a crucial element that can make things easy to accomplish—or impossible.

In thinking about the future, futurists tend to focus on the period from five to 50 years ahead. The reason for focusing on this period is that the immediate or near-term future (less than five years) constitutes what might be viewed as the domain of ordinary human concerns (although even five years from now would be regarded by many non-futurists as a very distant point in time!) In addition, one cannot do much to change the world that we will experience in the near-term future; there simply isn't enough time to decide upon and put into effect many basic changes. Nor can we do much useful planning for the period 50 years from now because so many unpredictable events and unknown factors will exert their influence that anything we tried to do would likely be erased in the intervening years.

Just as the Eskimos have developed names for different types of snow and the Arabs for the parts of a camel, futurists are beginning to develop names for various parts of the future. Earl Joseph, Editor of *Future Trends*, published by the Minnesota Futurists, has identified five basic periods of the future: (1) Now: the immediate future (up to one year from now), (2) the near-term future (one to five years from now), (3) the middle-range future (five to 20 years from now), (4) the long-range future (20 to 50 years from now), (5) the far future (50 or more years hence). (See Joseph's article in *THE FUTURIST*, August 1974.)

Joseph makes two points that are important in futurist thinking:

1. *The world that we will experience in five to 20 years is being shaped by decisions made now.* Today's decisions will not change very much the world that we experience during the next five years, but they may dramatically change the world that we experience five to 20 years from now! This curious fact results from the time lag between the making of a decision and its final impact. People new to government have often been frustrated by their inability to get their decisions implemented; U.S. President Harry S. Truman is said to have complained that he gave orders and absolutely nothing would happen! Yet the bureaucracy which responds so sluggishly to new commands may be changing pervasively in response to commands issued many months or years earlier but only now becoming fully implemented. In the U.S. Government, Republican decision-makers may preside somewhat helplessly over a bureaucracy steadily implementing policies and programs instituted by the previous Democratic administration! Later when the bureaucracy is finally implementing Republican policies, a Democratic administration may again be in power—and equally frustrated in its inability to get decisions implemented.

2. *Almost anything can be done in 20 years!* The statement is startling—until one recalls that, once the decisions were made, only four years were needed to unleash the awesome power of the atom and only eight years to put man on the moon!

These two points underlie the futurists' insistence on making the more distant future an integral part of current decision-making. The whole point of studying future possibilities, futurists emphasize, is to improve the quality of decisions that are being made *right now.* Today's decisions are shaping tomorrow's world, yet only too often we make decisions with little concern about their impact on the longer-term future.

The Importance of Ideas

Since the future does not exist, it must be invented; that is to say, ideas about what may happen in the future must be generated and studied. Such ideas or *futuribles* are critically important because our thinking is shaped both by our concepts of what happened in the past and our images of what we may see in the future.

Ideas are the tools of thought. Without them, no thought is possible. Ideas may be divided into two classes: concepts and theories. A concept is a kind of mental map or picture of something; a theory (in this sense) is an interlinkage of two or more concepts to indicate how they relate to each other. For example, one may have a concept of a house, a dog, or an educational system, and a theory that mosquitoes (concept) lead to malaria (concept). A theory may be compressed into a concept by striking out the space that separates two concepts and creating a new concept that incorporates them both. For example, the concept of "boy" may be given the attribution of "bad," so that the new concept of "bad boy" emerges.

Concepts and theories are our mental models of how the world operates. They enable us to recall what happened in the past and to imagine what may happen in the future. Thinking consists of manipulating our concepts and theories in various ways. When we daydream, we let concepts emerge into consciousness without attempting to focus them on a particular problem. When we want to solve a problem, we seek to summon to consciousness only those concepts and theories that relate to the problem. In thinking, we play with our concepts, moving them about in various ways. We are pleased when we discover a concept or theory that seems to correspond well with reality. A theory that promises to "work" rewards us, because we enjoy the feeling of power that it gives us; it is like having a new power tool or a new house. Even before we have done anything with the fine new concept or theory, we feel a sense of competence.

As we go through life, we constantly try to develop our tool chest of ideas. As we acquire new and more powerful tools, that is, as we develop knowledge and wisdom, we feel enriched and become more secure within ourselves. We feel better able to meet the challenges of the future.

The power of ideas is not always clearly recognized, because they are invisible and hard to evaluate, but they represent an extremely valuable resource and, from an economic standpoint, are often more important than raw materials, industrial plants, and manpower when it comes to earning money.

Businessmen tend to emphasize material rather than intellectual capital because material wealth can be easily calculated, and readily exchanged. Yet intellectual capital is generally more important. After World War II, Germany's material capital was in ruins, but within a few years the German people were prospering as never before, because the war had not destroyed their intellectual capital, that is, the ideas in their heads, which were their greatest resource. On the other hand, if today's Germans were, by some miracle, replaced by an equal number of illiterate tribesmen, the German economy would immediately collapse. Within a few months, the steel mills and pharmaceutical firms would be infested with rats and weeds.

About the Author

Edward Cornish, author of *The Study of the Future*, is president of the World Future Society and editor of *THE FUTURIST.*

Ideas have made civilization possible and keep it advancing. For example, the division of labor is one simple idea that has proved extraordinarily powerful through history. If we want to do a job, this idea offers a success formula: Divide the job into separate tasks and assign these tasks to specific individuals. In this way, each person can become proficient in his part of the work and everybody benefits. Without the division of labor, or specialization, civilization would be almost inconceivable.

"If we really give serious attention to the future, rather than continue to lurch from crisis to crisis, we can hope for enormous benefits in the years ahead."

From *The Study of the Future*

Another idea, Eli Whitney's notion of identical parts for a machine, provided the basis for the standardization of equipment and for assembly-line production methods. Other ideas, such as Copernicus' theory that the earth moves around the sun, rather than vice versa, displaced earlier concepts, which had proved unsatisfactory, and by so doing opened the way to new discoveries. Darwin's theory of evolution by means of natural selection was a similar powerhouse of an idea that could immediately be applied to solving all sorts of biological riddles. New ideas enable us to build more accurate and complete maps of reality. Useful ideas constitute an intellectual capital that we have available when needed. Education may be viewed as the mass reproduction and distribution of ideas that have proven their worth. The ideas are stored up in the brains of people so that they are available for later use.

If our ideas are powerful, we can dramatically change the world to make it a happier place. But if our ideas are weak, then we are extremely limited in what we can do. The power of ideas is itself a powerful idea. In recent years, government and business leaders in the advanced countries have come to realize that the major constraints on human achievement are not physical but conceptual, that is, the limitations are in our ideas rather than in the material resources at our disposal.

In social systems, more may depend on what people think will happen than on the "realities." A builder once explained how important it was for him to get people to think that a building was actually going to be built: If people believed that he was really going to build the building, then he would get the money from the bank and credit from suppliers and the building would indeed be built. The image of the future that people had in their heads played a crucial role in actually determining the future.

People often "cannot" do things because of a lack of ideas rather than a lack of muscle power, tools, or money. Armed with the right ideas about what to do, the "impossible" may quickly become possible. To get the right ideas, we can invest in the research required to develop them. In short, if we really want to do something that seems very difficult or "impossible," we invest time and effort in the development of ideas directed at achieving our goal. History is full of instances where an "impossibility" was simply a case where people did not see how something could be done. In recent years, governments have shown that the allocation of funds for research and development is an effective means of removing the obstacles that have made desired goals seem "unattainable."

Firmly convinced that ideas can move mountains, futurists are extremely interested in the systematic development of ideas. Better ideas will make it possible to improve the human condition. Armed with powerful ideas, the people of the poorest underdeveloped nation in the world might become the richest in less than a single generation. With the right ideas, the people of the world might soon throw war, poverty, famine, and disease into the ashcan of history.

Ideas about the future world—sometimes referred to as "images of the future"—may be especially important. People think that their actions are based on past events and present realities, but their images of the future may play an even more critical role. Images of the future are the blueprints that we use in constructing our lives, and the blueprints may be more important than the materials we work with (our bodies, families, financial resources, etc.) in determining our success and happiness.

Just as a building can be built if people believe it will be, a desirable world might be created if it can be imaged properly, that is, if people can develop a consensus about what a desirable world would be like and how it might be achieved. To develop such a consensus, futurists believe, ideas about the future world should be systematically generated and studied, and that implies the development of the study of the future as a major human activity.

FOR FURTHER READING

BOOKS

The Study of the Future: An Introduction to the Art and Science of Understanding and Shaping Tomorrow's World
by Edward Cornish. World Future Society. 1977. 308 pages. Paperback. $9.50.

This systematic introduction to futurism and future studies includes a history of the futurist movement, methods of forecasting, ways to introduce future-oriented thinking into organizations, detailed descriptions of the lives and ideas of many prominent futures thinkers, examples of current perceptions of future alternatives, and an annotated guide to further reading.

The Future: A Guide to Information Sources
Edward Cornish, editor. Revised 2nd edition. World Future Society. 1979. 722 pages. Paperback. $25.00.

A revised and expanded version of this indispensible guide to the futures field, first published in 1977. Contains the most complete and accurate information available on hundreds of individuals, organizations, periodicals, current research projects, educational courses and programs, books, films, videotapes, games, and other sources of information on future studies and alternatives.

Through the '80s: Thinking Globally, Acting Locally
Frank Feather, editor. World Future Society. 1980. 440 pages. Paperback. $12.50.

A selection of 61 papers prepared for the First Global Conference on the Future, held July 20-24, 1980, in Toronto, Canada. See inside back cover for complete listing of authors and topics.

Education and the Future
Lane Jennings and Sally Cornish, editors. World Future Society. 1980. 120 pages. Paperback. $4.95. (In the same format as *1999: The World of Tomorrow.*)

An anthology of articles on subjects related to the future of education and educating for the future, selected from the pages of THE FUTURIST and the *World Future Society Bulletin*. Authors include Harold Shane, Peter Wagschal, Jim Bowman, William Abbott, Joseph Coates, Fred Kierstead, and Gary Wooddell, with an introduction by Chris Dede.

Future Survey Annual 1979
Michael Marien, editor. World Future Society. 1980. 260 pages. Paperback. $25.00.

This unique publication, making its first appearance this year, provides concise, readable summaries of more than 1,600 new books and articles of special interest to futurists published during 1979. Prepared for the Society's monthly abstract journal, *Future Survey* (see below), these abstracts have been collected, integrated, identified by key-words and numbers, and supplemented with introductory essays and complete cross-indexes to subjects and authors. The volume includes full bibliographic information including publisher, address, and price for each book and article cited.

PERIODICALS

THE FUTURIST: A Journal of Forecasts, Trends and Ideas about the Future
Bimonthly journal published by the World Future Society. Subscription $18.00 per year for individuals, $21.00 for libraries.

THE FUTURIST is an exciting independent magazine that is always informative and often prophetic. Its primary objectives are to present readers with concrete information they can use to help evaluate, for themselves, alternative designs for change, and to alert them to the benefits and dangers of developments already underway.

World Future Society Bulletin
Bimonthly professional journal published by the World Future Society. Subscription $15.00 per year.

The *Bulletin* features technical and scholarly articles on the theory and practical applications of futurism and future study techniques. Also includes book reviews, news of futurist organizations worldwide, and information about the plans and activities of local Society chapters in the U.S. and in 18 other countries.

Future Survey
Monthly abstract journal published by the World Future Society. Subscription $24.00 per year for individuals, $32.00 for libraries.

The Society's newest journal, *Future Survey*, is designed to keep readers up to date on developments in every area of futures interest. Each 16- to 24-page issue contains up to 150 concise, jargon-free abstracts of current articles and new or forthcoming books. Each item is identified by number and key-word, and complete cross-referenced subject and author indexes appear in every issue.

NEWSLETTERS

The Society's three newsletters, *Business Tomorrow*, *Education Tomorrow*, and *Technology Tomorrow*, explore trends and current activities in these specific areas that are shaping the world of tomorrow. Each newsletter is published six times a year; the subscription cost per newsletter is $9.00 per year for World Future Society members, $12.00 for non-members.

CATALOG

Interested readers may obtain, free of charge, a catalog listing all items produced by or available from the World Future Society, including hundreds of books, audio cassettes, reprints, games, and other materials dealing with the future. To order, contact:

World Future Society
4916 St. Elmo Avenue
Washington, D.C. 20014, U.S.A.
Telephone: (301) 656-8274

WORLD FUTURE SOCIETY
An Association for the Study of Alternative Futures

The Society is an association of people interested in future social and technological developments. It is chartered as a non-profit scientific and educational organization in Washington, D.C., and is recognized as tax-exempt by the U.S. Internal Revenue Service. The World Future Society is independent, non-political and non-ideological.

The purpose of the World Future Society is to serve as an unbiased forum and clearinghouse for scientific and scholarly forecasts, investigations and intellectual explorations of the future. The Society's objectives, as stated in its charter, are as follows:

1. To contribute to a reasoned awareness of the future and the importance of its study, without advocating particular ideologies or engaging in political activities.
2. To advance responsible and serious investigation of the future.
3. To promote the development and improvement of methodologies for the study of the future.
4. To increase public understanding of future-oriented activities and studies.
5. To facilitate communication and cooperation among organizations and individuals interested in studying or planning for the future.

Membership is open to anyone seriously interested in the future. Since its founding in 1966, the Society has grown to more than 50,000 members in over 80 countries. Most members are U.S. residents, with growing numbers in Canada, Europe, Japan, and other countries. Members include many of the world's most distinguished scientists, scholars, business leaders and government officials.

SOCIETY PROGRAMS

THE FUTURIST: A Journal of Forecasts, Trends, and Ideas About the Future.

This unique bimonthly journal reports the forecasts made by scientists and others concerning the coming years. It explores the possible consequences of these developments on the individual, institutions and society,

and discusses actions people may take to improve the future.

Publications

The Society publishes books, reports, films, and other specialized documents on future-related areas, including works such as *The Study of the Future, The Future: A Guide to Information Sources, Through the '80s: Thinking Globally, Acting Locally,* and many other stimulating, useful guides to the future.

Book Service

World Future Society members can purchase books, audio tapes, games and other educational materials dealing with the future, at substantial savings. The Society's unique "Bookstore of the Future" carries about 300 titles.

Tape Recordings

The Society has a growing inventory of audio tapes, which are available at low cost to members. This cassette series includes coverage of most major areas and issues of the future, including science and technology, government, education, environment, and human values.

Chapter and Local Activities

Society chapters and local activities in many cities offer speakers, educational courses, seminars, discussion groups and other opportunities for members to get to know each other. They provide personal contacts with people interested in alternative futures.

Meetings

Meetings offer special opportunities for participation and interaction. The *General Assemblies* are large, multidisciplinary convocations where Society members can hear and meet frontier thinkers and doers. The Third General Assembly (The First Global Conference on the Future), held in Toronto, Canada, in July 1980, drew 5,000 participants. Specialized conferences are also held, such as a conference on "Communications and Society" in November 1977 and annual conferences on education since 1978.

Future Times

This informative publication covers meetings, activities, new books, tapes, films, and other information of interest to members. It is sent to all members regularly at no charge.

ᵀʰᵉ FUTURIST

A journal of forecasts, trends and ideas about the future.

Membership Application

I would like to join the World Future Society and receive THE FUTURIST as one benefit of my membership. Annual dues throughout the world are $18 in U.S. currency or its equivalent. (80% of dues is designated for subscription to THE FUTURIST.)

☐ Enclosed is my first year's dues of $18.
☐ Please bill me.
☐ Charge my credit card
  ☐ MasterCharge ☐ VISA
  Card No. _____
  Expiration Date _____

Name _____

Address _____

City _____   State or Province _____   ZIP or Country _____

For subscription to THE FUTURIST without membership, please check this box. ☐

ᵀʜᴇ FUTURIST

A journal of forecasts, trends and ideas about the future.

Membership Application

I would like to join the World Future Society and receive THE FUTURIST as one benefit of my membership. Annual dues throughout the world are $18 in U.S. currency or its equivalent. (80% of dues is designated for subscription to THE FUTURIST.)

☐ Enclosed is my first year's dues of $18.
☐ Please bill me.
☐ Charge my credit card
  ☐ MasterCharge ☐ VISA
  Card No. _____
  Expiration Date _____

Name _____

Address _____

City _____   State or Province _____   ZIP or Country _____

For subscription to THE FUTURIST without membership, please check this box. ☐

ᵀʜᴇ FUTURIST

A journal of forecasts, trends and ideas about the future.

Membership Application

I would like to join the World Future Society and receive THE FUTURIST as one benefit of my membership. Annual dues throughout the world are $18 in U.S. currency or its equivalent. (80% of dues is designated for subscription to THE FUTURIST.)

☐ Enclosed is my first year's dues of $18.
☐ Please bill me.
☐ Charge my credit card
  ☐ MasterCharge ☐ VISA
  Card No. _____
  Expiration Date _____

Name _____

Address _____

City _____   State or Province _____   ZIP or Country _____

For subscription to THE FUTURIST without membership, please check this box. ☐

BUSINESS REPLY CARD
FIRST CLASS   PERMIT NO. 10485   WASHINGTON, DC

POSTAGE WILL BE PAID BY ADDRESSEE

WORLD FUTURE SOCIETY
4916 St. Elmo Avenue
Washington, DC 20014
U.S.A.

BUSINESS REPLY CARD
FIRST CLASS   PERMIT NO. 10485   WASHINGTON, DC

POSTAGE WILL BE PAID BY ADDRESSEE

WORLD FUTURE SOCIETY
4916 St. Elmo Avenue
Washington, DC 20014
U.S.A.

BUSINESS REPLY CARD
FIRST CLASS   PERMIT NO. 10485   WASHINGTON, DC

POSTAGE WILL BE PAID BY ADDRESSEE

WORLD FUTURE SOCIETY
4916 St. Elmo Avenue
Washington, DC 20014
U.S.A.